G000296576

LETTERS FROM LAMBETH

THE CORRESPONDENCE OF THE
REYNOLDS FAMILY WITH
JOHN FREEMAN MILWARD DOVASTON
1808–1815

John Hamilton Reynolds
From the miniature by Joseph Severn

LETTERS FROM LAMBETH

*The correspondence of
the Reynolds family with
John Freeman Milward Dovaston
1808–1815*

Introduced and edited by
JOANNA RICHARDSON

*Published for
The Royal Society of Literature
by the Boydell Press*

Introduction and editorial matter © 1981 Joanna Richardson

First published 1981 for the Royal Society of Literature
by the Boydell Press, an imprint of Boydell & Brewer Ltd,
PO Box 9, Woodbridge, Suffolk IP12 3DF

Distributed in the USA by Biblio Distribution Services
81 Adams Drive, Totowa, NJ 07512

British Library Cataloguing in Publication Data

Reynolds (*Family*)
Letters from Lambeth.
1. Reynolds—Family—Correspondence
2. Dovaston, John Freeman Milward—
Correspondence
I. Title   II. Dovaston, John Freeman Milward
III. Richardson, Joanna
828.808   PR 5220

ISBN 0-85115-150-7

Photoset in Great Britain by
Rowland Phototypesetting Ltd, Bury St Edmunds, Suffolk
and printed by St Edmundsbury Press,
Bury St Edmunds, Suffolk

CONTENTS

ILLUSTRATIONS

INTRODUCTION

The Reynolds family figure largely in the life and letters of Keats; and to extend our knowledge of them is to extend our knowledge of the world in which he moved. Some months ago, in Shrewsbury, I found a substantial unpublished correspondence: two letters from George Reynolds, twenty-two letters from his wife, and forty-one letters and some poems written by their son, John Hamilton Reynolds, one of the most significant figures in the Keats circle. These letters, left on a barn floor when the owners emigrated, had long been kept in the County Record Office. I was the first to see this archive which virtually doubled the known correspondence of J. H. Reynolds. It illuminated his character and his career, and gave a lively, authentic impression of his family. It began in 1808, when he was still a pupil at St Paul's School, London; it ended in 1815, when he was a published author, and within a few months of meeting Keats. All the letters, from Reynolds and his parents, were addressed to John Freeman Milward Dovaston: a former pupil of Mr Reynolds who became, for a while, a close family friend. They are published now as a contribution to Keats studies.

Thomas Reynolds was a tanner in Tottenham. On 3 April 1733 his son, Noble Reynolds, was bound apprentice to a barber, and his fee of £5 was paid 'out of the public charity of the said parish.'[1] After a seven-years' apprenticeship, Noble was admitted to the freedom of the Barbers' Company; but he did not prosper, and he was not elected to the Livery of the Company for another twenty-four years. His circumstances had not, however, prevented his marriage—indeed he married twice. On 2 June 1761, at Samuel Pepys's church, St Olave's, Hart Street, he married his second wife, Susannah Beardsell. On 7 January 1765, their only son, George, was born; and on 20 January he was baptised in the same church. Noble Reynolds, who was a Freeman of the City of London, seems to have died, impoverished, in the 1770s. His son was educated at Christ's Hospital as a charity pupil from 1774 to 1779; and when, in 1781, the Court of the Barbers' Company allocated the Michael Tans charitable legacy to 'a poor Liveryman's widow,' they chose to give it to Susannah Reynolds.

We do not know what George Reynolds did when he left school at the age of fourteen; but within the next few years he had probably taken up the profession which he was to pursue for the rest of his life. He was no doubt a schoolmaster when, on his twenty-fifth birthday, 7 January 1790, at St Marylebone Parish Church, he embarked on his long and happy marriage. *The Gentleman's Magazine* was to list it among the Marriages of Considerable Persons: 'Mr Reynolds, of Wandsworth, Surrey, to Miss Charlotte Cox, of Mary-la-Bonne.'[2]

It was in some ways a surprising match. The former charity boy married a woman four years his senior. Charlotte Cox had been born on 5 November 1761. She seems to have had more sparkle and originality than her husband; one suspects that she also had the stronger character. They had, however, entire respect and affection for one another. When he was away for a fortnight she felt 'widowed'; when she left him, briefly, he pined 'like a lonely turtle.' For fifty-eight years, until her death, they were singularly content.[3]

Their contentment was all the more remarkable since Mrs Reynolds came from a much superior social background. She was a distant relation of the Coxes of Dunmanway, and thus of Sir Richard Cox (1650–1733) who had been Lord Chancellor of Ireland. One of the Coxes had married a Jane Hamilton, closely related to the Earls of Abercorn. Maria, daughter of the Hon George Hamilton, was the mother of William Beckford, who was the author of *Vathek*, the builder of Fonthill, and—so it was said—the richest commoner in England. William Beckford's cousin, Peter Beckford, was a scholar, and a classic writer on hunting and travel. Charlotte Reynolds showed her pride in her ancestry when she came to choose names for her children.[4]

The first of these, Jane, was born in London on 6 November 1791, and christened at St Marylebone Parish Church. Some time after her birth, the family moved to Shrewsbury, where Mr Reynolds taught at Shrewsbury School; and in that historic town his only son was born on 9 September 1794, and christened—to please his mother—John Hamilton Reynolds. Three other daughters were born in Shrewsbury: Marianne in 1797, Eliza Beckford in 1799, and Charlotte in 1802. In September 1798, when the Rev Samuel Butler became headmaster of Shrewsbury School, George Reynolds became the writing master, at a salary of £11 a year. When Eliza was baptised at St Mary's on 20 November 1799, his address was given as Castle Street. In 1802 he was described as 'School Master.'[5]

John Hamilton Reynolds spent much of his childhood in Shrewsbury: a town, he observed, 'proverbial for the pride and arrogance of its inhabitants, and for the excellence of its cakes.'[6] In 1803, when he was only seven, he entered Shrewsbury School. Like Peter Corcoran, the hero of his future work, *The Fancy*, he was 'permitted, at a very early age, to mingle with the world in little,—to tear grammars, break bounds, and pilfer orchards: to fight nearly as soon as he could walk,—and to swear almost as soon as he could speak. He has often given a lively history of his labours and adventures, as the boy-servant of an elder boy; . . . [and] how he escaped on a fine moonlight midnight to steal trout, or bathe in the chill and rapid stream of the Severn.'[7] Years later, he recalled these years with affection and regret:

I remember well the time,—the sweet school-boy time,—
  When all was careless thought with me, and summer was
    my sleep;
I wish I could recal[l] that schoolboy day of prime,
  For manhood is a sorry thing—and mine is plunged deep
    In faults that bid me weep . . .[8]

No doubt he would have liked to spend all his childhood and youth at Shrewsbury; but at midsummer 1805—driven, perhaps, by the expense of his large family—Mr Reynolds left his post at the school. Early in 1806 the Reynoldses moved to London, and settled in Lambeth, where Mr Reynolds became master of the Lambeth Boys' Parochial School, and writing master to the Female Asylum. In Lambeth the family stayed for the next few years—perhaps as late as 1816.

George Reynolds had high ambitions for his only son. On 4 March 1808, at the age of eleven, the boy was admitted to St Paul's School. Mr Reynolds himself earned his livelihood in a less exalted academic sphere. He was an early advocate of the Bell system of education, which had then become popular in

England. In 1807 Lord Radstock, an admirer of the system, suggested to the Archbishop of Canterbury that he should establish a school for two hundred boys in Lambeth; and soon after March 1807 Dr Andrew Bell moved to Lambeth to organize the institution. In this parish, as Robert Southey wrote, 'Dr Bell's labours were well seconded in every respect. With the master of the school, Mr Reynolds, he was particularly pleased, and used to allude to him as a memorable exception to the general run of schoolmasters.'[9] At about the same time the system was introduced into the Female Asylum at Lambeth; and in 1808 Dr Bell was appointed 'perpetual guardian' of the institution, so that he might have every facility to carry out his plans.

Mr Reynolds's labours in Lambeth did not exhaust all his energies. In 1809 he published *The Simple Rules of Arithmetic, in Questions and Answers, . . . on Dr Bell's Plan.* In 1810 he became an usher in the writing school at Christ's Hospital. He held the position until he was elected writing master in May 1817. He was a dedicated teacher; and, since he had a wife and five children to support, it is not surprising that he held more than one appointment. He still remained master to the Female Asylum, Lambeth, after his appointment to Christ's Hospital. He continued to publish school books, all of them on arithmetic except *The Madras School Grammar*, which appeared in 1813. On 9 July 1822 he was appointed master of the writing and arithmetic schools at Christ's Hospital. He remained a master there until March 1835, when he retired on a pension.

The move to London had not broken all the Reynolds's links with Shrewsbury. One of the strongest was their friendship with John Freeman Milward Dovaston. He was the only son of John Dovaston of West Felton, near Shrewsbury. The Dovastons came of good yeoman stock, they were not landed gentry, but the estate had been in the family since the reign of Queen Elizabeth. It had been 'almost swallowed up by mortgages and incumbrances,'[10] but Dovaston senior had redeemed them by two fruitful voyages to the West Indies, where he had developed a sugar plantation; he had secured his fortune by constant prudence and industry. In his youth he had been a close friend of the poet William Shenstone. Largely self-taught, he had become a scholar, bibliophile and inventor, and an inspired landscape gardener. He had built up his estate as a prosperous tree-nursery, and The Nursery became its name. He was a man of natural distinction, and he was determined that his son should enjoy the advantages which he himself had been denied. John

4

Freeman Milward Dovaston was born on 30 December 1782, and educated at Oswestry Grammar School before he entered Shrewsbury School on 1 October 1798. A pupil of George Reynolds, he later won an exhibition to Christ Church, Oxford; he graduated in 1804, and took his M.A. in 1807. On 12 June that year he was called to the Bar at the Middle Temple; and while he was living in London he became for a while drama critic for a morning paper. In 1808 his father died, and Dovaston inherited the family estate. For a time he still practised as a barrister; but henceforward he spent most of his life in country pursuits and in literary retirement.[11] It is clear that he had always wanted to do so.

> The bustle of the Bar . . .
> For thee I left,
> Sweet mountain Muse, daughter of Liberty.
> For thee I've borne
> The proud world's scorn;
> Reproach by Friendship thrown;
> And ev'n the tenderest Father's frown
> I've borne for thee . . .[12]

The Gentleman's Magazine was later to recall his way of life and character:

By the death of his father in 1808, he became possessed of an easy competency, and the small patrimonial estate at West-felton, where his progenitors had resided from the time of Queen Elizabeth. There, by judicious care and planting, he contributed greatly to improve the grounds surrounding his residence . . .

As an ardent admirer of Shakespeare, . . . he could readily quote with feeling and emotion most of the bright creations and beautiful images with which his productions abound.

Mr Dovaston was a gentleman of considerable learning and varied acquirements; his mind could diffuse itself in ample generalizations on most subjects of polite and ancient literature; his familiarity with the classics was vivid and correct. In the sciences of botany and ornithology he had considerable skill, and in music he evinced much critical taste, both in theory and practice. He was well versed in ancient book lore; to which his select and voluminous library gave full testimony.

In his mid-day of vigour and health he had an almost unlimited fund of discourse on all matters, seasoned with lively wit and humour, and his versatility in anecdotes and facetious stories, which were expressively told in a manner peculiar to himself, rendered his company very amusing and instructive. His political sympathies coincided with what is called the liberal party . . . In private life he exercised an honest and independent spirit, combined with a warmth of feeling and uprightness of intention. Contented in the retirement of his groves, and happy among his books and rural employments, 'home' was always a paradise to him.[13]

Dovaston was genuinely fond of the Reynolds family. His old schoolmaster remained attached to him. Mrs Reynolds delighted in his friendship, and there was a touching—sometimes excess-ive—eagerness about her correspondence. Despite the fact that Mr Reynolds was himself a teacher, the family welcomed Dovaston's counsel. As for John Hamilton Reynolds, Dovaston was twelve years his senior; he seemed an elder brother and a respected mentor. Reynolds hero-worshipped this pupil of his father's who took a condescending interest in him. He accepted Dovaston's advice about his reading and career; he eagerly reported his successes to him. At school, in Lambeth, and in the dingy offices where he was obliged to earn his living, he dreamed of his visits to The Nursery, of the elegant country life which Dovaston led, the literary conversations they indulged in, the annual Breidden Festival which Dovaston's father had estab-lished, when wine was drunk and poetry was read on Breidden Hill.

The letters which follow were written from the heart. They reveal the Reynolds family, which Keats and Thomas Hood were to know so well. Above all, they present John Hamilton Reynolds, whom Keats was to consider 'as a brother.' They present the poet of much talent who was flawed by nature. They show the eager, affectionate youth who was to be a disappointed man; they show the admiring friend of Dovaston whose enduring title to fame was that he became the friend of Keats.

I have in general kept the original text of the correspondence, but for the sake of clarity I have put the known or probable date of writing at the beginning of each letter. I have not corrected idiosyncratic spellings, but I have corrected mis-spellings and mistaken omissions. I have indicated illegible words, gaps in the text, or editorial supplements by square brackets. Numerals refer to the notes at the end of the book.

I am most grateful to the Council of The Royal Society of Literature, who generously agreed to publish this correspondence under the terms of the Dr Richards Trust. I am particularly glad to thank the Hon C. M. Woodhouse for his help with Greek and Latin references; Mr John Grey Murray, for advice on Byron matters; and Mr J. C. Trewin, for enlightening me on obscure points in theatrical history. I am much indebted to Mrs M. Halford, the Shropshire County Archivist, who first introduced me to these letters, and has given me continued help. I am happy to record my gratitude to Mr W. Brian Dovaston, who has allowed me to publish this correspondence. I much appreciate the kindness of Mrs G. D. Messell, great-great-granddaughter of George and Charlotte Reynolds, who has sent me notes on her family and, once again, let me reproduce Mrs Reynold's portrait. I must thank the Trustees of the National Portrait Gallery for permission to use the miniature of J. H. Reynolds; the Director of Libraries and Arts of the London Borough of Camden, for letting me reproduce the Reynolds silhouette; and the Chief Librarian and Local Studies Librarian of the City of Newcastle, who enabled me to use the silhouette of J. F. M. Dovaston.

JOANNA RICHARDSON

LETTERS FROM LAMBETH

From Mrs Reynolds

By my George's particular desire, & your request my good
friend, I undertake the pleasing task of answering your kind
letter—many a one would feel dismay'd in addressing you who
are so clever a fellow, dreading your criticism, I have no fears of
this kind knowing any thing I may write is wholly inferior
further notice than it informs you we are all well, & happy to
hear from you.[1]—the account you give of your father is not so
well as I wish it were, these cold cutting winds are much against
him, as they particularly affect the spirits—you should get him
now & then to drink a little mull'd Red Port, also a glass of *warm
Mountain*,[2] which is a very nourishing thing—one glass of
warm wine will have more effect than three cold.—made wine
will not serve him, what little he takes, should be real generous
good wine.—Calves foot Jelly, strong broths with the full juice
of the Meat boild into it would befriend him, & in all probability
with Gods help carry him thro' the remainder of this Month &
the whole of the next, then the Summer will do all the rest for
him I admire your zealous affection, & anxious care for this your
good Father, believe me in this age of dissipation & frivolity it is
rather uncommon.—I am at once pleas'd & oblig'd by your
sound advice, & judicious hints to Jane[3] as to her Music, she
was gradually falling from Hook,[4] & I think would have relin-
quishd him entirely but happily you sounded an alarm, &
Ma'am Jane turnd back to those very useful lessons. She
improves, but combats too many things at a time, she has
emptied her little purse of it's whole store, in the purchase of a
set of Scotch Songs, chiefly Allen Ramsey's, & Robert Burns,[5]
some I know are good, the rest waits your decision, I think they
cost her 12s, whether worth it or not I am not a judge. She
spends much of her time over Nicoli[6] which I know you dislike,
yet they have brought her on, she plays with rather more freedom.—John his Father & Mother are pleas'd at your expressing
a desire to interfere in his improvement & in offering to recommend him Books you think may be to his advancement, his
Father as far as he can, will ever be ready to let him have what
you advise the more eagerly, as the boy has that love for you, that
high Opinion of your knowledge, learning, & sense, he looks

up to you as an Oracle, & would do that with pleasure under your sanction, which would be labour to him administerd by any other Person. Mr R., Jane, John, and the noble Mary,[7] are gone to the Sanspariel[8] with orders, they regretted you were absent.—and now for a little news—by the time you visit London we expect to be in another House, the wiseacres after calling two or three Meeting's merely to call other meetings—at the last came to the resolusition [*sic*] to pull down all the Premises & erect us a new good House as well as Schoolroom,[9] which as soon as possible will be carried into effect—at present we have not met with any thing suitable. I fear for a time we shall feel much inconvenience, but whether a Palace or a Nutshell we shall be glad to see you.—the plan of our future dwelling is handsome & an exceeding good House, much better than the present one—if my family avoid suffering in health I shall be perfectly easy as to all the rest.—I who have been the Shuttlecock of that deceitful hag Dame fortune for so many years am not to be alarm'd at the fatigue & bustle of a moveing or such triffles, tho hang her I had rather remain quiet in this snug retird Comfortable apartment, if the Hussey would have permitted the triffling indulgence.—the rolling stone they say never gathers Moss—I think we verify the saying.—

Heaven defend us, what a Journey you had down to Shropshire, your dangers & difficulties were as [page torn] as a voyage to the East Indies.[10]—the Man you [page torn] Piccadilly was not killd, at least so say's the [page torn] how happy you must have felt when your foot press'd [page torn] fathers welcome threshold, after suffering the tedium & vexations of so wretched a peregrination. —With such a Father, a choice collection of Books, Music, & withal a delightful spot, both pleasant & useful to live on who would not be happy, on reflection I fear there are many who *would* not, shame on them. I thank God you are not to be rank'd with such wretches, & may your good sense still direct you to continue content with so desirable (I had like to have said so enviable) a lot. We have met with the words to Pinkey house, they are unworthy the Music, write some yourself, you who can so feelingly express the notes, could not fail to suit the words to the tune.[11]—I think my dear George misses your society & Music very much—sometimes I think he had reason to rejoice at your appearance as your wit, Play, anecdote, &c &c quell'd my inharmonious chatter, which to be sure for a continuance must be insufferably tiresome I acknowledge. My valued Mother[12] quitted here last night she is well & sends you her compliments—if I were to write all my dear

Children say of, & to you, it would fill a volume, their little happy countenances will speak more when they see you than my tir'd pen can express.—G. R. God bless him is well, but a little harrass'd with Business. I just the same as you left me in every respect. You are therefore well assur'd I in truth subscribe myself

your friend
CHARLOTTE REYNOLDS.
March 9th 1808.

Whoever corresponds with me must take all my faults as they stand I never waste time with excuses. I have written with the wind blowing about my head like thunder of which I am so naturally timid & so disorderd with, oweing to the unfortunate Nervous state of my health, that if my dear family are long before they return I shall be quite overcome by apprehension for their safety—tis a pity I am so great a fool, but *nature has been bountiful to me in this respect.*—all arrivd safe & well & the Sanspariel approvd of—Mr R. unites [with] me in compliments to your good father.

the Cakes came safe,[13] receipt & all proper & I thank your attention—

J. M. Dovaston Esq[r].
Nursery—
near Shrewsbury—
Salop—

2

From Mrs Reynolds

April 21st 1808

You would have heard from M[r] R. or myself my worthy friend sooner, but for his Business, and my sad unfortunate health with which I have been so afflicted these last five weeks as to render it doubtful whether I should recover.[1] I should not now attempt to write altho exceedingly better, but that M[r] R. returned from read[g] the papers on Friday night last, & brought home the painful intelligence of your loss,[2] which in truth affected me much—I confess I was not surprised, as I look'd for the affecting event from March till May [*sic*], your account of your poor Fathers ailments were such as to leave small hopes of him—but I will not dwell long on this melancholy subject, further than to say, I pity, I feel for you—but beg you to reflect that your loss is not from premature Death but according to the common course of humanity, your Father liv'd to a good old age, in the full action of his faculties, & to see you his only Child, by his kind attentions & labours, capable of passing your remaining days an honor to his life, & a credit to his Memory—which thoughts must I am sure have comforted & consol'd you both in this awful & solemn seperation.—Whenever you are inclin'd to indulge the sad reflection of your departed friend, & Father, which I know will now & then be the case—rouse directly from the pleasing Dream & seek employment of any rational sort to divert y^r melancholy, for what so trying to health as the indulgence of low Spirits.—I think I take a liberty in so freely advising you who are so capable of acting, but I mean it well & for your good, and need add no further admonitions, save these few words—*use your own good abilities properly*, & you will be more benefited than pages of my unmeaning stupid Opinions can possibly effect.—

I receiv'd your last sensible letter but was too ill to answer it—M^r R—never will write if he can by any means avoid it—we—I mean myself & bratlings have been teazing him these five days to write you, but he put if off till he provok'd me to torment you. Johns examin[ation] is on Monday,[3] he has offer'd up his prayers devoutly for your arrival, I fancy a little selfishly.—a little help was his hope, but it is better he should fight his way—poor fellow he is excessive fond of you without dispute & longs ardently for your return—I believe we shall all be made happy to see you, G. R. will I am sure.—Your Pinkey house is just the thing, you are certainly not a fool.—We are in our fresh habitation, situated opposite the Asylum late Williams's Auction Room which makes an excellent Schoolroom, the House is too small to be comfortable. Our old mansion is nearly raz'd to the ground. I have not seen the spot since I quitted it, when able to walk out I shall go that way to deplore my favorite home.—This is Childish, is it not, but you knew me before to-day & need not this fresh instance of proof.—

When you come to Town bring a four & sixpenny box of Shrewsbury Cakes & I will pay you again.—let us hear from you immediately & say when we are likely to see you & direct for us as above—Father & Jane are at Astley's.[4] I begin to get tir'd of waiting their return. John was not well enough to go with them[5] —I remember you told me you hated rem[em]brances in a letter, now what am I to do, I have the full injunctions of a good husband & five dear Children to send their affectionate & kind regards to you [.] I therefore beg to torment you with the afore-said Loves of the dear group just mentiond.—Jane is learning Handal's water peice[6]—we cannot get her to grace her music,[7] but I suppose that will fall of course after a time—she is going to have Handals Overture to, to [*sic*] I really do not know what. When she gets it you will know. I can only tell you that to my mind there is a glorious March in it, by this very *clear* account, perhaps you will know what I wish you concerning it.[8]—I am afraid the weather is dreadfully gloomy in the Country, a jaunt to London or some chearful spot would be to your Benefit. We are all solicitous to know whether we shall see more or less of you than hitherto—it will be no small privation to G. R. if you dis-continue your visits that usualy you have been accustomd to pay.—I can only assure you that whatever your future plans may be you will whenever agreeable to yourself be kindly received by G. Reynolds & your sincere friend

C. REYNOLDS.[9]

I have just heard from my dear Mother at Bristol who names you kindly—
John Dovaston Esq[r.]
The Nursery
near Shrewsbury
Salop.

George Reynolds
From an anonymous sketch

Mrs George Reynolds
From the portrait by William Hilton

3

From Mr and Mrs Reynolds

[9 June 1808]

D.ʳ Dovaston—

Naturally supposing you will think it strange that I never write to you—especially you will say—Whitsuntide—Holidays? the only excuse I can make—which is a lame one—my time much occupied with business—and *when* at leisure a great proportion of indolence—and that indolence arises from the indulgence of Mrs R.—who generally and readily writes for me and moreover 'she is a judge' of these matters—I have the pleasure to inform you that upon the whole She is much better than she has been for some time past—thro' taking the Extract of Iceland Moss—an excellent remedy for the Lungs[1]—Jane perseveres at her music and endeavors to profit from your valuable hints. I have lately bought her two Overtures—Ella Rosenberg and the Widow's Choice—also Shenkin—arranged for the Piano[2]—John has been very unwell for some time a bad Cold and obliged to stop from School—indeed all the family have been ill—with sore Throats &c.—our present Situation being so very confined—it does not agree with any of us—We hope to be out of here at Michaelmas as our building goes on very well—they having started the School Room and nearly erected the brick work of the house—the Elevation of the buildings here roughly sketch[ed]—

18

House in front is 23 feet—School 60 feet by 50—10 feet Garden whole length.[3]

Dr. Bell[4] visits us frequently—he has printed a large octavo Edition of his Analysis price 10/6 and changed the title to 'Elements of Tuition'[5]—He sent me one, with the following written by him in the first blankleaf—'To Mr Geo. Reynolds, Master of Lambeth School, in grateful acknowledgement of his Faithful, Able and Willing Services in the Cause of Education and religious Instruction on the Madras System from the Author.' He also mentions me in a printed note as follow[s]: 'Of which there is a memorable example in the Boys Charity School at Lambeth, where Mr Reynolds the Schoolmaster, found and made no difficulty but carried every instruction into immediate effect with equal ease and success'—I have just had an intimation (fortunate enough) that I must leave a space for other matters than dwelling on & quoting my own merits—its well— or I should have proceeded—however I must express a regret that I cannot possibly accept your kind offer of visiting Salop this Year—and very sorry that you have declined coming to London —be assured, you are highly esteemed in our Circle

    Yours sincerely
    GEO. REYNOLDS.
9$\underline{^{th}}$ June 1808.

G. Reynolds has said so much that little more can be said by his *better* half—however you, our friend Dov who know what a busybody I am will not be surpriz'd that I shall muster a few words in addition. Thanks for your last delightful letter—If I could write as you do, I would break forth on the world with something clever, & tis a pity you do not. There was a promise when you left London that you would collect some of your juvenile productions & send them to me—also a canzonet for Jane—wrap them in a sheet of brown paper & send them by the Coach I will cheerfully pay carriage—& write one of your sensible letters to tell when we shall have them.—John with his Mother is pleas'd & thanks you for your kind invitation but must defer it till next year.—he is distracted to be with you & [has] been very ingeneous in contrivances How to effect it but poor fellow he must have patience. We all much & truly regret that you will not come to London so frequent as you use'd. but whenever you do we shall heartily receive you, George & myself really like you well, because our Children love you.—how do you go on in the Organ way but I have not the least doubt your music will tell to your credit—I think Jane comes on, she seems to gain ground in the scientific part considering the small time she has been at it. Her Father has purchas'd her Busby's Musical Dictionary.[6] I believe a very useful Book. as you are not coming up the cakes are of no consequence—I shall not want them.— Your friend

CHARLOTTE REYNOLDS.

Jane beg[s] you not to forget your prose tales for her[7]—see postmans bell
J. M. Dovaston Esq.
The Nursery
Near Shrewsbury
Salop.

4

From Mrs Reynolds

August 24th 1808.

Dear Dov,

Illness has been the cause of our silence to you.—John our Dear John has been an Invalid above these two Months but [he is] now thank God on the return to his former self.[1] your kind letter to him has been an endless source of pleasure to him but we would not suffer him to attempt an answer till restord to his health—I cannot find a name for his complaints—first he had an attack in his Bowels, which was follow'd up by a vile cough so that every friend thought it must have finish'd him, added to which, he grew so fast, & so thin, that we were wretched to see him—not a bit of poor Jack remaind, not even his spirits, save his good heart. As soon as possible we sent him out of Town, where we find he is getting the better of all his cares. I am distressd to think he will lose full a quarters improvements in his Education but we were told we should lose him if he sustaind fatigue of any kind, so we gladly yeilded all advantages to benefit him in so serious a matter. Your letter will on his return home be I know a first concern.—I am happy you have had so agreeable a friend in the room of John. I fancy it is this same friend who has inserted in the Gentlemans Mag. your sweet lines of the sprig of Yew, from the Leasowes[2]—to tell you I think you a shab perhaps may provoke you, but as you knew C.B. before today & also know she will now & then say what she thinks—I repeat you are a shabby elf in not sending the Canzonet which you were to have sent to Jane—as to your excuses of want of ability, say no more, any other plea would have done better—your pleasing notes have been play'd over with all the Spirit Jane is Mistress of, & she approves & thanks you.—your prognostics as to my health were but too well founded, I have not been expected to come about again, but I have that true British spirit in me that brings me through in spite of the teeth of Death.—You give such a delightful description of your favord spot that it almost makes me envious, yet I dont think this vice belongs to me. I feel quite an appetite when you talk of your ale & Beef &c. &c.—I hope my *worst* half will some day come & scrape a trencher with you perhaps he & John may next year pay you a visit. The Boy is fond of you, I really believe sincerely so, & delights in talking of you—in one of your letters you say 'surely this spot was never meant for me alone' or words nearly to this effect.—I who am touch paper to every hint directly have concluded that some happy *she* is fix'd on to partake all your cares & comforts and as it is rather a natural conclusion excuse it accordingly only do let me put up one prayer in your favor—take care to make choice of a Lady of sense—for Gods sake avoid forming a conexion with a weak Woman. I have had one friend sacrific'd at the shrine of foolish Beauty & heaven avert I shall ever see another lost in the same miserable vortex.—however as you, like the rest of your wise sex, can't at all times call yourselves your own Masters I beleive you must take your chance but I shall be in a bit of a rage if you forget your old friends.—and now let me ask you when you mean to see London, whenever you do take a jaunt make our house your home—George quite regrets your absence—I don't know how it is, but your very nonsense is agreeable to him. I wish you would come, never mind the apples they will grow as well without you as with you. I hope, & indeed have not a doubt all your crops are good. The weather has been very unusually hot, not to say insufferably so, I never remember such a Summer before.—I am rather at this crisis disturbd in my cogitations, oweing to the sweet chaunts of my husband's Cherubims, who are most melodeously piping the Evening Hymn. Of course we shall soon have him up to Tea.—I am no Politician or should be telling you a multitude of News—

of the Spaniards drubbing the French &c. &c. but I leave these Matters to wiser heads than mine. I can only be glad in my heart that a check has been put on the hungry French[3]—I forgot nearly to tell you we have chang'd our Piano for one with additional keys which you will not be sorry to hear, we found it necessary for the Childs advantage. She has been to Mr Princes two or three times to play on his Organ & since then has playd on the Organ in a *Public Room.* 'Now you talk of Organs,' as your friend used to say, how does your neighbour succeed in his invention, & how does your new tune tell. We shall hear all about it some day—how came the Man to think of such a thing. I fancy you have suggested the Idea to him first, nay I even suspect you have been his instructor & have allowd him the Credit. I read in the Mag an account of your Father which afforded me pleasure.[4] I there learn'd many things respecting him which you modesty withheld but which your heart might be proud to boast. —My dear Mother is returnd from Bristol, is well, & ask'd particularly after you, I gave her the Character you deserve. She sends comp^{ts}. Our Children are well, I think you like them which is the cause I note them, indeed I beleive this is another reason and a very powerful one—that I love them so myself. I should not feel happy if I did not notice them to you, I scarce ever write a letter but they are brought in, in some way, however extreme [?], but you know 'Dame Reynolds' is an oldfashiond creature, firm in Love to her family, & her attachment to her friends & these very sentiments render her doubly so, as there is little stability in this age, but in charity & mercy to your long tried patience through this incorrigible Mass of stupidity I conclude with the warmest wishes of George & Charlotte for your happiness & health to enjoy those Blessings the almighty has so abundantly poured on your fortunate head, with the addition of the remembrances of us all I remain

    Your friend sincerely
    CHARLOTTE REYNOLDS.

George is pleas'd I have written at last to you, & so will poor Jack [be] as he teaz'd me all through his illness.

    Our house is not yet finishd but very near, then you must come. I wish you had been nearer to have had Jack with *you.*

    Jane begs you will get Calcots song 'When Mighty Mars'[5] if you know how, we would send it to you, she likes it.[6]

5

From Mrs Reynolds

[11 September, 1808]

This Day [Sunday] the 11th, I had fix'd to write to Dovaston, &
certainly will—God willing—fulfill the pleasure I had promis'd
myself. Unluckily I laid hands on a volume of Don Quixote, &
was so completely enjoying the Governorship of Sanco Panza
that I had like to have broken the above resolve,[1] I shall like
Sancho use a proverb that suits my purpose & begin with 'better
late than never'—for your hare so kindly sent I acknowledge Mr
R. & myself pleas'd & oblig'd, the Stuffing was excellent—Jane
relish'd it exceedingly, & had *play'd* her part well, & from all
accounts, I have led myself to believe that yours is a delightful
favord spot of earth—from the proofs I repeatedly receive I shall
begin to suspect it fairy land—first the Master, unlike the
Youths of the present Day, is a Man of Genius & many acquirements. Then Your Grounds are dispos'd with taste & Judgment,
your friends social, what can Man desire more—nothing—& I
believe you to be satisfied, which is above riches.—your Geese
are Poetical, your Hares are Musical, now is not this enough to
give us a high Idea of the Nursery.—I shall never see Shropshire
again, but hope George, or Boy Jack may.—Jane wrote your kind
expressions contain'd in your kind letter to him, he sends you
his '*kind best* love, that he is better, & hopes a time will come
when he will have the REAL HAPPINESS of seeing Dovaston.'
—This is exactly his words . . . he goes out Coursing, & shooting, & by his account, enters into all the Country sports but you
know he is a Lad of Spirit.—Your Music we admire—Jane, in
the best manner she can, plays it to us. The first is a tasty thing
—the next so [?] I don't know whether to say I like the notes you
speak of, added or not, but this much I do know that I delight in
the base, 'Lady all that live must die.'—Your account of Chester
Circuit is admirable, your interview delightful, & your return
Home, heart-whole, glorious, but in the name of wonder how
could you set it down so certain that I am not an admirer of
Beauty beleive me Master Dov you are in an error here, as I am
one that delighteth in it very much—but I don't like a fool.
Beauty & folly does not always go together thank Heaven—I
hope but seldom—however God preserve you from the latter &

send if ever you do wear the pleasing chain you may, like my George & myself, be able to say on the eve of the *ninteenth* year, you are happier than on the morn of the first.—Amen.—I like your Barrister Circuit better than the Chester one & daresay you was well amus'd. I have not seen him perform for many years but I know he is admir'd.—and now for that part of your letter which relates to your visiting London—George bids me say he shall feel particularly happy to see you, & is glad that you pay us the pleasing compliment to avow that it is in friendship to himself & family if you shall come at all. I am petition'd by the whole group to bid you come soon. George hopes you will make the next term (which is close at hand) the time of your excursion. I shall then begin to expect to see your snub poked in some day while we are settling round our fireside but sooner if you like it. The motive of this hurried letter is to thank you for the Hare & to say we admire the Notes—& to urge your quitting the Lasses & the Parsons & come away—I think there is less danger in the society of the former than the latter—there is a good deal of Mischief in some Parsons—a few agreeable clever Women will ever benefit those who associate with them—they give a Man a polish, soften his Manners & inform his Mind.—so much for *Church* & *State*. In my last I wrote to you that Jane had play'd on an Organ in a public Room.—there, did I expect you would be in a dreadful wonderment as to where, & how, & ask Me a Million of questions relating thereto—oh deuce take your want of curiosity—you defeated me in my plans intirely.—I meant to have taken you in bless you, & you would not let me, but I will be even with you.—George had not any paper in the House but foolscap, so that I am compell'd to pother your brains with more nonsense than there really is occasion for, to fill it up, but this is not the first foolscap my Head has fill'd by many.

The end of next week or the beginning of the week following we move to our comfortable new House where we hope to see you soon. Jack's heart will be 'light as thistledown' when he learns you have wisely resolv'd to jaunt it to this dearly belov'd place—London—tho the silly fellow prefers the Country. I dare say when you see my bratlings again you will perceive them much grown—to me they seem infinitely taller, but in my eyes they are ever improving, I am too partial, & too blind to their little defects—I will just tell you in what manner I am writing. Jane is reading the book I laid down when I began this letter—the consequence is that she every now & then breaks forth into such noisy laughter that I am in doubt whether she may not be a little beside herself—Eliza & Charlotte are in full speed after the Cat with a ball & Marianne[2] tormented with a vile cold which is attended with a perpetual sneezing. I leave you to judge with such a confusion of sounds what state this flimsy brain must be in for writing—Longer I could not defer it for the reasons above named such as moving &c. &c. George desired I would take it on me as he would not for some time be able—perhaps you will not hear again till we see you (tho I believe this is a bit of a Bull) however *I will take care* You shall hear them, unless unless [*sic*] it shall please God to afflict You with Deafness.—the day has been unusually Wet, I scarce ever saw so heavy a rain—but yet there are many People walking about, & a few Gigs—this afternoon we saw three people neatly canted into the Mud out of one of these ill contriv'd carriages.[3]—As the sun is too far gone to 'light your pipe' now—I very liberally contribute my lot of spills, by begging you to use this paper, twist it up ready for the purpose, & as Georges name is contain'd herein, then you & he will be smoking together, & *I* not the Sun giving spirit to the flame.—I had very near put the Sun out you see God forgive me for it—& I beg you will forgive me for the interruption this is to well spent time & believe my husband & self your friends, witness

CHARLOTTE REYNOLDS.

Sept.[r] 11th 1808, the 9th was John's birthday—14 years old. Write soon.[4]

6

From John Hamilton Reynolds
[23 September 1808.]

My dear Dovaston,
    It is a long time since I received your kind letter and I dare say you wonder at my silence but do not attribute it to Idleness but ill health. I have been really ill nor should I have recovered had it not been for the assistance of my kind friends in the country. I have been at Caldicott Hill[1] seven weeks which you know for me

25

is a long time but now I am perfectly well—You have no doubt heard of the dreadful fire at Covent Garden[2] I was there the morning it broke out and it was horrible to see them carry the dead bodies to S[t] Paul's, the women screaming one had lost a Husband another a brother such a sight I *never* wish to see again. It was at first supposed that Johnstone who acts the Irish parts[3] was burnt but it proves some one else—

When I was in the country I met with a M[r] Lawrence of Offington (whether I spell it right or not I'm not sure)[4] you may have some knowledge of him he is a pleasant sort of man though not one of sound sense—I think your canzonett is a most beautiful one indeed we all delight to hear it. I am just as fond as ever of 'Oft on a Plot of rising ground' and I think Jane improves in it—Talking of music Ware has lost by this fire a violin worth 300 Guineas—I hope (indeed we all hope) you will not refuse us the pleasure of your company soon though one Theatre's down yet there is another—as you desire I'll write you all the news I shall pause a little and see what will happen—Well I have waited a little & what *little* I have gathered I will here write down—Not long after you left us 'Hecate' set sail in her sieve[5]—but having too much *ballast* in her, she did not get down stairs quite so *straight* as usual we suppose she *follow'd you*—I have had an uncommon pleasant time in the country what with coursing & shooting (not that I fir'd my self for that would have been too great a risk) we had one week nothing but rain which was rather uncomfortable—Oh Dovaston! I have read (since I was in the country) Ovid's Metamorphoses in english—they are indeed beautiful.[6] After you went I got a very good Sallust but I can't rightly understand it. Well at last we are in the new House and it certainly is a very good one but it will be better when you are in it and whenever you are disposed to come I shall be ready with the *bolsters* 'one under each arm.'

I think Winter begins to appear (for on looking out at window I see people pass in great coats) 'Sullen & Sad with all his rising train'[7]—well winter don't pass so heavy with us as with many we have all something to amuse not that I intend ever continuing my magazines or newspapers I must find something—I thank you, really thank you for the good advice you sent me in [your] letter I read [it] over & over again I shall [endeavour] to profit by it I think it is you that have made me so fond of reading in some measure—I don't doubt but you'll be heartily tir'd of your kind offer by reading this letter I don't suppose I shall ever be any great letter writer but no matter.

26

If you see any one that I knew remember me to them and with
love to yourself I remain
    your affectionate young friend
      J. H. REYNOLDS.
Septr 23rd 1808.

7

From Mrs Reynolds

[15 December, 1808]

D^r friend

About three hours ago your neat Box (& of course its contents) arriv'd safe at Lambeth Green & was most acceptable in
every sense, never was Goose better cloth'd outside, or stuff'd
within,[1] the Apples are delightful, & beautiful to look at as
well—The Apple I meant was a particular sort that Sarah Blakemore[2] spoke of, she told me it was a very hard kind—you gave
her two of them, so that you was worse than the Serpent, as you
tempted her twofold. Give me leave to remark, I think you *line* a
Box, better than you make one, not that I wish to offend your
ingenuity either way—still with all this kindness, your friendly
letter &c. &c. there is *still* wanting your promis'd visit—George
had provided a Barrel of (not home Brew'd) but of tolerable Ale,
to whet your Whistle, and so prepossess'd was I that you would
be here, I had a fire two days in your sleeping Room with a View
to give you a thorough warm reception. A plague on Briefs,
Sessions, Bankruptcy's, & all the attendant employments of the
Law, if a Man may not be allow'd time to undertake a Jolting for
a few Miles to see a group of friends who have been anxiously
waiting his arrival these six forlorn weeks.—I can only add on
this score that George, Myself Jane & John were completely
disappointed, the latter also drew a long face that his name was
not mention'd all through your letter, but I reminded him he
had not answer'd your last which quieted the Gentleman, you
may expect to hear from [him] in his hollidays, which are at
hand. I give you credit for your Epilogue, it was well hit off & I
have not the least doubt but it was well receiv'd. A thing written

when in the mood, in a few Minutes, will frequently produce a happier effect than a labour'd production. We also admire the warmth with which you have defended 'the Bees' of your amiable friend D.ᴸ Evans,³ you seem to favor the Critic's as kindly as old Dame Reynolds.⁴ Many think these reptiles prevent the publishing a profundity of Ignorance. I think contrary—a sensible & feeling mind from dread of their lash, may be prevented becoming an author—but the Nonsensical race have not the minds to be affected by their sarcasms; & write on in spite of all their efforts to prevent them.—'Mighty Mars' you shall have, if we cannot get it, Jane shall write it. I have a great liking to it, & don't say you dislike it, as it will lower myself to myself, there's for you. Don't you admire the elegance of my expression. I shall very soon find an opportunity to send it to Shrewsbury. Now we name Shrewsbury, pray is old Mʳ Nelson⁵ alive I used to think him an intelligent old Gentleman. I wish I could say as much for my own writing heaven preserve you who have to make it out, for it is more than I can do. There is an old Story of a Cochnit writer—not that I know what such a person is.⁶—he was employ'd to write in some public office—which writing, when the clerk was call'd on to read he could not make a word of it and in consequence, the Man was sent for to read his *own* writing— after puzzling some time with the same success the Clerk had had he deliver'd him the paper back with this answer: 'I am Cochnit writer—not Cochnit reader.'—You must not ever look for news in my letters. I go out so seldom that I seem to get quite stupid, neither is my Memory what it was. These misfortunes steal on us by degrees, a circumstance by no means desireable yet we should feel very awkward if old Age *pop'd* on us all of a Sudden, these are the little hints that keep the Mind awake as to what is to follow. I always wish'd, if I ever liv'd to be old, that I might be able to render myself agreeable to my friends, alas I fear I shall fall short in this, as I feel at times a little tedious to what I was wont, I can't like you, speak of not allowing my temper to be ruffled, I wish [words missing under seal] but I commend much that you can be [word illegible] what you are—I have just question'd G.R. if he has any thing to say to you, he bids me say he is disappointed much you did not come but still looks for you at no distant period.—pray will it be treason if I say I don't much admire Mʳ Parkes's Prologue,⁷ it wants fire, the very end, is the best of it tho'.—Your Ep—is a good thing I like it better than at first reading.⁸ To remember my family singly is as bad as calling over the Names of a Jury they therefore send affectionate regards in the Lump to you & promise faithfully to play their parts well on the produce of your plentiful Habitation for which I again thank you. I am too tir'd, & I am afraid too idle to add more tonight, & tomorrow shall not be able for reason's not necessary here.—take then our sincere best wishes for an agreeable Christmas, & be assur'd your health shall be drunk with due honors over Ma'am Goosey & her eccelent companions, 'farewell rem[em]ber' *we*[9]

CHARLOTTE REYNOLDS.

Decr 15th 1808.[10]

8

From John Hamilton Reynolds

Saturday D^ec 31st 1808.

My Dear Friend,

I felt myself sensibly hurt when I heard you had given up all thought of coming up to town till the middle of January, but I hope when that time comes you will hesitate no longer but pop yourself in the stage and you are here in a jiffy.—By the by I have got a curious bit of news for you I have won a prize in the School Magazine for writing an essay[1] but they have not printed it so that they have given it me for nothing I was quite surprized at it—I like your epilogue much better than Mr Parkes's I don't think his reads easy—Pray have you read this new poem called the 'Fisher Boy' that is spoken so well of—one of the reviews say[s] it is equal to the Farmer's Boy—I should very much like to read it.[2]

I was lately taken by Mr Edwards (my master)[3] to the Surry Institution[4] they have a very good library and they also take in the daily papers and Magazines and at night there are lectures upon the different Sciences I heard one upon Electricity which was both useful and amusing he has offered me a ticket when I chuse which I think good of him.

You spoke in your last of my being too young to read Sallust I hope I had not the impudence to say I could? for I know he is above my understanding. You also speak (though it is something odd to talk of Theatricals now) of a treat at the opera house

Father & Jane were there (& *'they paid for a seat though they stood'*) to see the new opera & were much pleased at the sound of the voices for they could not even see the down of their feathers—

—The 7th of January is near at hand—Father's birthday—Mama's wedding day[5]—'sure such a day was never seen'! Therefore on that day we expect to see you—and before that day I expect to hear from you do not be so Idle as I am it is a miserable thing—upon such strong calls as these you cannot deny—I have got a latin line which if you have not seen you think curious—*'malo, malo, malo, quam vivere, malo, malo,' an answer is desired*[6]—Jane desires me to tell you that she ask'd at all the music shops in London for 'Mighty Mars' and it is out of print but she has written it out for you and waits the first opportunity of sending it to you *we have no such convenient packing cases as geese & c.* or you would have it presently—To-day the first stone of Covent Garden Theatre is laid by the Prince of Wales[7] and fine crushing and squeezing there will be no doubt—When I look back in my letter talking of going to all the shops in London is like what in music you call a *swell*—I suppose down your way business has been rather at a stop on account of the inclemency of the weather it puts me in mind of your break trace journey—I hear you don't like the Farmer's Boy I'm sorry you and I are not of the same opinion for you must know it is a great favourite of mine—You desire me to *Hear Ovid* tell his own tale—you are right in Latin he is most sublime in english he is elegant I have been reading the tale of Daedalus' swo[o]n into a river I think it most beautiful—[8]

My Father and Mother desire to be kindly remembered to you and my mother is very much obliged to you for your patience in corresponding with me and shall be very happy to pay the post for an early letter[9] on the same occasion—I must tell you I've got Burns Poems I begin now to understand them and truly delight in them[10]

I remain your
affectionate friend

JOHN REYNOLDS.

Compliments of Season to you
Mother says my letter is not grave enough I suppose she would have me write the Gospel—

9

From John Hamilton Reynolds

[10 February 1809] (1)

My Dear Friend,

You (at this present time) are calling me all the names of idleness you can think of. I own I am one of the worst fellows ever existed at writing letters at the last moment I work hard I am just arriv'd from school 'Write to Dovaston' echoes in my ears the finest opportunity you ever had a better one can't be M[r] Cowper[1] is going down—so I sat myself down & scribbled off this with the consolation that it would not cost any thing—we are quits—You say I am a fine pleader but I think if all pleading was to turn out as useless as mine has it would be poor work for the law you give me a bad inducement by disregarding my arguments.

What think you I have not been to the Theatre since you were with us nor shall I this season I suppose O what a fine description of a Play you gave in your letter to my Father it was delightful I was all upon the itch to have been there, what a difference to one we acted at my cousins but like you our Scenes were painted on purpose (by the finest painters in town '*ourselves*') upon brown paper, all our dresses were equally elegant. Pizarro was the performance[2]—My Father is overpowered with business has now in the School about 400 boys (egad I had like to have put another o to it with my running on) who when you get your head into it instantly makes your pate dizzy. I wonder how my father bears it—I sincerely lament with you in the loss of your apples and in the number you had I suppose it is a serious one—I told you about a prize I obtained in the School Magazine you mistook it for one in my own School but I have got another since I last wrote to you, I am sure I little expected my essays would ever prove so good to me—

Pray have you heard any news about your part if you have let me know it, I wonder how the pompous head master of the Free School gets on[3]—

I think you live somewhere near the Leasowes which by a description I read of (written by Dodsley) gives me a fine idea of the place[4] I should wish to see it very much—I have observed Dovaston how many fires there are always at this time of the year whether it is the wood is drier or what I can't tell but as I know you to be something of a philosopher I hope you will inform me—All our family desire to be remembered to you, but as Mama is writing at the same time I have no other particular message, therefore with remembrances to all I know I have any regard for I remain—Your affectionate friend—

J. H. REYNOLDS.

Feb.ᵞ 10th 1809.

10

From Mrs Reynolds

[10 February 1809] (2)

Dᵣ Friend

By the desire of my Husband, & request of your worthy self, I undertake the pleasing task of answering your very kind letter to him, which letter delighted Him to the heart, & which I shall notice the contents of, before I enter on any Nonsenses of my own—first you need never desire G.R.—to call his brats about him when a letter arrives from you, for the instant it comes the family instinctively assemble with full joy to listen to it's contents, & always shew great satisfaction.—ah welladay, & so all the Apples are wasted, why my Child what have you been at, that such a loss has befallen you, this comes of gadding after heiresses, & the law, & the Lord knows what beside.—I am sorry for you, & for your Apples, & trust you will take better care next year—not but this Winter has been severe enough to have frozen Yourself, for I think I do not remember any thing so keen these many a day.—& so to add to your winter amusements you have been surcharg'd, so has George but has got off well,—this is but rogueish sort of work but we are compeld to endure it, & may as well be quiet.—I am well pleas'd with your Porkington account,[1] you must have had literally a feast, & almost fancied yourself on fairy land. I should have enjoy'd to have been there, but pshaw, what have old Ladies to do with such gay scenes as these, 'now I think of it they'd better go sleep'—Don't you admire the elegance of my simile I thank you for your Love to me & my bunch of Grapes, Jane says you are the Fox.—The

32

Music I beleive goes well, the Latin Do, the old witch, I think Jack informd you, set sail soon after you;[2] & John is going this minute to give you an answer to your letter. It is his half holiday & he avails himself of this opportunity, so much for the different heads contained in your letter.—Mr William Cooper calld here yesterday & will obligingly convey this to Shrewsbury—I have enclosd 'when Mighty Mars' & you must positively like it. He (Cooper) informd us you made a very respectable appearance in pleading at the Hall, he said you was engag'd in very difficult business, & acquitted yourself to the astonishment of the whole Court. We were not surprized but delighted to hear it.—& now for a bit of news for you—you are Married.—don't be surpriz'd.[3] I think I am the first who have told it you & I hope you are not astonishd at the intelligence.—Cooper said he had heard so, but my George stoutly contradicted it—as a report without foundation—We have had a long dissertation on you at our Dinner today Jane said you & Mr Cooper were very much alike, Eliza said no, for that you had a nice rosy Cheek, & a fat Chubby head, now whether you conceive this a compliment is out of my power to determine, but I believe it was meant as such—I expect to hear sad accounts as to the floods in yr Country—I should suppose you can scarce get to Shrews^y to make your appeal, or rather to answer to your surcharge—I had a letter from a friend at Bath, with whom I have corresponded at least five & twenty years—she gives me a most melancholy account of the Devastation made by the Waters in those parts, & many have been lost by the flood coming on in the Nig[ht] & in so rapid a manner as to carry all before it, indeed in our part every house has been inundated, but thank God not attended with such fatal consequences as the above account—the Winds have been tremendeous, & I verily beleive have puff'd away my senses as I am by no means fit to write a letter. But you who know of old what sort of scribe I am, will from your friendship overlook the many errors contained herein. George by right should take this office on him, but he has so very much to do that I am uneasy lest he may be overpowerd; he bids me say he is happy to hear from you at all times & finds the great[est] amusement in your animated letters.—John has just deliverd his very foolish lines to me to enclose for you. To say truth I am ashamd of them, he is rather too heedless—all that he does, is the moment it is thought of—when a little reflection, joind to his naturally good understanding, & ready wit, might render him a very pleasant correspondent.—His letter I shall enclose with the Song, & beg you to

33

contrive to call or send to Mrs Pryse on College Hill Shrewsbury,[4] to whom I have sent it—her house is directly at the back of the Fox Inn[5]—if she should have movd since she wrote to me the folks at the Fox can tell you where, as they are intimate.—I pity you sincerely that such a sensible intelligent fellow as you are, should have to wade through such a mass of Ignorance as I & Jack have furnishd you with—but if you *will* have to do with fools, you must bear with their folly, & Heaven bring you well through it—the affectionate regards of the whole group to you.—beleive my Husband & self truly interested in your well doing & happiness & rest assur'd I am

    your sincere friend
    CHARLOTTE REYNOLDS.

II

From Mrs Reynolds

[March–April 1809]

What my good friend can you think of me, & my family, in apparently neglecting to answer your last kind, sensible & ingeneous letter. I scarce have patience to explain the cause, I feel so hurt—Soon after my good George receiv'd yours (which afforded us so much entertainment) Cooper the once Coachmasters Son call'd at our House.—he very politely offer'd to convey either letter or parcel for us to Shropshire.—he said he should go in two or three days—to work I went, & wrote as usual a sheet of true Reynolds nonsense.—John also scratch'd a few lines & Jane copied Mighty Mars, all of which were enclosed under cover to Mr W. Cooper, Cooks court near Lincolns Inn for him to deliver to Mrs Pryse of College Hill Shrew'y, of course this done we enjoy'd the hope that you wd soon return an answer—this is two Months ago.—At length we grew uneasy that we did not hear from you, when the thought struck my mind, that you had never receiv'd this parcel I sent off Yesterday to M^r C['s] lodging, & to my utter vexation had the packet returnd. He had gone without it. I must therefore seize some other opportunity to send the song.—I opend my letter to you with intent to destroy it, but I believe I will send it to prove you were not forgotten.—Mr Cooper told us you were Married which George & I stoutly denied, as your letter then was so recent you could not but have spoken of it.—but a person call'd here since who frequently hears from Oswestry, who spoke of it quite as a matter of course. Now whether it is so or not, or whether it is likely shortly to be so is nothing to me further, than that you have the heartiest, kindest & best wishes of George & Charlotte Reynolds for your enjoyment of every felicity this world can bestow in the conexion you I hope have happily form'd—enough of this till I hear from you.—Your account of Porkington was truly delightful, I fancy it owes much to your elegant description of it,[1] tho' I doubt not but it was an admirable entertainment—It is astonishing to me she—Miss Bonsby[2]—should remain single so long. Surely the Men in your part of the World are not so avaricious as in *all* other, or a Lady so captivating with a fortune so ample would long ere this have been led to the altar by one of your most finish'd Gentlemen.—Our Jack has a weeks holiday, he has accordingly pack'd up his Books & tatters & taken himself to Stanmore in Middlesex[3] for the time being.— Pray, how did you do these last assizes [,] I hope well.—Cooper gave us a most favorable account of your performances the time before—which pleas'd us all, for altho we knew you to be capable, yet we thought it too early for you to expect any Briefs yet—I promis'd you when you spoke the first time—or rather pleaded—I certainly would clap heartily now not being present at the time, nor ever likely to be present, I shall take away that promise—and replace it with another, & that is whenever you are pleas'd to bring yourself to Lambeth again I & my family will give you every applause such a performance deserves, & may every exertion of your future life be crown'd with as sincere & favorable encouragement as we shall then bestow. Is not this a fine prayer—you who are a little satirical, will laugh perhaps at it. With all my heart, you know I can bear it, especially when truth is the basis of my asseverations. I find Dr Calcot your favorite, & every body's favorite, is, poor Gentleman, quite lost in intelect, & that there is to be a subscription set on foot for the Benefit of his Family.[4] Should this be the case, how distressing that such abilities as he possess'd should have such a sorrowful termination. I fancy he has overstraind his faculties. How goes on the Nursery, I hope all your 'trees plants & flowers' are thriving amain but I suppose rather backward oweing to the severity of the past Winter, yet I expect they will succeed the better for it afterwards, if your Nursery should thrive like my *Nursery* you will have reason to be proud of it.—I am writing under an exceeding ill humour. I have been the two days waiting for the Paper hangers, & the wretches are not yet arriv'd, you may naturally suppose the provocation ferrets me a little, or I believe, I may say, a great deal, but patience you know, Johnny, Patience is a virtue, & I must endeavour to rummage a little spark of it if possible, from my irritable composition, & comfort myself therewith on this *very trying* occasion. Adieu let us hear soon, *very soon* – accept Mr Reynolds & my united kind regards & be assurd of the friendship of both—

    I remain yours sincerely

    CHARLOTTE REYNOLDS.

In my absence from the room the young kitten[5] took it into her head to have a taste of friendship & accordingly seiz'd on this letter as a sample & if I had not returnd, would have devourd the whole. She has sent her teeth or claws through the corner, which you must excuse as I am too indolent to write another.[6]

12

From Mrs Reynolds

[11 August, 1809]

And so friend Dovaston you in your great wisdom brought your mind to beleive the Reynolds a worthless set of beings, you conceiv'd the thought that they were incapable of a true & solid friendship, fie on you, could you suppose but for a moment that we should faulter where we have shewn such anxiety for your welldoing, & express'd sincerely such pleasure in the enjoyment of your sensible correspondence—Yet George & self are a little gratified at the solicitude you have display'd, it serves to convince you are not indifferent to our friendship:—and so the Mardol folk[1] set us down as Queer ones.—I thank them for saying nothing worse.—time was when I was spoken of in terms in that quarter that if it had been true I should have been unworthy the friendship of any one, but it was as false as the author herself, & reflected back on her—for whoever knows me— will discredit the idle, ignorant, low stuff, that falls indiscriminately on friend or foe from this capricious woman. I can only say that her Mansion, so far from being the Mansion of 'peace,' is the Mansion where *ingratitude* reigns triumphant. Be assur'd Dovaston you are held in the highest esteem by my husband, self, & Children, & we should be fools, to listen (either you, or ourselves) to any malicious inuendoes thrown out by the envemon'd tongue of envy.[2]—By these, our friendship with Sheils was rap'd,[3] & what shall we be doing to suffer this serpent to whisper away the respect which subsists between *us*.—Cheer up they must be wiser, wittier, & somewhat better than the party in question, that can make us alter our opinion of you. I wish with you some of my family could have visited you this year but it could not be, perhaps when least expected we shall sometime meet together, we all covet it much. I like your Breidden Hill bustle well, & if I had been there I could have borne the refrain in your song, why did not you send it?[4] I thank you for the judicious advice to John. I should have lik'd it better if you had said more on the subject as all you say is law to Jack.—'a little worm may canker the soundest nut,' 'if I was at your elbow I could shew you my fears were not groundless,' 'I write now with much agitation,' & such like sentences from your letter excite my curiosity, speak clear, for more lurks behind than I am aware of, or why such remarks as the above. You mistook me, with respect to Janes music, it was not Schroeters, but Shroders[5] we admire.—oh I long most heartily for your 300 satirical verses, let me have them or I shall be provok'd to death. I am all impatience, I wish you had sent them ere you had mention'd them, nothing is so tiresome as expectancy, & expect I will till they do come. I am determined. As to yr cutting a figure at Charing Cross, if we can see you in no other way, our compliments & we shall be glad to see you there & I will treat you with *Bacon to your Eggs.*——I have I think now answerd the most material items of your letter—now for a little of my own Genuine nonsense, for which I am so eminent.—I wish you, John, patience with all my heart to bring you thro' it. Nonsense did I say. I am stopd in my career, George is just arrivd full tilt from Fleet Street, where he has been to read the Shrews Chronicle.[6]—he has not had time of late to go there, but your hint has set him off Post.—he has read an account of your hiving bees so as to prevent their being destroyd, he tells me it is done by steam, if it succeeds, I shall think more highly of you than usual, both for your ingenuity & humanity—what little thought I have given

Bees has generally been that it appeard an ungrateful task to destroy any thing so industrious & useful,—then again I find you have been giving some account of the Spanish Chesnut tree, which seems to astonish George. I can only say

> The Man who can with so much ease
> Descant on rhyme, on Music, Trees
> And spare the lives of useful Bees

A very clever fellow he's . . . There's for you. Have I not fulfilled my promise to the very truth—aye I have, but I have not sullied my paper with falshood, & for the rest you must take your chance with 'Dame Reynolds.'—The Music enclos'd is sent with fear & trembling lest you should condemn the choice as you are rather a foe to Modern Music. Be that as it may they are considerd to be not quite trash.—& to send old Music would be somewhat like carrying Coal to Newcastle. Jane tells me tis rediculous to add Calcotts Glee[7] to the rest, but I say no—& that settles it. And now as I am drawing near the end of my sheet I must add that my husband & self request in future—if a longer time than usual passes without your hearing from Lambeth that instead of working your Ire, or turning your ear to the vague tale of slander, you make use of your own good sense, write, & demand the cause, & either G. R. or C. R. will give you a candid explanation. Believe me had I felt sore at any thing relating to you, before I resented it, I should freely tell you my thoughts & await your answer,—but I know not what can make a change in the sentiments of my dear family or self towards you. Therefore no more of this. John in the very centre of his letter has unexpectedly been fetch'd by a friend to set off for Stanmore, sooner by a day or two. I shall of course enclose it, & also the old letters which were to have been carried by Cooper, just because I promisd I would, God forgive me for assailing you with such trash, but when you are tir'd say hold—George advises me not to put this sheet in the Parcel as I shall be liable to a penalty of fifty pounds so off it goes with the post & the old letter. I shall send—as in fact they really are—waste paper. 'Farewell, remember me'[8] & mine & believe me your friend in truth

CHARLOTTE REYNOLDS.

August 11th 1809.

The Music will be with you the end of this or the beginning of next week.

John Freeman Milward Dovaston
From the silhouette by Thomas Bewick

13

From Mrs Reynolds

[18 August, 1809]

We have waited with the most anxious expectancy a letter from you our good friend, till at length our patience can hold no longer. I therefore am desired by the whole group of Reynolds's to enquire the cause of your so long silence. True I had the last letter from you but in it you express'd a wish that I should not send the long promis'd 'Mighty Mars' till you wrote again for me to get you some other Music, which, as soon as you determine I shall comply with your request to send it to you.—You are Idle I fear—yet I think again you are not.—The Summer is an interruption to letter writing, particularly in the Country. The Amusements & employments at this season imperceptably fill up your time, but thank God Winter is not far off, and then the dictating a letter to a friend is entered into with energy, and consider'd as a first rate solace to your dreary hours, when bad weather & as bad roads prevent your nearer friends from diverting your attention from your absent ones.—I have not lost, but mislaid your last, you will excuse me then, in not speaking as to particulars (if any) containd therein. I have been a Widow for a fortnight. M^r R—has been in Hertfordshire—or rather in the Town of Hertford to introduce Dr Bell's new System there—by desire of the Govenors of Christs Hospital.[1] I must rest a little here as it is too dark to proceed.—I resume my Pen & proceed to tell you that Father & Son spent a whole two week's from home, that *his*—George's—exertions at the Hospital were crowned with success, as the Masters enterd with spirit into the plan as well as the Boys, he has receiv'd since, the thanks of the Govenors. We have at length brought Jack to some determination as to his choice of business.[2] A Surveyor is the line he has fix'd on & of course as soon as possible his Father will endeavour to place him in that line, I am afraid it will be attended with more expense than can be at present accomplish'd, however this I suppose like many other things is to be conquerd & we must do the best we can.—Our conexions are good, the proffession I beleive a profitable & respectable one. The Boy possesses tolerable abilities &c. &c.—& I trust in God for a successful issue. The next holidays which I think is in a fortnight he quits S^t. Pauls—his Father intends to promote, or rather, instruct him for a time in those branches which fall within his line of instruction—also he is to learn Drawing for which Elegant & useful acquirement he displays a little Genius or taste whichever you please to term it. If I don't deceive myself, which Heaven knows Mothers are but to[o] apt to do. But even a Mothers fondness would not induce me to dwell so long on the praises & future plans of this Boy were I not assurd of your kind friendship, & solicitude for his welfare. Let us hear as soon as possible your thoughts on this subject. I tell you freely you are not to dissuade him from it, as he seems seriously to have made his mind to it,—but I have, his Father & himself have, so high an Opinion of your abilities on all things, that I look forward to many servic[e]able hints from friend Jonathan dont set me down as a selfish being for truly I am not so.—When you write, tell us how a parcel is to be got from Shrewsbury after it arrives there.—I fear the Apples at the Nursery will fall short this year as there are sad complaints of the scantiness of the Crops every where. Dont you think the Storms have been very tremendeous [?] I have not relishd this Summer at all. You ask how the Music goes on. As far as I can be a Judge well we all think Jane shews ability in it (now for Mother again) & I trust another year's instruction will enable her to perform well. She is an incessant slave to it & I hope her labours will succeed to her she has lately been learning some things of Shroeders which we all admire much—but you no doubt are acquainted with this Composer—say what you think of him. I like his freedom, & should fancy his Music good practice. Do come up to London & see how we are going on, a Journey would do you good, it would shake your bones, & senses into their right places. G. R. desires to know how the last assizes agreed with you, & whether you had any bri[e]fs we talked of you at the time, indeed we & our Young ones often do. Jane bids me ask have you got 'My Mother bids me bind my Hair.' *Haydn.*[3] [She] also reminds me of a passage in your letter wherein you desire if she is in need of *note*, she may at any time draw on you, I don't know how true or false her necessity is in this way, but she say's she is willing to accept your Notes. Only desires they may bear a short date. To speak clearly she shall think herself honord by using composition of yours . . . We are all well & John shall soon write there are two letters already written but have never been sent, I thought them rather carelessly written. G.R. C.R.

41

J.R. J.R. M.R. E.B.R. & C.R. all send kind remembrances to J. D. with good wishes.
  I remain your friend
    sincerely

CHARLOTTE REYNOLDS.

August 18th 1809.[4]

14

From John Hamilton Reynolds
[Late August or early September 1809]

My Good Friend,
  I feel ashamed that I have hitherto not answer'd your letter which deserv'd so much from my hands. Indeed I did write two or three letters at different times but my Mother expected them to be clever and as that is not in my line they were not permitted to make their appearance and I sit down now with strict orders to write a letter of *Sense*[1]—Yesterday we all left off St Pauls School for the Holidays I quitted for good and I must say I felt something rise in my throat when I shut the school door I was pleased to hear one master say he was sorry I was going and another that I had always behaved greatly to his satisfaction—I am now going to set tight to drawing Cyphering Writeing &c—nor do I mean to give up the Classics, but as the Winter will now be coming I shall study them with much delight in the evenings—Your observation in my mother's last letter I thank you for & I shall endeavour to fulfil you[r] good advice & I hope any letters you favor me with for the future shall be more punctually answer'd— I am going down to a country friend to spend a month where last Easter I dash'd off as a gentleman in a One horse ch[aise] *my first appearance in that character* the horse took fright and I got overturned[2] so *it had near been my last*—there's incident—I am now going for the sporting season so I have had a deal of advice not to touch a gun not even if it is not loaded because it might go off——The epitaph you sent me is a famous one. I declare I never saw a better. As to Malo Malo that you & Doctor Evans have found out and now it is found it is not worth finding.[3] O! that my Father would but allow me to come to you just to make a

42

finish it would delight me excessively—I am turn'd merchant already for I and a schoolfellow that was have taken to keeping pigeons & rabbits & greatly we get on with them. You have a capital dovehouse. I know you are in a great way of *business*. Give me leave to say a good word for my sister Jane I think she gets on well in her music and if you was to hear her you would find a wonderful improvement.

    JOHN REYNOLDS
sign'd by his Mother
    C. R—

15

From George Reynolds

Tuesday night. 10th Octr 1809.

Dear Friend,

    I went this day to the Temple and saw Mr Norris to whom (first apologising for your absence & stating the cause) I put the Questions you detailed in your letter—First & foremost: You owe to the Honorable Society £4. 6. 7. to this time. Should you wish your Name to remain—the payment is 19s 8d per Year—and they generally write to those, who may happen to be from London—about once in 4 or 5 Years for a remittance as its not worth their while for so small a sum to ask for it in less time.— You cannot take you name off, without taking up your bond—consequently cannot remain a member—You may take your name off by proxy—but Mr Norris advises you to remain a member as the payment of so small a sum can be of no object to You for in course of Years you may be a bencher[1]—whatever you may decide—I am willing to execute any further commands upon this subject—You will be surprised to hear that I have been publishing.[2] It is but a small affair—'Arithmetic for Children—educated on Dr Bells plan'—in 2 pts, only 9/6 per dozen—I have sold upwards of a thousand already——

    I have lately invented a *frame* for Schools on the D^{rs} plan which supersedes the use of any Books until Children are fit for the Testament—A Model of which I have sent to the Society of Arts & Sciences—it is very simple & the advantages resulting from it are as follows—The *great saving* in Books, as a set of frames & lessons will serve a School & last a number of Years from not being subject to wear & tear—The attention of the Boys is far more effectually rivetted to their lesson by the Teacher than when each had a Book in his hand—The Page of Syllables, containing about 5 lessons, cannot be put aside by the Teacher, imperfectly understood, without the inspection of the Master or whoever has the care of these lessons, as the [Teacher?] must obviously ask to have the Class examind, ere the frame can be replaced with another, besides it acts as a *check* upon the Teacher, highly necessary in a School upon a large Scale as mine is—It also, tho' perhaps a trivial consideration, causes the Boys, when engaged in studying their Lessons from the position of the frame, to carry themselves more upright—such is its simplicity [word illegible] the completest satisfaction and admiration by e[very] person who has seen it in operation—I hope some day that I may have the pleasure of shewing it to you—I am in the act of writing this—with Char[lott]e & Miss Morris (from Cheltenham formerly of Shrewsbury)[3] at Needle Work—the Children painting Scenery for a new Theatre John the principal Artist—round a comfortable fire—it being a very cold night—Jane out visiting at a neighbours—to amuse them with music[4]—They all beg me to say every thing thats kind to you &

I remain truly yours sincerely
GEO. REYNOLDS.

16

From John Hamilton Reynolds

Nov.ʳ 3ʳᵈ 1809.

My Good Friend,
    The reason I have delayed answering your Letter till the present time is because we have had Miss Morris[1] with us and as it was doubtful whether it would be next week that she meant leaving us. But she at length determin'd leaving us as [*sic*] this morning for Oxford which she did. My Father and Mother em-

ployed me immediately to inform you that as your letter implies your coming up at term time there is a Bed ready for you here aired by the aforesaid Miss Morris—And if you will come, you need not send an answer to intimate it as we shall always be ready to receive you. My Mother acknowledges her debt and is quite unable to answer your demands just yet but will patiently bear as much dunning as you think proper. You may depend upon good wages I (the *Manager*) k[n]owing you to be a good performer, and you shall come out in a £ump—This Letter that you have sent me now I like even more than any of the others and you may depend upon it I shall treasure up your advice most carefully it is a kind that suits me in particular. I am uncommonly glad to hear my friend Mr Shiel has obtain'd the tutorship of Ld Dungannon's family.[2] We set off on the Jubilee to see the illuminations which were some of the finest I ever saw,[3] I suppose you shewed yourself a Loyal man on that evening in particular. Jane was at the Theatre Yesterday Evening with a few friends and gives us a pretty description of the noise—almost every Man were O.P. in their hats—and 'Clifford for Ever' Who is one of your breed. (a Counsellor).[4]

—They all join me in the kindest remembrances to you and believe me your true and most affectionate.

    young friend

    J. H. REYNOLDS.

We shall expect you on Saturday for on Monday begins term—

17

From Mrs Reynolds

[18 November 1809.]

D^r friend,

Your letter this instant is arriv'd (three o'clock) & I am determind to send off an answer by the Postman of this Evg. I must therefore run on hand over head to send an answer—your last to me would have met attention from me had it not been that I had a visitor & exceeding ill in health—two, I think strong reasons for my silence. Time will not permit me to enter into particulars as to that letter, or there were things worthy notice therein. We have had no Snow here, till just as G.R. had finished reading yours a few minutes ago when it fell, & is falling as fast as it can come down. I hope you have not sent this instead of the Goose. I rather think from the black aspect of the Ev^g we shall have a great deal.—Thanks to this Oxford business 'Tis an ill wind that blows good to no one'—give your Vote to whom you will[1]—I care not, as I am a stranger in the whole affair—but give your society to my family as long as agreeable to you, & I shall feel happy in any cause that may have produced so desireable a pleasure—John and Jane are from Home till Monday the glad tidings will be acceptable I am convinc'd to both—I need not say how glad we shall all be to receive you. G. R. lost his accustom'd gravity when he found you were so near coming. I can only say in our plain friendly Homely way we are ready & willing to take you by the Hand & shall be on the look out every Hour for your arrival.—Thanks for the Goose & fowl whether they come or not, but I fancy we shall have them to Night according to the time you sent them off but you do not say what Coach. Lord I am glad to hear poor Sheils is better'd in his income & situation. I am mightily longing to hear particulars—but if this good fortune should enable him to marry, where will be his luck—common Soldiers pay would then be more advantage to him—I am going to write soon not because he has had success, no I am not of that mould—but that we all like him & that I am a letter in his debt—pray have you seen his lovely mass of flesh & bones since her arrival, has she returnd your London visit to her & her as lovely Sister yet—but more of this hereafter when we are met. The Music shall be tun'd, & all right & straight forward against you come. Jane will thank you for this, I have been grumbld at this Month to have it done. I do not wonder you like visiting at Dr Evans's—he is an amiable Sensible & kindhearted Man.[1] I have seen his tenderness to his little ones when he has not thought himself observd & I have not, nor ever shall forget it.—To visit at his House & mine will not bear a comparison he has an ample fortune to improve & indulge his family with.[2] We have nothing but our will to serve ours. Yet it is all very well & they are good Children.—Come on then if you are for play & mirth I have a dear delightful group at your service all waiting your arrival with happy countenances.—I am really so hurried that I can scarce tell what I write but take the intent for the deed.—G. R. thanks you for his letter & says the ale has been waiting for you. To Night he has made the bold the grand re-

solve to tap it, you may judge to what a pitch of joy he is wound up, to come to so valiant a resolution. No doubt he will drink a speedy & good journey to your Lordship, in which I shall heartily join. Adieu till we see you & believe me
　　　your friend sincerely
　　　　CHARLOTTE REYNOLDS.
Childrens love
Nov.ʳ 18th

This was scribbled on saturday as you may perceive but the Bellman did not pass which prevented our sending it—
　　The parcel is not yet come to hand which vexes me—not a little—send word particulars of it, but I fear all is spoild. Monday three o'clock.

18

From Mrs Reynolds

[14 February 1810]

I perceive my good friend the time you spent at Lambeth School produc'd but small improvement in your hand writing. believe me I could scarcely read your last letter I thought it a copy of pothooks & hangers on first opening it however I excuse it, as you justly say you have so much to do on your return Home. The account of your Journey was stupid enough or rather your journey, & *not* the account of it, was stupid. You dont say with whom you spent your hour or two the Evᵍ you got to Shrewsbury, which means you did not get Home that Night, I suppose Mʳ Nelson or Mʳ Parkes.[1] Why what a glorious girl is your Molly—prize her such a Servant as you describe her to be, is a jewel of the first water—How did she like her Gown, & Shawl, you need not hurry yourself to wive while she remain at West Felton. & so the consumption fled with the fog—very well, you seem to me as tho when you left London you shook off all your incumbrances, I suppose I shall be for following your example. But again, if I were to fly from this Misty spot, I should leave charms behind that would hang on my health & around my heart

47

so that clear air, & many other blessings would have no effect on me. Well reason'd Ma'am lotte[2] stay at home & be content. So much for jaunting out & staying at home. I have written to my valued friend Jane Mackay—I gave her your remembrance & also assur'd her that you was reconcil'd to the Mulberry Tree as you desir'd, I have not since heard but shall I know soon. With respect to Lancasters Book Mr Reynolds has it not—the papers you speak of were destroy'd—as to his causing much talk in your parts, that he does wherever his plan is introduc'd, but Doctor Bell's is making the surest progress—ours is the quiet side, & of course the business more solidly done[3]—you should get a book which has not been long out—'The New School, being an attempt to illustrate its principles, Detail, and advantages, by Thomas Barnard Esqr.' (but whether a lawful *Esqr* or not I cannot tell). It is a very impartial account of both Doctor Bells system, & Lancasters plan, at least G. Reynolds says so.[4]

G. R. has met with great encouragement for both his Arithmetic, & lessons, which has pleas'd him exceedingly. He has had a letter from Mrs Trimmer,[5] who means to encourage them, in it, she tells him she cannot but admire & approve them, & shall put them forward even tho they will completely do away her monosyllabic (duece take the word) spelling book which will be a loss to her. But she says she does not value that for she cannot but approve his publication—this is disinterested conduct, & like a *Woman*. Since I wrote the above I have been told that Lancaster is not pleas'd with Barnards opinions, but of this I cannot speak as to possible fact. If so Mr Reynolds has not taken the matter rightly—I know you like a letter fill'd to the seal—a very bumper—alas I feel Idle and not at all dispos'd to indulge you. I have written so many letters this week & under such a number of interruptions that I am cross to a most eminent degree. It is a happy thing that you are well lodg'd with Croney[6] and Molly[7] if you were here perhaps, I should be for rumageing you—I beg Molly pardon for placing Croney first, but as I think the sincerity more *certain* in the beast than the Maid I trust she will excuse it—if you can read this scrawl it will be well.—If not, we are even. M^r R—& John's remembrances to you the latter will write to you soon. A happy Valentines day to you—farwell—

CHARLOTTE REYNOLDS.

Fe^by 14th 1810.

19

From John Hamilton Reynolds
Begun on March 11 and ended on 14 1810.

My Dear Friend,
   Tell your antagonist Yates to look at the fourteenth letter of
Goldsmith where there is a strong argument in your favour as to
ornament & use.[1] I hope the hamper containing your busts did
not sustain any injury. I suppose now the poets have taken their
station on the brackets I'll give you a bit of advice, 'kick up as
great a dust as you are able it will be the better for your heads.' I
have had a famous bargain since you left, what do you think it is?
I fancy I hear you say 'Mass, I cannot tell'—'Cudgel thy brains
no more,'[2] it is 'Dodsley's edition of the Bath Guide.' I have also
bought Dinarbas 1/6 a very good edition.[3]—I went to King Lear
again last Monday night and was more pleas'd than when I went
with you, Kemble performed with more spirit.[4] He spake different to what I said, it is 'tooth' and not 'fang' I submit.[5]—I see
I hop from one subject to another faster than you can keep up
with me—but you know I am but a Colt in the field of literature
so you must not expect me to be so attentive.—Here goes,
another skip—I have to tell you that I and some friends have
opened a work among ourselves after the stile of the spectator
now what I want of you is to send me a few Essays and I will
insert them in the 'Inspector' (the name of our book) I have
written the first essay which is received with *universal applause*
—I have also opened my theatre *previous* to which I spoke an
address of my own writing, which my audience made shift to
bolt how they did it, Lord knows![6]
   I often say to myself *'would I were wi' my FRIEND and
CRONY'*[7] no doubt you find a difference [between] where you
are and the Strand—I went to Mr Walker[8] after you jogged off that
morning who enquired very kindly after you, I gave a true and
faithful account of your exit—My Mother made me sit down and
now I shall make myself get up and wait for more news.
   Again I take up my pen & subject but no thing new can I
say—except that I have published 5 numbers of my Essayist &
that they have been much liked I hope you'll send me a supply &
speedily, it is a kind of writing I like much & what I spend much
of my leisure time in I hope some time or other you will see
them—Since you left I attended a sale of books at Mr Squibb's

room,[9] where I bought G. Tonson's edition of the Spectator &
Guardian (and I think a bargain) at £1. 4. Both in excellent con-
dition—I also tried for Leonidas, (Dodsley's edition)[10] but that
went too high for me (pray tell me whether it is the same poem
you bought & if you want any books, send word to me & I will
hunt for them, and I assure you I am a most excellent hand at it).
Frank Squibb[11] was with us the other night. He said there was
no such thing as a swell in pillars[12]—of course argument en-
sued—I have examples—St Martin's—St Paul's Covent Garden
—Somerset House &c. &c. [Words illegible] not determined
with him, though I know I am right.—I offer'd to bet *8* shillings, he said he would lay *6*—no says I—*I never makes not no
two prices.* Punning is a thing I have given over as a bad job—
for I think a bad pun enough to tire the patience of *Job*[13]—Hem!
—I perceive I am getting near the bottom—So (as the Spectator
says) I remain
> (*with proper distances*)[14]
>> Your affectionate
>> and true friend,
>>> JOHN HAMILTON REYNOLDS.

P.S. Do not mistake the price of the Spectator (viz. *£1. 4s. for
£1. 4d. similis*[15] *£1. 6s. for £1. 6d.—Maiden Lane.*)
Latin—Pater et Mater mittunt amorem[16]
English—We have heard from Miss Makay who made particular
enquiries & desired to be remembered to you.

20

From John Hamilton Reynolds

[10 May 1810]

My dear Friend
    The arrival of the Shrewsbury Chronicle[1] has spurred up my
head & collected the few grains of wisdom that wandered about
my spacious Scull into one *large grain* & from that LARGE
GRAIN you are to expect whatever comes upon this Paper. I
have perused your Ode to Shakespear & like it excessively there

is one thing I think good and that is the irregularity of the metre.[2] Let others talk of 9 *words in line* I say more meaning & more Genius appear if not, there is also more difficulty in writing irregular poetry. No doubt you are engaged with Wood in his Paper if you could make an opening for me in any way [as] a London Correspondent it would be assisting me to a situation which I should like & also to something for my pocket at present I belong to the Day Newspaper[3] not as a writer but as a Clerk yet in that place I have acquired a perfect knowledge of the business of a writer. Dovaston: I really am at present in a post most unpleasant & though perhaps I am too young for the place I have mentioned I wish for it most ardently a desire for doing something [h]as urged me to accept the present undertaking, thoug[h] God knows how I long for something superior, my mind is determin'd & whatever unpleasant may occur I will obtain a respectable & settled situation.[4]

I am sorry I have trespassed upon your time with my petty troubles but I assure you they rest upon my mind heavily——

The eighteen penny picture remains there nor do I think it will ever depart at least for £1. 6——after the manner of Peters[5] —heavy Cloud that—Natural sea—pretty wreck—no doubt you recollect these sentences I do perfectly—how I wish I could visit your beauty spot—the thoughts of '*the trees green*'—'*the flowers blown*'—'*Birds singing*'—and others equally delightful crowd upon me—they come in vain, summer appears not to me—the dusty windows of an Office files of Papers are all that come to [my] eyes. We have had a letter from Miss Mackay she desires remembrance to you—I have been to King Lear again since you saw me and liked it more & more tonight I hope to go to the play '*King Henry the eigghth*'[sic]—

Dram. Pers.
Cardinal Woolsey——Mr Kemble
King Henry——Mr Cork

Mrs Siddons——Queen Katharine[6]
[Part of the letter seems to be missing]
My Mother has been so ill she has neglected writing to all her friends but she will answer yours soon

All Send Regards[7]

21

From Mrs Reynolds

[12 June 1810]

Dͬ friend,

    I am not very willing to think ill of a friend at any time, & I hope a friend will be as lenient to me, if not, what will become of me, as I certainly have not of late used you well. But you who know the wretched state of my health, the many occupations I follow in the Domestic employments for my dear family, & the thousand other things I have on my mind must take the good naturd side & think the best you can of a poor repentant Sinner. I find my Son has been scribbling to you, I did not see his letters, but I fancy they were triffles as you have not answerd them. He has been employ'd these last three Months in the Office for the Day paper but we are disatisfied with the situation now we are better acquainted with it. We do not like the conexion & we have sent in a resignation but he has offerd himself to a Conveyancer & has gained the place—whether this will suit I cannot yet tell as I am as ignorant as a post as to the employment.¹ He is to enter on it in July I think, when I am better informed I will let you know particulars. Sheil is in London & likes it well, he frequently is here of course, but this can be no news to you. I know how you are passing your time either watching your Bees, peeping into a flower or sitting in your Hall smoking a Pipe & drinking your ale with your friend Yates at your side & faithful Crony at your feet. These are too great enjoyments at your time of life, you cannot have enough to do, indulgence will in a few years bring on the gout, the Palsy & the Physic—but Lord what am I talking of, I shall frighten you into the horrors, & you had better hang yourself than that you would then fancy (all the good old Heads which you view with such delight now) a set of blue Devils come to torment you, or horrid Monsters to devour you. I conceit I hear you exclaim for Heavens sake Mother hold your pen you frighten me to death. In kind compassion I have done Johnny, & hope you will live many years to enjoy the blessings that surround you in spight of the fearful picture I have spread before you. I have been refreshing my Memory with your last letter—which to my shame bears the date of the 26ᵗʰ of March but ere I answer one word of it I beg to inform you that your letter to John is just arrivd, a double reproach to me for not sending to you sooner. You will see by this that I had begun to write before it came to hand, I had written part on Saturday & twas lucky I had not sent. I can scarce ever set a whole letter out without interruption & this was rather a fortunate one. But to return to the subject of yours to me of the 26th March how does your West Felton School proceed I hope well, do you follow the Bell System, or the farcical Lancastrian plan, I have my fears the latter will take with your folk as it look's more, tho it accomplishes less—& Country People in general are easily deluded, & too, too many of them of the dissentering persuasion for which God forgive them—Pray how do you go on with your Poetical Romance.[2] I shall expect to see & hear that you have made progress in it. The very little taste of it you sent to me I like, but do not possess either sense or boldness sufficient to give it other opinion than that I hope to see more of it & shall be exceedingly disappointed if I do not. Your other poetical effusion does very well. I fancy Mr Yates thinks so to[o]. Jane Mackay when she last wrote was well & sent compt^s to the Esqr of West Felton.[3] So much in answer to March 26th. I have to remind you (when you write again to me) that I am not a widow, I have a very good, odd sort of Husband that you have omitted to name when you have written twice . . . beware oh John of the third time or I shall have a hump as big as King Dick's. What think you of the attempt to assassinate one of our Princes, it seems to have struck most folk here with horror.[4] That, & some of the late disturbances have opend the Eyes of many of the misled. It was a diabolical business altogether. I thank you for your kind invitation to our good fellow John, who (however he and all parties may desire so agreeable a visit) must decline accept^g it for the present, as his time is fill'd to the utmost & he would lose a situation (we much Covet) by his absence. You will admit the propriety of this consideration I know—he & I have had some conversation on this Head since the letter came, & he is to save a little out of every quarters Salary till he has *amass'd* a sufficient sum to convey him to the borders of Wales, which when it does arrive I am convincd will be the height of all his glory.—I thank you for you admonitions to him he did wrong & I was not pleas'd with him and you express'd yr disapprobation just as I had mine, which of course must convince him of his Error. I have this instant receivd a letter from my ever dear Jane Mackay who begs to be rememberd to you it is a letter in her best way, sensible, witty, & so forth. We told Sheil your Message, who

53

sends kind remembrances & intends writing soon. Adieu
Husband & *bratts send* love, I good wishes, & remain as ever

CHARLOTTE REYNOLDS.

June 12th 1810.[5]

22

From John Hamilton Reynolds

[1 August 1810]

—One, —Two, —Three Months past and no notice taken by that
young ill mannered Brute, John* B——n feast[1] finished no
arrival—now I must be supposed to hear all this then be it
known this is our Answer
  'That it was not in our royal power to come on account of our
office (you must understand that I am in the Amicable Assurance)[2] having been there only a Month could not have the
impudence to ask for leave of Absence, that next year we hope to
spend a Month with you as I now lay by something every quarter
to pay passage given under our hand this 1$\underline{^{st}}$ Day of August
1810.—J. H. REYNOLDS.'
  Having answered the first part I shall proceed to the usual
Letter talk—I have the pleasure to tell you your Essay excited
such univeral satisfaction that I cannot refrain from begging
another as soon as convenient. My papers have encreased
amazingly through the help of one friend and ano$\underline{^{r}}$.
  I, the other day, saw your *friend Walker* standing at his door
who desired his remembrance when I sent to you.
  I have been reading Coleman's Play of the 'Iron Chest'[3] and I
really think [it] a very excellent one permit (stiff word) me to
recommend it to you. As I shall not be able to come to you send
me the *little Gun* and Croney and I'll see what I can do at *'Kenn-
ington Marsh,' Clapham fields* &c. &c.—One more request &
that shall be the last (I fancy I hear you say: 'Another yet—I'll
see no more')[4] which is that you will send me a copy of what you
have finished of *'Whittington Castle.'*[5] I long to read it, the bit
you gave me to taste only made me long for the whole——
  I have not seen the inside of Mr Scott's Lady of the Lake[6]
though many outs it is quite *'Bang up'* here—W$\underline{^m}$ & Frank

Squibb[7] desire to be rememberd kindly to Mrs Bruin[8] and hope this weather has not set her all in a *Muck*—You ought to be in London now to see

The Blood Red Knight

at Astley's Royal Amphitheatre,[9] the last Scene a Battle upon real Horses in Armour I and my Father expended two shillings upon him the other night 'Half Price'—much pleased—Blue light.

I suppose you was at the Installation at Oxford[10] by the account given in the papers it was a very grand affair. I should like to have heard some of the Speeches we had extracts [from] them. I suppose the Corn looks well around you since these Showers which have fallen lately I knew when it was coming for my *Corn* ached most confoundedly but if it was to ache ever so much—nay even mortify—My Bowels ache, my head ache—I was troubled with the Gout—the Rhe[umati]sm[11] &c. &c. I should still remain

your affectionate friend
J. H. REYNOLDS.

*Sooner than make a Blunder in my spelling I put a dash.
All send Kind Remembrance

23

From John Hamilton Reynolds

[27 September, 1810]

My good Friend,

I have been very inattentive in not answering a Letter which has given me more pleasure than any other in the whole course of your interesting correspondence but delay the nearest relative to Idleness had so taken possession of me that it was but by main force I seized this opportunity of writing—The Task you desire me to undertake is one of so difficult a nature and also one that requires such a nice conception of works in general that I shall show my sense more by not adopting it—what I allude to is that of criticising your poem. One thing I have no hesitation in asserting [is] that it equals any parts of Walter Scott.[1] I perceive it is a style of writing you are rather partial to for instance the ode to Shakespeare was written like it—I hope you will not neglect continuing it my Dad and Mam like it amazingly and so do all Friends that know what good things are pray send me it as you continue it—your works hold a front place in our Shelves[2] nor does the last work diminish your popularity in our family you might I think favor me with a few of your wild flowers they will not loose their sweetness by coming to London for those you account dead at your house will be treasured as blooming and live ones at ours if you would send me a packet nay a little packet of your tales and scraps to scatter the gloom which Winter spreads around us I will send you thanks warm from my heart— You should have been here at the reign of OP the second which was twice as powerful as OP the first[3] tomorrow I and Dad are going to see 'All in the Wrong,'[4] I expect much pleasure.——

I am now in a situation of the most comfortable kind plenty to do yet not too much the Governor is a good man easily satisfied yet punctual to Business I will thank you to direct your Letters to me in manner following

> J. H. Reynolds
>> Amicable Assurance Office
>>> Serjeants Inn
>>> Fleet Street

by which means I get my letters at 8 o'clock in the Morning instead of 3 in the Afternoon—We are going to perform another play at Squibb's this Winter which I believe is to be one of Colman's your performance of M[rs] Bruin is often talked of with pleasure[5] indeed I think it was a *masterly* piece of acting—M[r] Elliston has made a very pleasant kind of entertainment at the circus consisting of Plays versified which by means of a good delivery passes well he lately got up a Grand Pageant being a principal scene from nineteen of Shakespeare's Plays[6] it was very free—all was carried on in dumb show whereby the beauty of the Author (his language) w[as lost]. I have just seen in the paper an account of the death of [a] friend who was overturned in the Margate Coach I should almost be afraid to Travel so many Accident[s] happen of late.[7]

—I beg you will not follow my example in delaying the writing of Letters—[8]

> Yours truly
>> J. H. REYNOLDS.

All at home beg kind remembrances

24

From Mrs Reynolds

I should have answerd your last letter without dispute before now, but have been prevented by a multitude of vexations, & some few pleasures—first I was too ill to write, then I went to the Country for my health & at my return found myself so much better I began to think I had taken a new lease—but alas this was one of my air built Castles for I was scarcely enjoying the happy thought ere my dear family arousd me to attend them on the bed of sickness. Eliza & Charlotte[1] were attack'd by a fever—which had nearly terminated the life of poor delicate Eliza tho she is now getting well fast. The consequence of my attendance on these dear Children (what with fatigue aided by infection) was being laid up myself—& after all Mr Reynolds. I leave you to judge whether I have been [able] to pay attention to friend or foe. Not that I will tell a falshood by saying I have not written in all this time, but your letter puzzeld me a little. There is a sentence or two I am at a loss to comprehend. You seem to apprehend 'the daily diminution of your powers to please at Lambeth.' Why should you pester your brains with Ideas such as these, unless when you examine your Bosom you call to recollection any conduct for which you can blame yourself, if you can, or do, I believe you think more of it than any one here does, for we remain the same happy united family we were before you press'd our threshold, & I trust shall ever remain so, & you seem to wish us to beleive you the same friend, then, what occasion for all these doubts & fears —as to John spending the time with You instead of the Office he first engagd in, it was wholly impossible. He was at an age to be doing something, & the that something was attended with mani-fold disadvantages to him & a world of anxiety to his good Father & myself, yet, it was better than being wholly unemployd. He was so fortunate however by his situation there to meet with one which he now enjoys that we are all satisfied with, but as he wrote you last week, he no doubt has told you particulars. Heaven knows what he said to you. I did not see the letter—Your Poetry I like much particularly one or two passages but as I have seen it but once or twice I cannot speak as freely as I should do, but even then I should not think myself competent to judge as you desire. I admire it in truth. That you have, at least that the good folk in your part have adopted Lancasters plan does not surprise me at all[2]—poor Man he would Lecture to little purpose if no one were to encourage him—That you heard his lectures described in a ludicrous way I can readily beleive—so did we. Lord Radstock[3] brought some folk here & is going to adopt a School on our System. Two ladies came who had heard Lancaster Lecture somewhere in the Country where he cut a very sneaking appearance, but Lord it stands to reason if it answerd to him, he need not go about like a pauper to hold forth for sixpence or a shilling a head. He would remain at home & attend his School. I suppose most of your heads of your School are dissenters in which case they are right to take their lessons from such a quarter. I wish you success in the undertaking. Mr. Reynolds is just off to the Magdelen,[4] part of my family are in the Country & I nearly alone. I thought, & indeed told George so that I might as well, nay better—chat away an hour with you than not twas agreed on, and you see plainly, that whether alone or surrounded by my Children, lively or sad, or however situated I am, I am still the same dolt I have ever been at making out a letter. Postpond till tomorrow. Monday the 8th. of Oct[r]—I have this instant receiv'd a letter from my highly esteem'd friend J. Mackay who writes in good Spirits—she sends her Comp[ts] to you—you tell me Sheil sent you a letter while in London without a date, look at it again & see if you cannot find one. He spent some of his leisure time with us, He is certainly a worthy being if you see him remember us to him.

I think you told me when in London you were not a Sportsman, perhaps by this time you are become one—if not you have friends that are, do rummage among them for a Hare & a brace of partriges & send them by way of a treat to poor starv'd Charlotte Reynolds.[5] —I shall relish them exceedingly & the more so if they come from Dovaston. I have just receivd a hint that the above request is not a very modest one—you knew me before today & must take it as it is meant—at any rate in true English I wish you may be able to send them. I had nearly forgot to observe one part of your letter—'an old Lady from London with you which makes your House cheerful.' oh oh Mr Johnny have you not made a little bit of a Mistake, & is it not a *Young* one? Single Men seldom think we old ladies agreeable.[6] I strangely suspect you have made a little erratta here—Mr Reynolds sends Compts. I the same John is at office. Box is just come in. I can just have time to subscribe myself your well wisher & friend

CHARLOTTE REYNOLDS.

Oct[r] 8th 1810.

Write very soon.

25

From Mrs Reynolds

[November 1810]

Dr Friend,

All your letters abound so with Ideas of my incorrigible severity towards you that I almost begin to think I am not a degree behind the famous old Mother Brownrig for cruelty.[1] In the name of patience & wonder my good fellow cease these wailings. I am what I ever was, a reasonable sort of woman firm in my friendships, but perhaps rather too free in speaking my opinions, this however has been my line of conduct ever, & tho it may be blameable, I am too old to mend or become a *Modern friend*. In this case good Mr Counsellor, assist me with your advice & tho perhaps I may not wholly follow it, I may glean some scraps of useful knowledge—but I dont pledge myself that this will positively be the case, therefore dont be disappointed. After *all* I remain the same humdrum creature I was at my outset.—Indeed I beleive it were better I kept up the bustle as you seem to be doubly kind for a little snubbing—what an acceptable basket of poultry &c. Thanks for its contents, in my life I scarce ever saw or partook of such fowls. I think they are the Dorking breed. The partridges excellent—the Leveret a tit bit for the Gods—no Apologies I beg—proceed I pray you. And yesterday came your second letter, today your second Hare for while I am writing this Jane has brought up the Noble fellow from the porter—well all I can say is go on & prosper——& so you think me illiberal to Lancaster, *I* don't think I am, but it may be, that to speak truth at all times is not to act wisely, so let the Man rest. In answer to what you say of Sheils letter—I have done—I have struggled to restore a broken friendship from respect to both, but one artful Woman will work more mischief in an hour than an amiable one can counteract in Years.[2] Tho last not least in our Dear love next comes the subject of my Dutiful, amiable Son—who is at present all a Mother's fondest wishes can desire—you seem not to agree with me in his employments—believe me Dovaston I should have preferred if possible that his Occupations in life should have been widely different to what they are—but this was the only thing offer'd, & had he continued at home he would have lost ground in every respect. His Father could not attend to him, & I still hold that to be employ'd at his age is of the utmost consequence to his future good.

Not a word of Music, is it yourself or your Instrument that is out of tune 'John Anderson my Joe'[3]—or have you met with some 'Lady fair' who's 'e'en of bonny blue' has stolen your heart away from the enchanting subject. 'Heaven thee save' should this be the case, for Dame Reynolds will hold herself ready to sound, not 'Loves alarms,' but her shrill pipes to awaken you from your lethargy. We seem to proceed well in this way—but the old instrument is an endless grievance—our Eliza promises to be a very tolerable player. Mr Whittle[4] whom you have seen here din'd with us on Sunday, as did Mr Goddard,[5] your Health was drunk—oh, by the bye I am told you are *in* again at the Lawrenc[es],[6] how did the old Lassie receive you, was you not a bit afeard at the first meeting . . . Miss Blakemore[7] call'd here about a Month or so ago. I have not seen her since & very probably shall not see her again. I did intend to have written a much longer letter than I have done but upon my word—as usual I have met so many interruptions that the thread is broken past splicing & as John wrote you as soon as the acceptable & kind presents arriv'd I have rather suffer'd myself to be a little idle which I know you will think lightly of, when you consider that I am getting quite an old Lady—& not so apt and ready as I was at a scribbling bout. We are all well, at least except myself. The group join me in kind & good wishes for a good & mer[r]y C[h]ristmas, & a very happy new Year

I remain your sincere friend

CHARLOTTE REYNOLDS.[8]

26

From John Hamilton Reynolds

My good Friend,

There is a custom that generally prevails and one that I would not wish should be broken by me of acknowledging a present the first Opportunity. My Mother having been very busy these last few days has commissioned me to make this same acknowledgment, & with many thanks for the kind & friendly way in which her request to you has been executed. The basket of Grog arrived safe at our Mansion as likewise did the hare with Nature's Passport. The fowls were the largest I ever saw & the finest—*I am a Judge!*

I admire your poem though must say it is rather severe. I would ask you to send '*Prometheus*'[1] to me but you say it would be much trouble to copy it yet I would describe a way by which you might accomplish it write a few lines every evenᵍ. *A wonderful good Idea* of mine. Your Motto is a very good one for those who require it. Thank Heaven I hope & truly beleive our family have no subject for which it would suit. Howeve[r] I have presented it where I conclude you intended to direct it.

We have got up a play at our house with new Scenery, &c. &c. 'Tobin's HoneyMoon' I did the Duke Aranza, or rather did for him[2]—we intend performing it next Xmas again with some farce (I wish you were with us)—

I see by your Letters you enjoy yourself in a way which will hereafter repay you few pleasures I beleive contribute to future good—yours do—that of planting Trees—I must say it would be no very great pleasure to me I would rather sit in your Library & study present comfort. I am *a selfish* young dog *you* know.

I have no doubt you have read the 'Lady of the Lake.'[3] It is much talked of here. I do not like it so well as any other of his poems. It certainly possesses what very few Authors works possess novelty of Incident. I should like to hear your opinion—*you understands them things—you's a Critic!*—

I wish you would write oftener.[4] Your Letters have very good *credit* here—they are held in high esteem—they have a very great *circulation*. Few things are received with greater pleasure than a letter from Dovaston. Alway[s] direct to me at the 'Ami-

cable Society' I get the Letter soon[er]. You will have no excuse
for not writing when you see how soon I answer you. Imitate my
length of time but not of writing—I indite this at my Office so
cannot tell whether they have any thing to say [at home]—Shall
not close till I have asked them.

    I remain truly yours
    J. H. REYNOLDS.

I find that since I have been out my Mother has been writing so
you will either have a letter by the same post or a day or two
after—

27

From John Hamilton Reynolds
[24 December 1810]

My Dear Friend,
    I am ordered by my Mother and Father to return you their
unfeigned thanks for noticeing the Slovenly & noncencical
Letters of Jack Reynolds. I always had a confounded bad opinion
of his writings and your remark has confirmed it, though had a
correction been intimated to me from any other Person than you
I should have been hurt as it is, I am pleased, & shall take all
pains to improve—On friday next we perform our play of the
Honey Moon—The Duke JHR—to which will be added the in
terlude of 'Sylvester Daggerwood' The Hero JHR.[1] The whole to
conclude with the farce of 'Who's the Dupe' Old Doiley by JHR
so you see I mean to cut a dash though absent you would assist
me greatly if you would write a prolouge [*sic*] for the Farce.[2] I
own this is hurrying you too much to write it and send it by
friday but I know your Genius that way so if you can and will
direct to me as usual at the Society I will thank you—
    I am sorry this day to see a very bad account of the King not
only as to his mental derangement but also his bodily health. To
lose him at the present critical juncture would be a heavy shock
to the Nation. I pray heartily for his recovery. All eyes are now
bent towards the Prince, a natural anxiety prevails among all
ranks but we must hope alls for the best.[3]—This time last

eason you was with us it was a happy time I wish it was to come
over again. Last Sunday I saw a Mr Whittele,[4] whom you must
recollect he desired his Compts to you when next I wrote he is to
spend the Xmas with us—Frank Squibbs is gone to Exeter for 2
Years Land Surveying[5] before [he] went he begged kindly to be
remembered to you indeed all who knew you desire the same—
     You have taken up a sentence in my last letter about pleasure.
I am hurried now or should answer your remarks so shall postpone them till the next when I hope to convince you my asser-
tion is right—I expect a Frank for a letter next week[6] when I
mean to send you a long epistle & one of my best you must
excuse me now writing more I should not leave off or short but I
expect the Postman every minute & if it misses going to night it
won't arrive with you in time for you to send a prolouge by
riday—do oblige.
          Your affectionate friend
          JOHN H. REYNOLDS.
Am Soc^y
5 OClock
24th Dec^r

A Happy Xmas to you and your Friends.

28

From Mrs Reynolds

[13 May, 1811.]

I have no doubt my good friend but a thousand fanciful Ideas
have possessd your Mind, that the Lambeth folk are fickle
beings, hard to please, &c. &c. I cannot positively tell you your
thoughts (if as above conjectured) are vague & groundless, but I
think they are.—The fatigue of nursing my family when ill in
the winter, brought on a return of my complaint & has left me in
so weak & nervous a state that I am little beyond an Ideot, or
Infant. Indeed it is a farce for me to attempt writing to any one,
but I know you so well, that you would protest it were all a
falshood, that I were Idle, wanting in friendship, & so on—

However my letters will support the above statement.—I generally, when I sit down to write to you, manage so as to mislay your last *foolish* Epistle, & puzzle myself to recollect whether there is any particular subject incumbent on me to answer. This is positively the case now, but I am determind to find your late favor ere I finish this, & ere I place it among your many sensible productions to say nothing of the foolish ones.—Just as I wrote the last sentence, I arous'd & sought your letter that I might make good my resolves, alas it was not to be found, I think John must have had it, & that will vex me not a little as I have all the others safe. You know I keep whatever letters I receive unless some mischance like the present deprive me of them. By the bye, speaking of John, yesterday was the Aniversary at his Office, & of course the first public Dinner Son John ever made his appearance at. Whatever pleasure the antissipation or enjoyment of it might afford him, to me it was a day of the utmost anxiety, as he is infinitely too young to enter into such amusements, (or rather such Miseries). He arrivd back at 10 at Night most compleatly finishd. This morn$^\mathrm{g}$ he returnd to business. I expect him back at four, very ill no doubt, nor shall I feel sorry as it will give him a disgust, I hope to the repetition of such scenes.[1] True, this was not to be got rid of & I thank God it occurs but once a Year. He continues the same good pleasant fellow you left, if possible you would love him better than ever. He is all a Mother can wish, or a Sister want. Pray have you collected any seals—you promised a little good Girl of mine you would send her some curious ones.[2] If you have kept your word which I cannot doubt take some method to let her have them, & Marianne will thank you for them. I fancy to myself I hear you say what a selfish creature this old Dame Reynolds is, she writes but seldom & then tis for what she can get—dont tell stories friend Dove she is not a selfish Woman, & whenever you are dispos'd to ask of her if it is in her power to oblige you she is ready. So much for all that. Pray how do you go on with your welsh Borders. & now for a bit of *your* old stile: now for it. I remember the time when you woud have forwarded such things without a hint from me—as your brain produc'd good things, they would have been communicated to Lambeth—they would not have been snug'd up in your fusty library but sent off with all the energy of an author, instead of which how alter'd is the scene. A short letter, about the middle of which is enter'd six or eight lines of your Poem, with a host of complaints of the change of affairs &c. Now are not the above complaints exactly as

64

you go on. I cannot but laugh at you, bless you, you are not neglected nor are things so much amiss as you are feign to paint them. 'Tis true you do not write so often or so well quite as you were wont—but it cannot be expected of a Man who is sometimes mounted on Pegasus one day, another at the top of a high hill or sporting with the Lasses on its summit, sometimes a commissioner—always a Counsellor. This much consider'd, I make allowances that you do not write as you have done, & you do so by me. All except myself are amongst the tolerables, I am an intolerable creature & scarce worth the room I fill . . . Your last to John was a *bit* of a cutter,[3] he thought so—but it was not one of your worst I must say. The whole string of the Reynolds send kind remembrances—my dear Jenny Mackay as is usual with her sends compts to Jackey—It appears hardly credible that this insignificant paper was to have been sent off by last Night's Post, but delay'd by a triffling event. When lo this morning old Nick arriv'd & set us all grinning at your expence. I suppose he was displeas'd I should make such complaints of the indolence of your Muse & has boldly step'd forth in your behalf—his Devilship never appear'd to me so pleasant as on the present occasion, I hope he will stir you up to do something more. We all think the thing wittily & well done, I should have no objection, to mount the Hill on the 21st of June, tho for myself I should not be able to accomplish so arduous an undertaking the '*Kissing Stone*' would be the extent of my journey I fancy.[4] We wish you all happiness, fine weather, fine ladies, and all the rest will follow—our kind remembrances to you—write after this day is over and say how it pass'd[5]—adieu

CHARLOTTE REYNOLDS.

April 13th 1811.

May I mean

29

From John Hamilton Reynolds

My Dear Friend,

If you were to see my phiz now you would see a very awkward shamefaced fellow the reason both I and You know the only excuse—'Idleness'—

First I have to thank you for your most excellent verses for Breidden—I had the impudence also to take them as an invitation to the sport—I'm tied hand and leg—hand tied to the pen—and I'm tied or rather untied by the leg having snapt a small leader cf the foot at Cricket—[1]

Scott has a small poem in the press and another in hand of large dimensions[2]—he is going (I am informed) to the Isle of Wight to cull Scenery for the undertaking[3] I am excessive fond of all his works but like Marmion the best—I wish I was $^1/_{16}$ as clever as he is I think I shold go ¾ mad with joy—what a misery it is to be born a fool with just wisdom enough to know that you are one—I have not seen a tree that bears any thing like a green color for ½ year I thing [*for* think] I'm getting a most compleat Cockney Clerk that thinks it a blessing to be allowed a Walk upon sundays—sweats at the pen like a Bull all the week for 100£ !!! a Year with no rest save that at Bed time—Devil take it!—

I now and then read of some pleasure that you enjoy at West Felton in the Gentlemans Mag[4]—by the by if you have a copy (without any trouble to yourself) which you can well spare of 'Prometheus'[5] pray send it me I pride myself upon being acquainted with one Poet and consequently do all in my Power to possess myself of most of his works. A Lady I know has fallen over (devil take the pen) head and ears in love with Old Nick from your extraordinary description of him—One Sin and a *Wapper* upon your head—My Mother (to whom you owe a Letter and who desires kind remembrance) has written a very good address for our Anniversary[6] which as soon as it is printed I will take care you shall have a copy of—Mr Hudson (whom you must recollect) is dead and has left a large Family in rather a distressed state.[7] Miss Box (your most accomplished and favourite)[8] is not married yet so you may still have hopes of possessing a good Wife.

—Upon looking back I perceive a jumble of nonsensical remarks and uninteresting intelligence put together without care or ability—I am confident of my want of power at Letter writing and the only good my epistles are of is in drawing sensible ones from you—pray write soon Yours most faithfully

J. H. REYNOLDS.

Amicable Society's Office
Fleet Street 14 June 1811

30

From John Hamilton Reynolds

[2 September 1811] [1]
Am Soc Off

My Dear Friend,

I will endeavour to atone for my abominable neglect by writing an unusually long letter as for excuses upon the subject of not writing sooner you must be so well acquainted with the generality of them that I will pass them over—The first thing I shall converse upon is a play! we are going to perform one 'The Rivals'[1]—your humble Servant is to personate *two* Characters (small enough Heaven knows for one) viz. Sir A Absolute and Faulkland the one a Testy Old Gentleman the other a Sentimental Whining Lover.—Now as you were so kind last year even at a minute's notice to favor me with a Prologue and one that deserved every praise for its genuine Wit I make so bold as again to request one for my delivering if therefore you will write one *as soon* as you are at leisure and drop it in the post directed to me at my Office I shall be particularly obliged—My Mother is writing a letter to you in which she will talk to you upon coming up this Winter I shall be *very happy* to see you—I have read and have been highly delighted with a poem of Campbell's named 'Gertrude of Wyoming' let me recommend it to you as a poem worthy of attention.[2] I must not forget to tell you that I am turned Fisherman-Angler-Troller the few spare days I can get are employed at the Water—I should like some sport at West Felton but Heaven knows when I shall be able to accomplish my wishes—

I have since the commencement of my letter been able to get a Frank therefore if possible I mean to persuade my Mother to write with this. She I am sorry to say has been very ill lately and with respect to letters is in debt to most of her Friends—you amongst the rest—We have had grand work at the Theatres with the horses I cant say I felt much pleasure at seeing them the papers were all up in arms attempting to vindicate the wrongs of the Stage and vainly endeav^g to *recal public* taste and the summer Theatres were all burlesquing as much as possible the pieces of the Winter ones Asses instead of Horses—Colman's the best that I have seen it abounds with wit and is written as a rehearsal after the manner of Sheridan's Critic[3]—You seemed to hint in your last letter that you had some intentions of publishing your poem[4] I hope you still keep in the same Mind—Frank Squibb is near your Country he is in Wales and I understand is very highly delighted with the place—I don't think I told you that William is taken in partner[ship] with the Gentleman he was brought up with lucky fellow![5] We expect Miss Mackay up with us very soon I wish you could m[ake] it convenient to meet her—you [are] a great favourite—I believe I have told you all the News of London and shall conclude with expressing myself your most sincere Friend

J. H. REYNOLDS.

All join me in most heartfelt remembrances
   dont forget the [prologue].

31

From Mrs Reynolds

[2 September, 1811] [2]

D^r freind,

   John has got a frank which is to go from here at five, it is now 4 & I leave you to judge what can be said in so short & hurried a period of time. I have been in appearance very remiss to you, as your last letter certainly deserv'd an immediate answer but half the time I have been without a Servant the other half plagued to death with them, & the whole of the time so ill that I feel quite incapable to write at all. All the civilities of your Epistle I kindly thank you for.—With respect to your visit to London I must say a little on this score—a bed I have not to offer you as Jane has enter'd into business for herself which has depriv'd me of every possibility to accommodate you as to sleeping, having resignd that Room as a School room to her.[1]—But if you can creep up the sleeve of some good Hostess for a Nest, Mr R. & self will feel happy to see you at our humble Dwelling as often as you like to partake our homely but welcome fare—When I say this you are to understand you will be kindly receiv'd without any fuss or ado—the sound of the Postmans Bell[2] has put me aside from useing more pressing or powerful arguments than the forgoing.—We all unite in kind & good wishes to you

  & I remain your freind
   as usual C. REYNOLDS.
Septr 2^d 1811.

32

From John Hamilton Reynolds

           Novr 4th 1811

My Dear Friend,

I am astonished at your silence, it is now 2 Months at least since I wrote to you & according to the *etiquette* of writing I should not send this Letter but as I should be hurt at losing any Friend without enquiring the cause of his withdrawing his Esteem and as I should be particularly hurt at forfeiting *your* Friendship—I waive all form—and Write again. My Mother thinks that my frivolous manner of correspond[in]g has disgusted [you] but you should think with Sheridan that 'when Friendship guides the pen he must be a brute who finds fault with the Style.'[1] I hope to hear *soon* from you.

We have had fine work with Bell & Lancaster. A furious correspondence has been kept up in the Papers Lancaster has retir'd to his position in the Borough with a determination to war no more. I am sick of both.

Last Night 'Measure for Measure' was got up at Covent Garden

Theatre. Mrs Siddons performed Isabella—Kemble the Duke—
I'll warrant the play was well acted—Mrs Siddons will retire
from the Stage this Season—

> 'like a bright Exhalation in the Evening
> and no man see her more'—[2]

upon which account Coriolanus—The Winter's Tale and
'Venice Preserved' are preparing for her to shine in. I saw her
performance of Isabella in The Fatal Marriage lately and was
much affected.[3] Kemble played Biron—'excellent well,' though
in my opinion his performance of Penruddock in The Wheel of
Fortune is his Masterpiece of acting there the studious manner
of deportment becomes him and that pedantick formality which
is so disgusting in most of his characters in that is admirable.[4]

I am going to learn Greek by a new method which is by using
an English & Greek Grammar instead of a Latin & Gk. one
whereby the Rules are more easily understood and a person may
learn Greek without understanding Latin it is certainly a clearer
& shorter way and consequently the best.[5] I hope you still keep
in the same mind about coming up to Town at Christmas I and
all at home shall be happy to see you. I am sorry to say my
Mother has been very ill and is far from well now so that you
must not stand upon form in corresponding with her for she has
not half the spirits she had—My Father is over head & ears in
business I think he applies himself too close and that so strict an
attention will not be beneficial to his health in the main, he
desires his kind remembrance to you—When I last wrote to you
I took the liberty of requesting a prolouge for our play but from
not receiving it I conclude you was too busy to attend to my
desire—I hope you will write to me soon and believe me

    your faithful Friend

    J. H. Reynolds.

Amicable Office
  Serj^{ts} Inn
   4th Novr 1811.

33

From Mrs Reynolds

[2 February, 1812]

D⁺ friend,

That I am a Sinner according to the common acceptation of the word I am very willing to admit & trust to be forgiven. But that I have sinned against friendship (in appearance) I blush to acknowledge, & know not that I can reasonably look for pardon. Were I to acquaint you with all the particulars why & wherefore I have so long been silent to you, it would swell a letter to a volume of uninteresting stupid matter—by way of explanation I can only tell you, that a train of Sickness, vexations, & events have deprivd me of paying you the attentions your sensible & entertaining Letters demand from my hand. I have just rummag'd the last—which, to my utter shame bears date June 23ᵈ 1811—but recollect I sent a few lines as an acknowledgement since, which breaks off the force of my neglect. You there speak of your delightful exploits & enjoyment in terms that would tempt an anchorite to wish to have made one of the party—that you rode thro' the Vyrnwy¹ on your return Home by mistake I do not wonder at after so recently quitting the '*Kissing Stone*'—by the bye you tell me that the Breidden Glee & Chorus are to be engraved & remitted to Lambeth. I fancy you have tasted 'Lethe' instead of any one of us you also wish an *Enemy* pick'd from the Lambeth group to speak seriously the faults of your Border Ballad, now in very truth I tell you I dont think you have one foe in my family—nor one friend eaqual to pass an opinion on your work so as to render it one Jot more valuable in the worlds Eye—of this you must be aware when you used the expression alluded to, but you have many friends at Lambeth who would be delighted to hear the praise it deserves bestowd upon it that they think it Merrits—not that I or any of us can speak can Judge properly even as far as our lame abilities extend, or we have only yet been favor'd with Stanza's from it—you forget to indulge us with the whole—but this omission has proceeded I know from your fancying yourself—*fancying* yourself—neglected on my part—O thou foolatum—I did not expect John Dovaston of the 'Boxen Bower' was such a Ninny²—but this you may take for granted whether you are friend or foe I look to the fulfilment of your promise that you forward the border Ballad & the Briedden

Glees to your old friends *at Lambeth*—I forbear to say much on our Bell system which is now arriv'd at the Zenith—as I know you are on the other, or rather on the wrong side—for this I pity you as I should have lik'd you to be one of us on this Head, but perhaps *you* like many of your side the question are a convert; if so I hail you as an ornament to our cause—if not & you still remain in darkness, I regret you as a ray of light separated by a cloud. Heaven knows how I can make myself understood for Jane John and a few friends are singing & playing the whole time & my attention is calld away every instant, for altho I am almost an old granny yet I have still a delight in Music. I need not tell you this I suppose. My Daughter has chang'd her instrument & got a very delightful ton'd one. Mr Reynolds solaces an hour now & then of a night by listening to it—he is well, but a little worn & fatigued with business he has scarce time to breath[e]. John was going to write to you two or three times which I prevented, thinking to send myself sooner than I have done, but I suppose you [will] have a letter ere it be long—he is just as Kemble mad as ever, the last Saturday he saw the delightful Young in Hamlet which has charm'd him very much[3]—he thinks him infinitely superior to K—in this Character as being more suitable to his age &c.—but if the Public continue to be fool'd as they are at present by the performance of an Elephant for a Kemble, a Horse for Young. an Ap[e] for Grimaldi & so on, Exeter change will then be preferable to Covent Garden Theatre & a more *reasonable* or rather the cheaper entertainment of the two—Kemble himself cannot rant louder or astonish the wondering audience more than the roaring of the poor goaded Elephant[4]—the great Beast contrary to the great Man I daresay would feel highly honord to be hissd off the Stage, but the generous Public choose to applaud, and the Manager as generously complies with their desires so this poor animal is feasted with Rice & apples when once they have compeld him on to keep him in any way decorous till he is forc'd off again for he is sometimes as Stobourn to depart as he is at others to enter. But enough of Performers of all Descriptions, you no doubt will be too tir'd to arrive so far as this part of my Sheet if you have patience I beg you will accept the kindest remembrances of Mr Reynolds myself & dear family to you—your friend

CHARLOTTE REYNOLDS.

Feb$^{\underline{ry}}$ 2$^{\underline{d}}$ 1812

can I have the assurance to say write soon[5]

34

From John Hamilton Reynolds

Amicable Office
23 June 1812

My dear Friend,

You must think me endued with the impudence of the very Devil himself when you see my scrawl once more after an ungrateful neglect of more than 4 Months bit I find that the longer I delay answering any friend the more inclined I feel myself to contrive the postponement not from any want of friendship but from an unaccountable idleness that increases upon me—

We have had Mr Shiel with us these last 2 days he is now settled at Burntwood in Essex[1] a distance of only 18 Miles from us. I wish most heartily that you lived as near.

I shall endeavour (though I am afraid without effect) to pay you a visit at the Nursery the end of this summer it would give me very particular pleasure I assure you the distance is certainly very great but I flatter myself I should meet with a welcome at the end of it—

I am going to see Mrs Siddons in Lady Macbeth on Monday next being the *last* time of her appearing upon the Stage.[2] I have witnessed her representation of every Character which She acts and hardly know which to admire most.[3] We have no prospects at her retiring of any one capable of filling up her place in Tragedy—I have seen Julius Caesar which has been got up with great splendor at Covent Garden and certainly reflects great Credit upon the managers. Kemble in Brutus and Young in Cassius are excellent.[4] The former kept up that Philosophical dignity that so nobly distinguished the Roman Patriot. The latter was equally good in the delineation of the hot and crafty Cassius—the Quarrel Scene drew repeated Plaudits from the Audience and I left the Theatre highly satisfied with the Evening's Entertain[men]t.

My sister has been in very ill health and is now in Cheltenham recruiting her strength[5] it is an unfortunate fact that ever since we have been at Lambeth one or other of the Family has been ill—

I am *still* prosecuting my study of the Greek language with *unabated* vigour—and have already made considerable advancement in it. I think it a most delightful language and shall feel great satisfaction when I become able to read Homer in his own garb (the grand point at which I aim)—You blame me for attempting by the English road to arrive at Greece but I assure you I find it so smooth and easy to travel upon that I should be inclined to recommend it to all others who have the same place in view.—The Latin Rules cannot impress themselves upon the memory or appear half so clear to the understanding as Rules written in the very language we are accustomed to speak.[6]

I hope you have not forgotten a promise you made of transcribing some of your poetical pieces at your leisure. I also hope you have not given up your intention of publishing the Poem (part of which I have received, read, and admired) written after the Style of Scott.[7]—you hinted that the said Poem might be the occasion of bringing you to Town pray let our house be the first place that holds you after quitting the Coach—

My Father is over head and ears in business as usual and hardly finds time for his meals he desires to me [*for* be] most kindly remembered to you as do my Mother & Sisters that are at home

> believe me yours truly
> and affectionately
> J. H. REYNOLDS.

I did not get the frank that brings this till 4 o'Clock PM so have been quite unprepared.[8]

35

From John Hamilton Reynolds

[2 July, 1812]

My Dear Friend,

I have delay'd writing as long as possible in hopes of accomplishing what I have so long wished but I am sorry to say there is still a bar to my coming immediately—Upon receiving your letter I applied to Mr Pensam[1] for leave of absence now instead of Sept^r (the time I mentioned to you as likely for my visit) but he informed me that owing to present business he should not be able to spare me till after the 10th of August and as that is a Month you expect to be from home I shall forego the pleasure of visiting you till next Year—The friendly & pressing manner in which you have invited me has given me most heartfelt pleasure, it has acted in like manner towards My Father & Mother who beg to be most kindly remembered to you with thanks for your kindness. If you should be at home in August (though I beg you will not put off any engagement for me) and will let me know I shall then be with you to a certainty—You must excuse my writing any thing like a proper letter of length & substance as I expect the Post to pass every moment so must conclude & make up my letter as the Spectator says with expressing myself at *proper distance* (which by the by I did expect to have expressed *near*)²

      Your most
        affectionate Friend
          J. H. REYNOLDS.

Pray let me hear from you by return of Post as it will satisfy me that you have received this.
2nd July 1812.

36

From John Hamilton Reynolds

[11 July, 1812]

My Dear Friend,

    I have been anxiously looking for an answer to a Letter I sent this day week and from not receiving one I very much fear mine has miscarried—I shall therefore give you the heads of it in this—Your very pressing & friendly letter came to hand about 10 days ago in which you request my company immediately—when I hinted in the letter (to which yours was an answer) of my paying you a visit this summer it was without any at home knowing of it and without any very clear prospect of leave of absence from [the] Office however your Letter has compleatly obtained my Father & Mother's sanction from its friendly and truly hospitable manner—I also shewed it to Mr Pensam and requested his permission which he told me I should readily have had but for the great flow of business at present in the Office he however has given me leave for a fortnight any time after the 11th of August but which time I fear will not suit you since you mention an intention of taking an Out[ing] at that time—Now though the pleasure I should receive from a visit to you would be beyond everything still I request you will not inconvenience yourself or give up any pleasure for me, but if on the contrary, you should have nothing to call you from home I shall at last have it in my power of accomplishing my long hoped for wish——

I had some thoughts of taking in an Edition of Shakespeare which is now publishing in Numbers from the Text of Steevens but as there is some probability of my knowing a little more as to the goodness of the several Editions now extant I shall postpone it. It is very likely that I may be wrong but Warburton's Shakespeare suits my taste most he does not attempt (like Malone & o̅r̅s) to find out the errors of every page but points out the beauties with a nice eye—[1]

I progress to be a *great Fisherman* & shall therefore bring down my tackle and if you are near any Water destroy accordingly—but you will smile to hear me build my Castles in the air—

I was at Covent Garden the Night of Mrs Siddons' retirement and was highly delighted at her acting.[2]

Pray write soon and *put me out of my misery.*

Father & Mother & Sisters send their kind remembrances and believe me very faithfully yours

J. H. REYNOLDS.

Serj^{ts} Inn
11 July 1812.

37

From John Hamilton Reynolds

[July–August 1812]

My Dear Friend,

I received your kind letter yesterday and shall instantly set off for your hospitable roof—

I shall start from London by the Mail on Sunday Even^g which will carry me to Shrewsbury where I should very much like you to meet me with Doll[1] and the Gig as I shall be a stranger to the Plan of getting on to Oswestry you know doubtless where the Mail arrives and at what time—

The Books I shall make a point of buying and bringing with me—Southey's Curse of Kehama is a most beautiful Poem I have read it upon the recommendation of Miss Mackay and admire it exceedingly.[2]

I am very glad to see fine weather preparing for my journey it seems as if the Sun had resolved to cheer me on my way though were the journey double the length I should perform it with ease by bearing in mind how well the pleasure of seeing my friend would repay me—

I had almost given up all hopes of seeing you this summer from the tenour of your last letter but one yet I must say never did any one pay so strict an attention to time as you have done— My Father & Mother & Sisters desire their most kind remembrance to you and thank you for the *very friendly* manner in which you have acted

'till I meet you upon Shropshire ground farewell'—[3]

J. H. REYNOLDS.

This is a kind of *ex officio information*

38

From Mrs Reynolds

D.ʳ friend,

As usual I have mislaid y.ʳ last letter to me, & cannot answer
many items I wish'd—it is not far off I know as I never destroy
any of them but it chooses to be absent on the present occasion
& my memory (which is not worth a rush) will not serve me at
all—*being* a selfish *being* I just recollect something like a
promise of some Music I ther[e]fore give you a touch on this
score—John our dear John will place this in your hands, & I
cannot but say I should like to make up the Trio—take care of
him for he is a good fellow. I dont like his travelling outside but
he prefers it. I expect about eleven at Night his usual drowsy fit
will overtake him & his Lordship will fall from his seat, Heaven
forbid such a misfortune, but he is engaged in it & I trust he will
arrive safe, & not meet with any thing that shall disturb the
pleasure he promisses himself in your society, a feast he has
long, very long anticipated——I wonder'd at M.ʳ Gribbles[1]
calling on you as he did not ask us for a letter of introduction,
but particulars John will inform you of. And 'tho last not least' I
now come to a theme particularly agreeable to me & that is your
Border Poem[2] which I look with a greedy eye for—quotations
from it are very well to read, but you are in the dark as to the
ingenuity & Plan of the whole Poem. I ther[e]fore shall have a
hump (if you do not send me two books) as big as the Breiden
Hill[3]—why I ask two is, that my belovd friend Jane Mackay may
have the compliment of one, for she is so fond of any scrap of wit
of yours that I would forgo the gratification of haveing it myself
that she should have it, & pray add from the author in your own
hand writing. I shall forward it to her with delight whenever you
come to London she intends coming also, Jane spent near a
fortnight with her & is but just returnd——I liked your last
Breiden bit well, that has been copied & sent to Bath, you may
feel yourself somewhat taller when such a Woman as my Jane
Mac enjoys your writings, beleive me Dov she is a very superior
being[4] & I wonder not a little that she has kept up such a long &
solid friendship, with such a grub as your humble servant—yet
so it is & I trust so it will be to the end of the Chapter for I love

her next to my Husband & bratts. I am just disturbd by Son John's sudden start of 'God Mother theres the Guns'—which are firing away for the brave news from Portugal, it has a little interrupted the eulogium on my friend but she will excuse me on so joyous an occasion—the Spaniards will adore Wellington—& the English will Hail him as their Saviour.[5] I am glad the boy sets sail with such Glorious news in his budget—the Bells have treated us with a merry Peal & I who am an invalid in the true sense of the word feel renovated—there never sure was a female who felt more for the success of their Country than my poor feeble self. If it had pleas'd heaven to have made mee [*sic*] a Lord of the Creation I think I should have been a brave one—but Lord, perhaps not, I might then, not even have had more Courage than I possess now—it may be very possible not as much—remember you talk'd of something in your letter like a Breiden Glee let us have it or any thing in that way—the kindest regards of our domestic party are sent to you G. R. sends his compts.—not our good King but *my* good Husband *so no more at present* from your sincere friend

CHARLOTTE REYNOLDS.

August 16th
  1812

39

From John Hamilton Reynolds
[August–September, 1812] [1]

Vain pomp & glory of the world, I hate you![1]
    Never did I return with greater disgust to 'the fog & filthy air'[2] of London as now—accustomed to the undisturbed pleasures of the Country Crowded streets will of course have few if any charms for me 'how great is the transition from silence & content to bustle & confusion where all without is noise & all within are anarchy & tumult.' The word tumult reminds me that I ought to give you a *small* account of my journey.[3]
    The Passengers were far from agreeable & that I very quickly found out. The Men were all knaves & the women fools for such

company you know I have an utter abhorrence—We all rode along in *silent* horror for the distance of about four miles the Coach then seemed to be jolting us into a humour for talking. One directed a Question at his right hand traveller about the harvest but without allowing time for an answer whisked his empty head to the left and tortured another with the same question. The Coachmans conversation was vulgarly sharp & cunning—thus passed the whole day upon the *top* of the Coach but the night was more horrible for though I found means to get inside 'rest were impossible' an Irishman was bringing his Wife (who laboured under fits of derangement) to town in hopes of curing her by change of *air*. Every five minutes she was talking loud & incoherent—he was swearing—We were grumbling; so that by the Morning every passenger 'was as mad as she.' I arrived in town by six o'Clock last evening melancholy mad but the pleasure of seeing all at home brightened up my ugly visage and cheered my gloomy soul. After some refreshment I read them those poems which they had never seen viz: 'Echo'— 'Kynaston's' &c.[4]—also Rylance's Summer & Winter Songs[5] with all of which they are highly delighted—by the bye pray send me up one more copy of Kynaston's Cave if you can spare it by Rylance when he comes to Town—Walter Scott is going to publish another poem price 2 Gñas Quarto as usual called [blank space left in letter]. His Works always come into the World very pompously drest at first; but time crops their pride & size at the same time.—Longman & Co. are now publishing a very elegant Edition of Shakespeare large Octavo. I have some thoughts of buying it if not too expensive—the notes are selected from those of Steevens Malone Warburton &c.—a good edition of Shakespeare I want. There is another Number of that *damned* book the Edinburgh Review just published I must procure a sight of it and read the *list of deaths* for the last Quarter—Pope should not have written that line of 'Oh! Grave where is thy victory, Oh! Death where is thy sting?'[6] because any one that has ever read the book will be able to answer him immediately—I have put that letter of yours to the Revd J. Nightingale[7] into the Post as I find it will be impossible for me to get there to see him in any reasonable time but as to Rylance's Letter to his Mother, I shall deliver that in propria persona, the meaning of which (as you don't understand Latin *any better* than your friend) is 'I shall see her and not trust to others to deliver it for me considering that any thing I can do is but a poor return for the delight Mr Rylance's conversation has afforded me'—(a free translation) but to you I am 'doubly bound' not only for your pleasant and enlightened company but also for the hospitality & attention I experienced under your roof[8] & pray my dear Dovaston whenever you have any business that wants transacting in Town make use of me—employ me any way you shall find me not forgetful of your kindness —I have procured Spenser's Translation of Leonora[9] and still (without any predetermination) after a full consideration of its beauties—after a fair comparison with the other versions I think it infinitely better—the language is more Elegant, the Style more chaste—but I am talking (alias writing) to one who has been *a Critic* and is more able to form an opinion of its Merits—I shall copy it immediately and think it can be got into one sheet, if so, will you have it sent by post? or would you rather have it left at Crosby's to be sent to Wotton [?]. You can mention, in your answer to this, your opinion—Don't forget that Rylance & you are to write me a joint Letter,[10] I beg you will get the largest sheet of Paper you can and begin directly—I anticipate great pleasure from it well knowing the merits of the Actors—'Oh answer me, let me not burst in *ignorance.*'[11] Pray have you been to the Giants Grave—the Ogo—the—&c. &c. I *pant* to know what Rylance will think of the scenery round there,[12] I for my part was highly delighted with the views in [word missing]. Nature has been lavish of her beauties about the [word missing] Hills. NB. If you have not been—but are going pray call at the Trusten[13] as I think the Persons who keep the Inn there are very worthy people and ought to be encouraged—Mr Pensam is out of Town had I but known it I could have stayd two or three days longer which would have been fortunate—but 'Heaven thought otherwise'—

My Father & Mother desire their kindest remembrance and thanks for your goodness—Sisters ditto—ditto to what the last two have said—I myself desire the same and remain your affectionate and grateful friend J. H. REYNOLDS otherwise Wm WIMBLE.[14]

⁎ Service to Mr Shortface

Tell Mrs Turner that I shall deliver her sons letter myself to-day—direct my letter to Office
I have written this Letter without any mention of the Theatres to show you that I can scribble upon paper without calling them into use—My style was always bad—I'll reform it altogether— My letters shall not in future be mere play Bills.

40

From John Hamilton Reynolds

Folks say (and I don't know but that there is truth in the saying) 'it is best to strike when the iron is hot'—Now, as I have just received your Letter and have made up my mind to *write* one more scrawl before Rylance quits the 'Felton Groves' it will be most advisable to work away while the subject is *hot* in my mind.—These few words above are written by way of preface or rather as a sentence explanatory of my reasons for addressing you again. I shall now treat with you separately.

'Rylance a word with you'

your Hawking Pen appears to be well trained and also to be possessed of great natural capacity; I admire its choice of prey very much—in fact the only use of this present Letter is to 'lure my tassel-gentle back again'[1]—its performances never need *pounceing*; so far it differs from beings of its own nature.— Don't frighten yourself about Coach companions, you will no doubt be classed with a better species; Some you know are born with silver spoons in their Mouths, and others with Wooden ladles, I was crammed with one of the latter, aye, & an oaken one if I may guess by its hardness—You tell me that I omitted mentioning any account of the Bookstalls; the reason was that I wrote the letter almost immediately upon my arrival in town— consequently I had not seen many; I have however taken a peep at them since and have poppd upon the scent of Burton's Anatomy.[2] The Woman says she has an *old Copy* somewhere and that she will look it out I'll get one in spite of the Spoon.— Beresford's *Miseries of Life*[3] are not upon the Stalls yet, I think. —When you come to Town I will go with you the Book circuit; I shall be very glad when that takes place though I know how difficult it will be for *you* who are your own Lord and Master to resolve upon leaving Felton & Dovaston—My answer to your Q^y about B.M. and B.H. is Ballad Monger & Beauty Hunter— damme I know I should puzzle the knowing ones—why did not you translate it Bard of Hotspur?—I am very anxious that you should begin your poem of 'St. Magdalene's Eve'[4]—your idea of opening with a description of the battle is good—it would have a fine effect—you would also have the *rough* work over at once and work on *smoothly* to the end—pray carry this, your intention into effect.—

I am pleased to 'hear' that you have exerted our oratorical powers in defence of Clarice[5] at the last meeting of the House of Representatives;—you know my opinion of that lady,—you know how warmly I am her friend—I would deliver a written speech in her favor (it would not be at all agst my character as a Member of Parliament) did I not well know how able you are to support her rights;—I think the next time she is debated upon there ought to be a call of the house.—

I delivered your Letter to your Mother myself—She was drinking tea at a friend's opposite of the name of Cromeck; some relation of Cromeek who collected Burns' remaining Works[5] it struck me. Your quotation there is very, very excellent, but not true—

> The service and the loyalty I owe,
> in doing it, pays itself.—Your Highness' part
> is to receive our duties.—[7]

Kemble I believe is in Town but as yet unengaged with either Theatre—The Chronicle of today says that he is in treaty with Drury Lane—Another says Cov^t Garden. There is a new farce 'in Rehearsal and will speedily be produced with new Scenery Machinery Dresses Music & Decorations' at the Haymarket—I have not been to the Theatre since my return to Town.—

I have now I believe 'kill'd every question by rule' as Ollapod[8] says and have nothing particular further to add except how much I am your really obliged and faithful friend—J. H. REYNOLDS.

One down and the other come on—Now that I have well *worded* Rylance about the Eyes—Heads & Ears little remains for me to do than to serve you my dear friend in the same manner—so have at you but I am afraid I have expended so much of my strength upon Ry. that a sufficiency will hardly remain to enable me to combat you; however—I'll try—I'll try—aye & quickly, ill deeds are seldom slow, nor single—in the first place I have copied Leonora (egad the tale is as long as her name), I will pack it up together with Robin Adair[9] which I have got written out for you and leave them at Crosby's for Watton immediately—You are right,—Rokeby is the name of Scott's poem[10]—I had left a space for the name I recollect, and forgot to put it in afterwards—but I see talking to you upon this is nonsense—its like sending news of the Army—to Spain.

What a devil of a blow up you appear to be making, amongst the small game—'leave them alone can't you'—it was a pity to destroy the nest in your Orchard they could not hurt anything there

> 'Oh yet I do repent me of my fury,
> that I did kill them.'[11]

Bid Rylance be bloody bold & resolute, laugh to scorn, the power of wasps, for none of hornets born—shall harm him[12]—I never think of the Nursery without a degree of pleasure—I never spent a happier fortnight in my life than that at West Felton 'I sin in envying your nobility, and were I any thing, but what I am, I'd wish me only you.'[13]—Some one mentioned to me yesterday that Moore is about to publish more poems I hope he will—for his lines are truly poetical[14]—Covent Garden opens today with Romeo & Juliet.—I like the Theatres to commence with a Play of Shakespeare's—the name is almost a charm against a bad season—I cannot go on any further as Will Wimble is rather anxious to insert a few words to his Friends Sir Roger and The Spectator[15]—Father Mother & Sisters desire kind remembrances to you, and believe me your grateful & faithful friend J. H. REYNOLDS.

Dear Shortface,

I suppose this will find thee blowing of hornets or drinking of ale—I *wood* I were with you—I know my Letters are not composed of proper stuff for your learnd head—not thorough bred;—but really Mr Spec. they are genuine. Pray be particular to take the comb completely out or you will be doing little good —I have *thought* of a new way of destroying them which I shall take an early opportunity of adopting and remain with great respect your obed$^\text{t}$ humble Serv$^\text{t}$

W$^\text{m}$ WIMBLE.

$\star_\star^\star$ pray show the bottom part to Mr Knight—

My dear Sir Roger

Pray save me a pup of the Spaniel Bitch as I have a great admiration for the breed—it strikes me if you look in the Barley Stubble you will yet find the Guinea hen—it was with great concern that I observed the last time I was with you that your Gun wanted a new flint—I shall therefore bring some with me

84

the next time I visit Felton—Pray tell Mr Spectator when he rides Mr Davenport's Poney not to curb him tight—I make this request to you as I know you can inform him more learnedly, understanding his ways——I have seen that part of your visitor Mr Rylance's letter where he talks about Hawkes' squirrells—& small game—and like it hugely—he is I dare say a very shrewd man—pray is he a good shot?

I should very much like to see him—please to tell Mrs Turner that I delivered her letter safe and saw Mr T. he was quite well—NB he has got a very pretty terrier puppy which I think promises to be a good ratter. I hope you will take care of yourself the next winter and pray look sharp as I hear of two Men of the name of Addison & Steel—the first I am told means to *kill* you that the other mayn't *murder* you—have your house well guarded—I dare say they are *Mohocks*.[16]

 I remain dear Sir Roger
  thine eternally
   Wm WIMBLE.

P.S.—Service to Mr Salter

I beg Dovaston you will upon the Receipt of this take one of your Whole Sheets of Paper and call in Rylance's aid to write me a good terrific Epistle, 'shed ink enough, oh! how You please me'—You will have this letter by 10 oClock Tuesday Evening you can write an answer so as put in the Post by Wednesday Evening and I shall get it by Friday Morning—so all's settled—

Something more—My Father & Mother will be glad to see Mr Rylance to dinner on Monday next at four o'Clock if he should be in Town.[17]

41

From Mrs Reynolds

Sepr 2d 1812.
[2–3 September, 1812.]

My Dear Friend,

Our Son is safe arriv'd, & his countenance speaks (if nothing else) the kindness you have shewn him while with you. To whom does it belong to speak of gratitude? You have long talkd to me of it & I always thought you said too much, now tis my task, & I find how pleasing it is to express the feelings of a heart overflowing with the above delightful sensations. I thank you for the friendship & hospitable treatment of my Boy, it would appear overmuch to say all I think, you would call me flatterer, chatterer and such like Nonsense names, to avoid which I plainly tell you I am more than commonly pleas'd, & only wait to see you once again at Lambeth, where if good Friendship, Beef & Beer, will have any avail you shall not lack either also a snug nest to repose in—& I trust the Period not far distant when G. R. & myself & family shall greet you—at six last night Jack bolted in, & from then till eleven he read & talkd, till I began to think he would die of fatigue—of you, your friend, & the wonders of Wales, he incessantly prated, also of your charming Poem which I am more than half mad to read & which as soon as compleated I beg you will order The Publisher to send me two books & I will immediately remit him the Money—I am aware I took a liberty in asking you to supply me, but you have heretofore spoild me—I intended to have sent this letter last Night but on John's return to Dinner I learn'd he had dispatchd one to you, upon which I chang'd my mind & thought it more adviseable to postpone writing till some other opportunity, but today I turnd the matter over again woman like, & determind you should have it whether or no.—Jack tells me you need not be troubled about getting the Books for me as he says they are to be sold in London & he will have them directly they appear—he promised to bring us a Welsh tune which he, by his own account was too well engagd to copy. I will trouble you to do it & I trust from the amiable character of your friend Mr Rylance that he will take charge of it for us to London—this is I own taking a freedom but if we shall have the pleasure to see him I will atone as far as possible for the liberty—My Son is delighted with him

& much covets a continuance of his acquaintance—if he can endure it with such a will-o'wisp & harum scarum as my Boy—tell me if you think him improv'd—not in Person but understanding—I shall look to you for truth on this point. I fond as I am of him can bear to hear your opinions & advice let them be ever so frankly spoken—& indeed if you were to flatter him I should soon perceive it. Is he not a little too volatile?—but I ask you to give me your thoughts & am very near taking the task out of your hands—He bids me say the space left in his letter to you relating to Scott's new work is to be filled with the word *Rokeby*—I am so broke, & my eyesight fails me so rapidly that I shall never be able to write to you much & I am so sensible of the lamentable change that I feel mortified, as it deprives me of receiving many sensible letters from you & which ever conduc'd greatly to my pleasure & that of my family.—I regret not that I am going down hill, but I should like to retain my good Spirits & there are many that do, but I fear this will not be my case.—but this is a language you cannot understand I therefore wa[i]ve it—some thirty summers hence you may begin to comprehend it—'all my little ones' are gone to Elistons Benifit[1] & John follows at half Price I shall sit alone till twelve—cannot see to write, read, or work—dont you think my time will be very entertainingly spent? What would you do my active minded friend in so pitiable a case? I fancy to myself I hear you say, why damme I would think, & get some one to write for me—true this might do John Dove with you, but I can't even think . . . for I not only want eyes but head—but least you should expect I am quite a Joan—I must tell you I have not yet taken to my Pipe, or a walking stick—Mr R. & family desire me to say every civil thing to you I can suggest & compts to your friend Mr Rylance—The Musical Glasses we hear much of—thou art a clever fellow. 'adieu, adieu, adieu, remember me.'[2]

    yr friend

    CHARLOTTE REYNOLDS.

Septr 3d 1812.

Who can I better ask to 'tell me where is Fancy bred'[3] I request you to let me have this elegant thing with the Music. I am angry that John was too Idle to copy such a feast for his family.

42

From John Hamilton Reynolds

[15 September 1812]

I saw Rylance yesterday, and he told me that he was going to
write to you. I have obtained the Frank and offered him the use
of it which he has accepted—but as the cover itself will not be
used inwardly—I shall take the opportunity of saying a few
words to you upon it.

Our very clever Friend dined yesterday with My Father and
Mother at Lambeth—A Gentleman that has travelled a great deal
but very honestly brought little away from the various places he
has seen was of the Party.—I was anxious that Rylance should be
suited—which I think he was, in the company of an Uncle of
Mine (a very clever man) and one who has a tolerable share of
Taste for the ancient & modern classics.[1]—My Mother admires
Rylance very much upon a first view which is a great thing—for
he is not a Man that appears to advantage at the beginning of an
acquaintance, but the more he is known, the more he is liked;—
He has made great progress with his Poem, I delight in the Lady
Cecilia's Song,[2] it possesses all the enchanting simplicity of the
English ballad;—His opening is also good, it commands atten-
tion, by introducing a prominent character in a fine situation at
once. I was glad to hear that Morris[3] makes greater haste with
FitzGwarine[4] the manner in which he composed it while I was
with you was as injurious to you as it was to himself—The
Public which are now in expectation of speedily seeing your
Poem out should be satisfied by its appearing early—I'll insure
that they are satisfied after its appearance. Rylance and I have
talked it over thoroughly together.—We find no conversation so
pleasant as that which touches upon West Felton and the [word
illegible] thereunto be[longing]. I think if Rylance had begun
his Poem earlier when he was at the Nursery it would have been
better[5]—for it is impossible to find a Place more suited to the
purpose.—I am going to purchase Child Harold as it is now
published in Octavo.[6] I have heard it strongly recommended as a
Poem combining all the beauties of the Muses in its pages. You
should have it I think.—Leonora[7] I suppose is by this time
arrived in Shropshire, as I left her at Crosby's more than a week
ago; how do you like her dress? is she clad better than her antag-
onists? tell me truly.—Squibbs are going to give a very grand

entertainment at their house at Ealing upon Frank coming of age—or as they call it more properly, his birthday.[8] A Breakfast at 3 oClock, Afternoon! and a Ball in the Evening.—I shall enjoy the Dance much.—

The Zetesophians[9] get on nobly, I am to be one of the elected at their next meeting, I mean to brush up my Latin and make it fresh in my mind—it is a pity what little belongs to me should die—Greek will also meet with my particular attention. Write soon and according to our promised plan—

 this from you faithful friend
  J. H. REYNOLDS.

I have just seen Rylance—he dines today at the Coffee House with a Mr Lewis.
Septr. 15th. 1812.

43

From John Hamilton Reynolds

Am Socᵞ Off. 9 Apˡ 1813

Dear Dovaston,

 The delay of Rylance's intended Felton journey may be said to be the cause of my long silence,—it was my intention to have sent a few lines in his pocket to you, but as he finds it impossible to proceed until the 20th or thereabouts I have altered my mind and write accordingly.

 I have been puzzled at a sentence on one of the slips of your last letter which mentions an advertisement of your work as a Quarto. The proposal has never met my eye, neither can I imagine how or where it appeared or by whom it was written. Inform me of these particulars.

 I am going to deliver an Essay to the Zetesophians on Wednesday next;—I have given it the following title 'Reflections on Posthumous Fame, and its effect upon the minds of the Ancients.'[1] I have taken some pains with it and am particularly anxious that it should be well received; but perhaps 'there, where I had garner'd up my hopes'[2] I may fail . . . I called on Mr Walker[3] the other day and mentioned your Poems to him, and at the same time intimated to him that perhaps you would be pleased to hear that he had promoted the sale of them. I took care to mention to him however that you had no other view than that of fame as the profits were entirely the property of another.

I believe it is in my power to convey a copy of your Work to the Editor of the British Critic[4] by means of Mr Hatchard[5] who is particularly kind and attentive to my Father; But I have no other copy than my own which I purchased, and as the Review is only a Monthly one I think it is hardly worth seeing about.

We have had but a sick House of it latterly; My Mother's health is still bad, and mine far from what may be called good; I have some ideas that I shall never die 'full of Years'—but I must 'defy augury.'[6]

I hope the Sun will shine as gloriously on the 23^d Ap^l as it does at the present moment. Are we to expect an Ode on that Day from you?—Will Rylance exert his poetical powers on the Occasion? I hope both he and you will;—The Spirit of Shakespeare will not smile on your festivities unless an offering is made to him from Genius and Worth . . . An elegy on his death, or an ode on his Birth is a tribute that is surely due annually.[7] —Let the Day come as she will her appearance must be suitable; —if Bright and Cheerful, her countenance is joyful in commemoration of the Birth of Shakespeare, if gloomy, it is but an aspect mournful for his death. The 23^d of April may be *similied* to the 21st of October, on the former day Nature obtained a compleat conquest but at the same time lost her hero; on the last England was blessed with a [glor]ious victory but was likewise deprived of her wa[rrio]r . . .[8] I think Mr Shiel is a very eleg[ant] Latin Poet; I have in my possession some [of his?] manuscript verses, they please me very much.[9] Why do you not rouse the Latian Muse? 'You [who] like to do such things'—

I perceive you are very methodical in your correspondence and will not pay a line more than what is due: else why have you been so silent these four weeks past?—let me beg of you when an idle moment is stealing on you, kill it by writing to me.

I am your very Affectionate
Friend J. H. Reynolds.

44

Dear Dov,

It has been a matter of great grief to me to find that our late worthy Friend, R. Rylance, has departed this Life;[1] I had hoped to have seen his merits duly appreciated by an admiring world, but Death has nipped his blossoms in the bud, blossoms that promised the fairest fruit!—He cut a good pen—and dead! wrote a good sentence,—and Dead!—

> Lord Rylance for *thy Life*
> Would I had lost *my hand*.[2]

Has the devoted son of the Muses left a Will? Has he, my Dearest Friend, left any papers in y^r hand?—I believe it was his intention to have put his hand to the 2^d Canto of a Poem yclep'd St Magdalene's Eve;[3] if any should be done, (which I question) pray forward it to me, as I intend publishing every scrap of prose & poetry of his that I can find, with a short account of his life prefixed. It is a *melancholy* duty, but yet it is one; if his spirit should be looking over your shoulder when you read this, it will recollect a promise which I made to his fleshly case to this effect.

I understand he was very well 'till his decease, that he sat at the Table near the Sun Dial laving his clay and puffing at the Evening Sky with great sociability. Alas! poor soul he little thought, his Spirit was more than half seas over! or that each whiff of tobacco was the nearly [*sic*] the last gasp of Life! . . . I shall certainly write a very careful Epitaph, and perpetuate his memory in the——Lady's Museum.[4] Is it true that he dropped his last tear in a mug of Stingo? and that he breathed his last Sigh through a Brozely?[5]

I am sure you will excuse my dwelling so long upon this unfortunate subject, but I esteemed him much, and your own feeling will accord with every syllable that Memory has uttered. I will endeavour in the next Page to break through the current of my grief and give you some London Information, but you must pardon me if I should break off suddenly and talk of Arthur's Death . . . So good a Son—so upright a man—

The Observed of all Observers.[6]

The Edinburgh Review is come to London. The Editor apologizes for its delay, 'occasioned by circumstances that can be of *no* interest to the Reader'—What? I suppose the Scots have struck for Wages, and refuse to put their broad shoulders to the Wheel (Qu. Rack) without additional pay—Oh Scotland, Scotland!—Southey's Life of Nelson comes out tomorrow,[7] together with Campbell's beauties of English Poetry—[8] Montgomery's new Poem of 'The World before the Flood' is published,[9] he [is] a very clever though *sombre* Man.—

One of our Zetesophians was at Cambridge a year and a half ago—he saw the Woman who used to attend H^y K. White[10] and on shewing some eagerness for information respecting him—she said—'Ah! that Mr White!—People make a great fuss about him, for my part I think he was little better than he should be—he wrote a book of Rhymery, I think he might as well have let it alone and learnt to behave proper to folks about him.'—Poverty you see stood in his way, every moment of his life. May it never stand in the way of John Dovaston's—Dead Ralph's or——

JOHN H. REYNOLDS.

This is a plaguy Wolfish Letter.[11]

45

From John Hamilton Reynolds

[24 May, 1813]

I generally have cause to apologize for my long silence; you know that it is useless to sit down to a Letter unless the Mind accompanies you and as I so seldom enjoy that, it will account in some measure for my delay. However I promise that spare hours shall be employed in conversing with you, my good Friend.

Your last Letter was written well, but the one penned in partnership was rather wolfish! I am rather vexed that you hindered Rylance sending the account of the 23^d,[1] for tho' it might have been written in unison with my own feelings, I should have found pleasure in the perusal . . . Clods! say you?:—by Jove you are wrong;—Crabbe is a poet; When I read his Tale of the Patron it affected me considerably.[2] I will venture to say you could not open a single leaf without seeing an abundance of Poetical Beauties—When the Young Man in the afores^{d} tale finds all his hopes of fame blasted Crabbe writes—

> —'His mind resembled a bleak wintry scene,
> Sad tho' unclouded, dismal though serene.'

This description of a mind compleatly defeated in every prospect yet bearing its defeat with a mild melancholy appears to me all that is natural, poetical & chaste.

With respect to your uncertainty of mind between Ballad and Blank, I should advise you to follow the dictates of Fancy. If I were to recommend any Style for you to pursue, it would be the *Spenserian*;—The Stanza is particularly harmonious—The Sense may with ease be *compleated* in every Stanza,—the double Rhyme in the middle is very sweet,—The Alexandrine winds up the whole with great force and Beauty,—No Poet has ever failed in it yet—And to crown the whole your Poem upon your Birthday (I mean the τὶ δ' ἔρεξα)[3] is an admirable Specimen of your ability in this metre.

I myself have had the boldness to attempt something of the *Tale* sort in this Style; founded upon an anecdote in Ker Porter's Travelling Sketches in Russia[4] ('the attempt and not the Deed confounds us').[5] I have reached the 34th Stanza there the *Work* stops—and there I think it likely to stop.[6]

A Brother Zetesophian has lent me the Irish Melodies,[7] with which I am particularly pleased:—every additional line of Moores that I read, establishes him firmer in my favor—He is indeed a Poet.—By the Bye in perusing them the other day, I was surprized to meet with a Ballad entitled 'Lough Neay' written upon the very same story, your 'Llunc Lys' is—except that his pool is situated in Ireland and yours on the Border of Wales[8] . . . I was in hopes our Friend Rylance would have added somewhat to his Ballad:—I am truly sorry that he is going to Edinburgh, it will neither gain fame or profit for him I fear.—

The first of your Sonnets I am not so much pleased with as the second (to the Æolian Harp)[9] which I admire very much. But I should rather hear that your Talent were employed in some work of consequence; I fear you are letting some of those fine Ideas evaporate in Sonnets which would dignify a 'bolder Song' —Your Genius for Poetry is too good to remain unemployed, and its ability is not justified when you employ it on light subjects:—leave trivial works for such limping Rhymesters as myself . . . The following Stanzas are humbly submitted to your consideration and Your Opinion is requested; Whether the paper upon which they are written, is not compleatly qualified for a Chandler's Shop?—

I

Can a rosy lip or a sparkling eye
    rivet the lover's heart;
Will not at last their memories die
    and their fading charms depart:
For oh! when a mind is wanting there,
    Will Beauty requite? ah never!
The remembrance of lips tho' sweet & fair,
    Time will sever.

2

Oh many a flower of color bright,
    Delights the eye while thriving;
But it only pleases the passing sight,
    And only attracts while living;
The Rose still remains admir'd when dead
    And its fragrance serves to discover
That virtue lives when Beauty is fled
    And Life is over.

The above Stanzas were written for a slow Movement of Haydn. The music is sweet; I would the words were deserving of such good company.[10]

Pray do not always wait for my answer before you write; whenever leisure suits, I shall always be thankful for a line.[11]

Yours sincerely,
JOHN H. REYNOLDS.
24th May 1813
ASO. S.I.F.S.L.[12]

94

46

From John Hamilton Reynolds

[8 June, 1813]

My Good Dovaston,

I saw the Letter to my Mother yesterday; for what reason do you give over every intention of advising me for the future? Heaven knows I need your attentions. It has occurred to me that I have assumed a part not at all becoming or decent, when I desired you not to write so many Sonnets:—If truth is to be believed, my very dear Friend, My expressions were not intended as advice but uttered as wishes—Every line you write is received by me with attention & pleasure, and what I said or wrote only expressed my desire as to the alteration of your plan of composing from Sonnets to Poetry of a higher Order, which your Mind is *fully* Capable of . . . vide Roscoe.[1] Pray—Pray continue the same Plan of Letter writing you have ever done.—For though I grow older—you grow older also.

The Essay of mine you ask for, I will take an opportunity of copying for you; but the 34 Stanzas are neither worth the trouble of transcribing or carriage,—uncorrected & unconnected as they are . . . —

Lord Byron has published a Fragment of a Turkis[h] Tale, something in the metre of Scott, called 'Giaour.' There are very fine poetical passages in it, and I think [it] wo^d please you—If you will commission me I will get it [for] you.[2]

Will you suggest any correction in the text of the following stanzas, that may occur to you—They are absolutely copied as they were written, and your eye will be the first that has seen them, save the Author's—

Sappho

I

Fair was the Night, the Western breeze was still,
   The Moonlight slept upon the glossy wave;
When Sappho on the dark o'erhanging Hill,
   To the wide air her gentle sorrow gave;
All,—All was silent as the gloomy grave,
Save when the Seabird dipt its heavy wing

Deep in the dark blue flood beneath, & save,
Its mournful shriek, and Echo's answering:—
Love thus enforc'd the Maid,—the beauteous Maid to sing.

2

'Sweet Star of Eve!—Sweet Mistress of the Night!
    Hear!—Hear thy Sappho's supplicating prayer;
Shed on my Watry grave thy softest light,
    When from Life's Page my mournful name I tear;
    And make my Memory thy fondest care,
When Strangers view my Deathbed from above;
    Point out the tomb of a forsaken fair,
And as across the Waves thy light beams move,
Smile on the hallow'd Spot where rests heartbroken Love.'

3

'Oh should my tale in future Song be told,
    Let it be said for Love that Sappho died;
Love!—that first warm'd her heart, then made it cold,
    Love!—Her best solace & her dearest pride;—
    And now receive me Oh! ye gloomy tide
Destroy at once the tumults of my breast:'—
    Thus having mourn'd the beauteous Sappho sigh'd
    The name of Phaon, and his memory bless'd
Then plung'd from off the Rock, & sank to silent Rest.[3]

Rylance is gone;—He left here last Sunday Week, so doubtless he has reached Scotland by now. It will I should think be
out of his power to send you the Breidden Song, however when I
write to him it shall be mentioned in my letter.[4] Rylance has a
noble heart, I would to Heaven Fortune had placed him in a
situation more worthy his deserts. His genius is unbounded; is
it not hard, that he cannot find time to employ it properly [?]

You once *I think* said to me, that at any time I needed a trifle,
you would accommodate me. If you can now lend me £5, I shall
consider myself truly obliged:—The repayment I will make you
in the course of two or three Months, when my salary will [have
come]. Pray do not mention any thing of it in your [letter] if you
cannot assist me to it . . .[5]

    Your very faithful friend
    JOHN HAMILTON REYNOLDS.

From my profits which will arise from a Magazine, which I am
now to be rewarded for contributing to, I hope to be able to see

you for a Week or ten days this Summer. If you will be *bored* by
my company for so long a time.
  I shall be glad to hear soon
Serj^{ts} Inn
  8 June 1813

47

From John Hamilton Reynolds

[Late June 1813]

My very Excellent Friend,
  The kindness the very great kindness with which you have
acted has impressed me with very grateful feelings. Your
MANNER of conferring a favor convinces me of the genuine
friendship that inhabits your bosom; I can only at present thank
you, and that most truly.[1]
  Your observations upon my Stanzas to Sappho, evince the
delicacy of your taste; I have adopted every amendment except
the one of shortening it into two stanzas; unfortunately I have
even lengthened it into 4, by adding another . . . I will make a
fair copy of it, and send it you by Wood & Walton's Parcel at the
end of the month, with my additions and alterations, and your
amendments . . . If you have not a copy of Hodgson's 'Lady Jane
Grey, a Poem with others, Latin & English,' I happen to have a
duplicate copy, and will send it you:—His verses I think very
spirited and original. 'A *gentle* Alter[n]ative to Reviewers' has
highly pleased me.[2]
  Have you seen the illiberal notice of your FitzGwarine in the
Monthly Review[3]—That Enemy to Genius and Youth?—Their
opinions will have no weight on account of their inveteracy.
This is the Review that attacked Kirk[e] White, which drew down
the odium of all Mankind upon them . . . You see '*some damned
good natured Friend*' is sure to tell you the news . . .
  The Quarterly Review will be published tomorrow, I am
anxious to see it, as it is likely you may be *judged*.

The *Reflections* of Mirth,
on the Eve of the Breidden Festival.

I

Tomorrow's dawn shall scarcely light,
The grassy brow of Breidden's height,
   Ere souls of wit & worth,
Will press to sip at pleasure's rill,
And to make that 'Heaven kissing Hill,'
   A kissing Hill of *Earth*.

2

The morn shall find each roseate streak,
Reflected bright in many a cheek,
   Its light in many an eye;
The gladsome smiles of day shall grace
The festive scene, and every face
   Will smile as brilliantly.

3

Wit & song the scene shall crown,
Wine the sighs of care shall drown,
   And give to Mirth a zest;
The Sun shall view the generous feast,
When first he rises in the East,
   And when he leaves the West.

4

Time shall throw aside his Scythe then,
Time shall join the throng at Breidden,
   And bid the goblet pass;
Time shall lose his flying power,
Shall disregard the *sandy hour*,
   And only use the *glass*.

5

Then quickly fly ye shades of night,
And quickly come Oh! Morning light,
   In all thy colors fair;
Every lov'd one, Every Friend,
Shall round the bowl of Life attend,
   And I will take the Chair.

Finis.

Do not imagine my Dear Friend that I have the vanity to suppose the above will serve for the Muses' annual Tribute; But perhaps the Reflections may be read as a Make-weight by you;— that is if you think them worthy of a public perusal. I assure you that it will not at all either vex or astonish me, if you should put them aside altogether . . . Do not at any rate read [them] without a correction.

I have not heard from Rylance!! What am I [to] think of his silence?—He agreed to write at least within two days after his arrival at Scotland,—he has been absent these three weeks,— and silent all the time!

It will give me infinite pleasure, if at your leisure you will transcribe me what you have written of Owen Glendower.[4]— Rylance told me you had some intentions of 'calling *his* spirit from the vasty deep'[5]—So doubtless you have thrown a few flourishes—pray let me have them.

Most faithfully Your Friend
JOHN H. REYNOLDS.

I mean to annoy you with my lines occasionally.

48

From John Hamilton Reynolds

[July 1813]

My Dear Dovaston

As it is my intention to send Lady Jane Grey[1] by Wood & Walton's Parcel tomorrow, I have been wavering whether to write to you by this conveyance or by Post. But as it is likely a considerable delay may attend the former, I have thought it adviseable to adopt the latter.

You have (of course) gratified me much by approving the little tribute to the Breiddenites;—I would it were more worthy your praise & their attention. From what you mentioned a few Letters ago, I have reason to believe the day is at hand, or over:—Will you give me an acco^t (if the latter is the case) of your entertainment?²

Your Remark upon my lines to Sappho, would have induced me to hazard even another verse, had I not seen the thought beautifully described by Lord Byron in his New Poem of 'The Giaour':

> 'Sullen it plung'd, & slowly sank,
> The calm wave rippled to the bank, &c. &c.'

It is curious to observe how apt, feeling & ingenious Minds are to possess similar ideas;—The Episode in K. White's Clifton Grove is sweetly told,³ in truth what line of his teems not with deli[cacy] and beauty:—I read him continually. Understanding, disposition, and all that could dignify the human breast, he fully possessed. What a picture of peace are these two last lines of the passage you noticed . . .

The last N^o of the Quarterly is 'stale, flat (& I think the book-sellers will find it) unprofitable.'⁴ Books of a Year's standing and some much longer are noticed in it only. The poetical article is 'Rogers' Poems' a new Edition with additions; of course The Pleasures of Memory is past over; after which is a frag[ment] of a Poem on the Discovery of America. This is praised highly & certainly not unjustly . . .⁵ I read the other day in one of Miss Baillie's Plays, a beautiful song on the subject of the Warrior's Return after a long absence;⁶—it so much delighted me, that I co^d not rest 'tll I had eased myself of the following verses:— videlice[t]⁷

The Warrior's Departure

I

Beadsmen for the War-tide praying,
Soldiers shouting, Chargers neighing,
Armour in the Sun Rays beaming,
Bright blue eyes in Sorrow streaming:—
The laurel wreaths await on brows to bloom,
Of those who for the battle, quit their Native Home.

2

Beauty on the Warrior mourning,
Trembling for his safe returning,
Tearful eyes, & bosoms heaving,
Infants to their Parents cleaving:—

Blessings from worn & aged patriarchs come,
To those, who for the Battle quit their Native Home.

3

Nodding plumes & warriors mounting,
Age, the feats of youth recounting,
Lovely Maidens fearful listening,
Paly cheeks with tear drops glistening;—
Some on the eager gaze; and weeping, some
Turn from the Mournful sight of Heroes leaving Home.

4

Cheering smiles with anguish blending,
Farewell sobs the sky ascending,
Music to the breezes playing,
Ban-dogs at the tumult baying:—
The trumpet's brazen sound,—the hollow drum,
Loudly proclaims at last,—The Heroes leaving Home.[8]

Upon a perusal—'I do repent me of my fury, that I have sent it you'—you'll say 'Why did you?'—to which I answer 'Who can be wise, amazed, & temperate in a moment? No man.'[9]

Ideas confused. Rhymes miserable. Metre *see-sawish*, & tame execution mark every line of this trifle, as—Moore says—'doubtless few will have inclination to read it, and I sincerely repent that I have had leisure to write it.'[10]—I think song-writing is miserably neglected, it would surely be admired if properly cultivated. A Song to be a good one, should be delicate & feeling, with no poetic liberties in the verse & above all it should be short: not one of which requisites mine possesses . . . It would please me much to see a few lines from your pen, pray employ it.

Have you written any thing, since I last heard from you? Remember every line of Poetry is acceptable . . . Not one of my correspondents, save you & Rylance, care[s] a jot for the Muses: —What is it *aMuses* their minds in a solitary hour?—or what can even make verbal scenes to them delightful? . . .

I have had a very long Letter from my good Fr[iend Ryl]ance; He seems to have passed a journey of weari[some] insipidity. The Scenes so beautifully pictured in Marmion were the only objects particularly pleasing. He bids me say you will speedily have a Letter from him;—The Tea for M[rs] Turner[11] was sent by Yockney in a regular way by the Shrewsbury Waggon; if it is not in hand, enquire for it at the Warehouse, where R. thinks it must be.

I believe (if the state of finance will permit) that in the Month of August, I shall pass a week with you. Say if you should be out of the way, & do not put anything aside for me;—I have some idea that it is the time you visit Needwood Forest,—is it? . . .

Rylance has spoken to me, in high terms, of your worthy & ingenious friend Mr T. Yates;[12]—I beg to be named to him. He knows not that such a creature as myself, breathes on this uneven Globe . . . To Mr Davenport,[13] 'speak of me as I am.'[14] To yourself: come all health, wealth & happiness.—This is the fervent wish of your faithful friend

JOHN H. REYNOLDS.

49

From John Hamilton Reynolds

[2 August, 1813]

Dear Dovaston,

I have at last so arranged Matters as [to] be able to start for West Felton on Saturday by the Ancient Briton from Holborn at 3 oClock.[1] I mention these particulars because you will be able to calculate what time it passes your habitation—I hope my journey will not interfere with any plan of yours if it should write & put me off.

I have enquired what Hayley's Life of Cowper 8vo come to & find it will be 2 Gñas. Will you have it?[2]—The System of Nature[3] is an old Book, I despair of getting it—I will call at Walker's and ask him whether he will agree to your proposal about Tales from Shakespeare.[4]

Will you have Ld Byron's Poem of the Giaour, it is oneof the most elegant & fanciful Tales (in Poetry) I ever read—Price 4/6.

I heard from Rylance yesterday, he mentions no words of coming home—

My Mother will write by post, that is by me . . . I will bring

down a few of my best & worst lines & read you to sleep of an
afternoon——
    Farewell till I see you
      Yours very truly
        JOHN H. REYNOLDS.
Serj⁻ᵗˢ Inn
  2 Aug⁻ᵗ 1813
    Within earshot of the Postman's Bell.

Write me back by return of Post all the particulars viz whether
you are disengaged.⁵ What am I to do in the *Book* case, &c. &c.

50

From Mrs Reynolds

August 8th 18[13]

Dʳ friend,
    Long before you receive this I hope my Jack & [you] have met
& talked away many a cheerful hour. I am afraid his visits to you
are to[o] frequent to be convenient,¹ should this be the case be
candid & tell him so, for nothing but a flat denial on your part
can prevent him (whenever opportunity falls in his way) from
taking a Journey to you. I took it kind your writing to me under
the many discourageing circumstances you have. I very naturally
concluded that when all the failures of youth were stealing o'er
me,² and the many tedious associates of old age fastening on me,
such as bad sight, want of memory, a spiritless way of writing &
a still more spiritless way of conversing—that I should experience also a neglect on the part of those friends who were
younger & in possession of their faculties, but your letter &
attention contradicted the supposition, & I was flatterd there-
by.—The Notes you sent were not quite so much admir'd by us
as your choice of Music is in general but perhaps we want taste
in playing them, pray do you not think John improv'd in his
writing, he rather gains credit of his London friends, but I like
to know your thoughts on this subject. I am very sorry we are so

long depriv'd the sensible converse of our friend Rylance. I have a high opinion of his Understanding & well informd mind and am sorry he is compeld to drudge thro life for existence when had he time to use his powers at pleasure I have not a doubt but he would cut a figure in the litterary World. He is a good hearted soul as ever breath'd, in short too good in every respect to spend his time in Scotland & we all wish his return most ardently here—

John will tell you all news so that I am rather at a loss how I shall fill my letter & I could not accomplish to write by him as I was rather hurried before his departure—nor am I blest with the gift of half filling a letter—as you are—with a Sonnet, or some well-hit similes, a good Pun, or a well introduc'd quotation, neither a Breidden festival to describe—the account of which revives ones very heart to hear—no, I am tied to the old tune, George is well & I am well—& so are my Children & I hope you are the same, nor do I think you would do much better if you were fixd in this stupid Lambeth, as I am, where there is bare occasion for either Eyes or ears—I am sorry you do not keep moving in the Poetical way, that is writing something of greater scope for your abilities than Sonnets.[3] I hope some day to read a tale or Poem that shall reflect credit on your fame, it is a shame you should not proceed, as you are gifted by Nature & Education, your time is your own, your genius is not disturbed by the cravings of hunger or the crying of your babes, the vagaries of a Wife (or I hope) the qualms of your Conscience. Then let me ask you why you are not (under all the above happy circumstances) some hundred stanzas deep on the woes of the Desdemona you spoke of some time back, or one of your really elegant descriptive peices on some of the retir'd parts of that romantic Country whose verge you reside on. Tell my dear John we miss him sadly. Jane looks like a Widow, so forlorn at his loss.[4] I hope he will acquit himself well in all respects while with you— of one I am assur'd he will well & duly perform his part, that of reducing the contents of your Larder. Your skinny folk are ever immoderate eaters, of this discription I fear is Son John but I know he is welcome at your Board. Give him our affectionate love & tell him to return so as to spend one day with his good old Mother. He had left his great Coat—will you say—at Mr Squibbs[5]—his Umbrella we cannot find. This it is, to be a Man of *thought*. I wish it possible he would manage his journey to Mr Gribbles when you are absent at the assizes as that will be losing as little of your Society as possible. I beg you will let me have a

letter by him when he returns.[6] Home remembrances of us all to
you both—

C. REYNOLDS.

August 10th

George Squibb & Frank Fladgate were here last night—the
former bids me tell John he has commenc'd Doctor & has seen a
Lady's liver. I don't know whether this may be any particular
relish for John, but G. S. seemed to speak of it as a valuable
morsel. F. F. thinks they shall go to Brighton instead of Wales
—[7] last Night great news came by Telegraph from Wellington, I
beleave he has rather beaten & disturbd Soult, but the whole is
expected this Ev^g—the account seems to infer that the Battle has
been a warm one, we have driven him from St Sebastian & tis
asserted that the place is surrender'd as their Forces are so
weak[ene]d.[8]

51

From John Hamilton Reynolds

Saturday 4 Sept.[r] 1813

My Dear Friend,

I had packed up Boccacio,[1] the Waltz and a Bolero to be sent to
you by the Watton parcel but upon taking it to Longmans I
found that they had closed their Book-packing, so it must remain
untill the end of the Month . . . Walker says the 3^d Vol. of the
Calamities of Authors[2] is not yet published; he will procure the
Reflector[3] for me, there are four numbers only.

I was not in Shrewsbury time enough for any Coach that day I
left you, so of course I remained there all night, during the
evening I called on Morris[4] who was out. I also called on
Walton[5] & procured a Newspaper with the Breidden Acco.[t] in it;
his Young Man informed me that M[r] W. has intentions of publishing E. Lloyd,[6] I hope under your *Editorial Jurisdiction*.

Pray did you dine with Mr Yates last Sunday? If you did, and if
you read him any of my lines you will be obliging me by writing
his opinion of them:—I am terribly afraid as H. K. White said

that I have only the longing, without the *Afflatus*.[7] Have you copied those ill-natured couplets of mine? I will thank you to return them to me. Upon *my honour* I am hurt that you have had my permission to copy them; they will stand lasting memorials of my ill-natured severity.[8] Get a Frank and return them as soon as possible. I am tempted strongly to burn the remainder that I have written, at least I am determined to write no more.

I have purchased of Walker Bland's Translations of the Greek Writers (Minor)[9] and am quite satisfied with them: He has preserved much of their simplicity and much of their elegance. I have not found any english version of 'Εὐδαίμων ὁ βλέπων σε etc.'[10]—so I rather think it is an extract of some of the *Major* Poets. By the bye take these two attempts as *paraphrasing* it. The one is seriously written, with a close observance of the greek;— the other is loosely composed, in which an endeavour is made to give something of the point, spirit, & whim of the original.[11] Give me your verses from it.

1st.

Oh! Blest is he on whom thy beauties break,
Blest! Ah thrice Blest! is he who hears thee speak,
Happy that one whose looks thy charms approve:—
But he's immortal who can boast thy love.

2nd.

To see thee is to cheer me,
To love thee's but to hear thee,
Tis life's charm to be near to thee
And Heaven to be dear to thee.

There is a 4th Edition of the Giaour with *considerable* additions. I think this a scandalous affair, for those who purchase the earlier copies, get imperfect ones.[12] Have you seen the Edinburgh Review? What servility!—What crouching!—They are now content 'to lick the dust beneath young Byron's feet'—He has taken the sting from these vipers with respect to himself, but at his departure from this Kingdom they will be as venomous as ever. 'He has *Scotch'd* the Snake, not kill'd it.'[13]—However it will be easy for any one of spirit to make an impression on heads already bruised, and to weaken hands, already how unnerved!

I have been mighty busy about your Work.[14] Longman had no opportunity of sending a Copy to Gilchrist[15] but a Young Man there told me of a Person who sends to him weekly from Ironmonger Lane, thither I went with one packed in a Sheet of White

Paper, and O. G. has it by now. Ask for Rylance's Letters of Mr Yates. I have not heard from our friend Ralph[16] yet;—have you? Write a very close letter to me soon, on such a sheet as we wrote to Rylance on;[17] and give me all the News literary and commonplace; also the heads of the Letter from him who is sojourning in Scotland . . .

The Ninth Statue remains at present in *Statu quo.*[18] Tho' I have the plan much riper in my head, and many lines ready for stacking on paper. I intend to proceed on my first plans, and not adopt the Spenserian Measure.

Have you in your unmolested retirement since I left written anything of Owen Glendower?—I have been thinking you might make a fine Canto of a chorus of Witches and their mystic rites in which they might foretell the fate of the Hero.[19] You might certainly take the most interesting incidents of his life & combine them without regarding the unity of Time. I am not one of those who are strict in that respect, as you will see:—for this single sheet records the actions of a Week.

Remember me very kindly to Mr. Yates.
JOHN H. REYNOLDS.

52

From John Hamilton Reynolds

[30 September 1813]

Dear Dovaston,

This is not to be accounted a Letter for I intend writing you one of a more regular habit. Longman & Co. have not room for all so I have sent a part now and will send the rest next Month—One Number of the Reflector I have detained as there is a paper in it I wish to Copy—it shall come next Month together with the Decameron.[1]

I have had a Letter from Rylance cheerful & witty. He talks now of returning.

As to the Letters you talk of keeping I can only say that they are *prized particularly by me* and I cannot on any account allow you to keep them.[2] If I had not thought much of them they would not have been carried about with me. Pray return them:—

I will (if you cannot get a Frank) willingly pay the postage—The Loss of them *I assure you* would very *much hurt me.*

I have given an Essay upon Flowers to the Zetesophians and yet no Botanist.[3] You'll wonder what I could make of them.—I think you would like it.

Miss Williams[4] sent my half sheet of virulence by a Friend;—she said, had she not been engaged in preparing to return into Bucks she would have called herself. I wish she had, for I understand she is clever, and a clever woman is a great treat.

Write to me soon.—do not stand upon bandying Letters backwards & forwards regularly.——

Give me some account of your literary prospects and what you may have written since I left.

J. H. REYNOLDS.

30 Sept. 1813.

53

From John Hamilton Reynolds

[23 October 1813][1]

I find that my ability for Letter-writing is gradually decaying, for I now can seldom bring my mind to a state of quiet fit to communicate with a learned Friend. Idleness in Letter writing is the root of every error, and it has flourished in my soil prodigiously.

First and foremost—I have obtained leave of Mr Asperne the Proprietor of the European Magazine to review your work, but the space allowed me is limited. The Article I have drawn up is undoubtedly the most spirited prose performance I ever accomplished.[2] I have reviewed you most impartially, for the opinions are absolutely what I think; they are the unbiassed examinations of a Critic and not the partial observations of a Friend:—The beauties I have mentioned are what really please me and the faults I must confess are what to me appear objectionable. I have first made some remarks on the Style with some allusions to Mr Scotts; then I have extracted;—and also pointed out a trivial error at least as it appears to me. It appears to me very absurd in many Reviewers of the Day, to object to any new method of amusing the public, and to uphold those harsh rules that have been so long considered the necessary beauties of Poetry. Probability is certainly necessary, and where the Unities can be preserved without enfeebling the Language or the Spirit, it is undoubtedly desirable:—But I cannot consent for the sake of regularity that Genius should be strictly curbed and the strength of the imagination entrammelled. Your work would stand but *a bad chance* under the hands of the Edinburgh Gentlemen:— They are professed admirers and supporters of the Ancient Laws of Poetry. You have followed the Steps of Scott who has suffered his Genius to range unchecked.[3]

My Essay on Flowers is written in a very flowery manner; I have treated the subject in a way you little expect, if possible a copy shall come in Crosby's next Parcel.

Rylance has just been here and begs me to say that he has called upon Miss Williams and has seen her: He attended to your directions (he says) with regard to the length of his stay there.

You have rather astonished me with your mournful Reflections on the State of Poetry in your own Mind.—What has cast these clouds of dissatisfaction over your Hopes? If tis the ill-natured opinions of Acquaintance,—Never mind them. Remember that the greater the Genius, the greater the difficulties & drawbacks;—There are always those in the World who are ready to attack Merit;[4] and the more humble it is, the more open it is to injury. The opportunity, the ability, the classical acquirements, the Retirement and the Scenery you are blessed with, render you peculiarly fitted to produce some work of importance.—I cannot but think the behaviour of Morris ought to enliven you. Be assured that your Literary Reputation is dear to me, and that the neglect of Talents so great on account of a trivial dissatisfaction is to be deeply deplored.

Many thanks for your Music, it is much admired; in fact it is an old air My Mother sang in her Girlish days, so its favourable reception in that quarter was not to be doubted. The Notes of what we have once admired, vibrate on our Memory with redoubled pleasure, since they bring with them recollections of former amusements & earlier happiness.

The British Reviewers of October have attacked Ld Byron in a bold manner, though it is evident they do [not] forget his Lordship has written the English Bards & Sco[tch Reviewers].

I have entirely remoulded my Poem of the [word missing] in the following manner. First I have written 11 Spenser[ian] Stanzas by way of Introduction, and my intention is now to strike off into a livelier Measure—the effect will be greater both ways, For the Stanzas will acquire greater dignity by the Sprightly Measure that follows and the Measure itself will appear easier by the heavy Metre that precedes it. Do you approve my plan? . . . I am glad you have written me so good and kind a letter as the last, for to speak truly I have been somewhat dissatisfied with a few things I have lately observed——But enough of this. You shall have the £5 soon, I am hurt that my pocket has not allowed me to send it to you sooner.—

Pray remember me kindly, very kindly to Yates. I like him much.

The first leisure moment you have may be employed in writing to me, if your inclination so prompts you.

> Yours very truly
> JOHN REYNOLDS.

54

From Mrs Reynolds

[20 November, 1813]

I have before me a letter from friend Dove dated August 22^{d}, written when John was at West Felton & which according to Old usage should have been answerd at the moment, or very soon after it came to Hand—excuses & Apologies are nonsense, the reasons why I am not so quick in my answers are accounted for in a former letter, & as they are of so serious a Nature as to leave me without hope of ever again writing any letter but that I may blush for, you must content yourself to take them as they are or resign them altogether. But that you urge to hear from me, & take the trouble to write *now* & *then* to me, I should I verily think yeild my Pen, my stupid pen for ever.

To answer the different parts of yours as circumstances then stood, were a folly, it would be somewhat like preaching a Sermon on a Fast day that four Months before had been given on a Festival, & proves I am not quite so ready with an answer as Looney MacTwalter.[1] We have got back—from that wretched barren Country Scotland—our Fertile friend Rylance, he is a wondrous favorite with me . . . he was here last night I saw a letter he had recently had from you,[2] I find John has disappointed you with respect to some Books you required him to send you, are you not too hasty in your expressions of anger, be 'slow to anger,' learn Patience I daresay his business prevented him, but I find he has written to you, & he can better answer for his transgressions than I can. I can only say he is a[s] good a fellow as ever liv'd. I perceive in all your letters you talk of giveing over the fascinating employ of Poetry—for why? Give me a reason? You are not so old that your Genius is blunted, for you are but thirty last Birth day, the very Zenith of your life.— You do not want time, that is all your own, you do not want learning or Abilities, these Gifts God has bestow'd on you bountifully, then—as John Kemble said—'what is it you do want'[3]—alas, I fear the *will*—but I cannot beleive you, & shall certainly be looking forward to some elegant & well written Poem at a very early period.—I'll tell you what—you are too much alone—your mind wants recreation. Mount your Horse, or if Lame—mount your Neighbours—ride out, take air & exercise, revive your spirits—then sit down & write like a Lord—tho it were better you never wrote, than write like some Lords, and on the other hand it were *well* you wrote like others.[4] I perceive you are not an admirer much of my Jacks productions[5]—yet he rather gains praise—I think you a good *Judge* you see I have brought you all at once to the height of your professions (& had rather you could, with justice to your conscience, have found some room for praise)—yet I like that you do not speak better than you conceive they deserve—candour I highly commend, & do not the less like you for it however I might have been delighted had it been otherwise. I have told him not to pester you with his Poetical effusions but whether I shall be attended to I cannot say. He has got himself a Dog, a beautiful Spaniel Named after your old favorite, Croney[6]—We thank you for the last beautiful Scotch Air which is admirable, the words lovely, whose are they? Would you think I had written this as long ago as last Sunday—yet so it is. I plac'd it in the Table drawer, & so trecherous is my Memory that by mere chance I found my error. John has got the Spanish Bolero,[7] at least the Notes to send you. I fancy they will please you. When he will pass them on to you I cannot say—— Our compts, good wishes, &c. &c. to you. He has in fun put the point of the Poker through the one glass of my spectacles (which by the bye did not suit my sight) & has rendered me almost incapable of concluding the slovenly work herein begun. Write soon,[8] & think me your friend

CHARLOTTE REYNOLDS.

Novr 20th 1813.

III

55

From Mrs Reynolds

[29 November, 1813]

'Pray can you tell me if one Mʳ Dovaston do live here' & if you to whom I am addressing myself be he. I have received a letter dated Novᵗ 22d. bearing your signature, that I cannot conceive came from your hand but for this same positive proof in it you imply great meaning to many sentences, which to me are a riddle to comprehend. In the beginning you talk of the many visits & revisits you partake of from both sexes not on account of '*property (the usual cause)* but Poetry.'[1] Much do I commend their taste for their preference to the latter charm, for if they have as great a contempt of the former as I have (unless accompanied with Mind and moderation, and manners suited to it) it were better to be a beggar. I remember to have spoken of you as a Man of property, but to the Person or Persons I so have spoken I am sure I never in the least intimated that I valued you one sixpence worth the more or less for it. It was the solidity of your mental powers that I ever valued, & that I still value & ever shall—for the rest you may be assured I care not.—I somehow do not think this same jolting & jumbling in Coaches (that you talk of) agrees with you—it seems to have stird up spleen, wrath, satire and a few other combustibles not quite so agreeable to an old Friend, & one who has been accustomed to letters of a quite contrary description—the satire with which you treat on my 'four Months early let[er]' is what I can smile at,[2] but, when I see the intent is merely an inference, that I accommodated my writing to that of my Sons from *motive*, I withdraw the smile a little innocent satire might create, & flatly deny the inenuendo implied. Dont you Mr John Dov think so meanly of me as that because John Reynolds is my Son I would defend him right or wrong—*no*—in truth I have observ'd of late a something like irritation between you & really beleiv'd his visits became too frequent to you & of course his society tiresome;[3] but I still know you lov'd him in friendship—but you have led me to expect something remains for me to know or you could not talk of returning his letter which to remain you say would 'exist but to his disgrace' these are strong terms & I like them not, & so well do I know Johns mind that tho I may now be a stranger to the meaning of all this, I shall yet know the extent of his error which has blown up the embers of your anger into so strong a flame—& which has burnt with such Acrimony in your letter to me. I have ever requir'd at your hands candour of opinion & freedom of advice to my beloved Son, & I think very few Men so capable to act the part of adviser & friend as yourself—under such an impression I naturally feel astonishment at the union of *John* & *'Insolence'* therefore explain—another sentence I am curious to understand 'as I lately told his better friend to whom he owes all he now enjoys, he will find he has wrong done.' Who is this better friend, & in what is he indebted to him? I question *you* as a friend & I look for your serious & honest answer. I know not of such friend as you speak—perhaps John has bare'd his bosom to you—he lov'd you well enough so to do but *I* who am his first, best friend must come to you for a solution of the Mystery attachd to this business—he will shew me his returnd letter—I should abhor his submitting to insult from any one, I also should with anger condemn his offering *Insolence* to any one, much more the friend of his Childhood, Boyhood, his entrance into Manhood & I trust his future life—it would pain me that the tendril which was twin'd round you & has gaind strength from the succour of your support should be rudely torn from its adherence, because one small blight has touchd its stem—no— rather put gently forth a fostering hand—let advice with temper be that fostering hand let John be the tendril—enough nay if I read you right more than enough—with respect to your writing Poetry please yourself, if you will fritter away your abilities in Gods name do—only let us have a regular take leave of the Ladies nine[4]—I will add you need not blush at the words to the Scotch air—I was interrupted last Night from closing this, just as I had intended to have observed to you that I fancy your letter to me, not exactly a justifiable one but the subject I shall wa[i]ve as to myself. I have again read it and am less satisfied with what relates to John than before as it appears to me rather to covet an open rupture than any thing else—if he is as wrong as you say, he deserves your resentment nor shall I defend him, but that does not auger that I should be affronted when I know not the cause of your quarrel—if he has done amiss I am convinced he will acknowledge it. He has ever so acted to me, for he is amiable, & well & unchangingly belov'd by all who know him[5] —when I have acquainted myself as to particulars, I will perhaps write, as I could not like you should remain at variance—& I will then prove to you that altho a Mother, I am not a fool—I have been engag'd in the sick room (near a week night & day) of one of my dear Children whose life has been in the most eminent danger so that I am ill calculated to write—I remain the same friend to you I have ever been but I think I perceive you have a little faultered—your last wants candour. I suppose something had put you aside elsewhere—I am at a loss whether to direct to Hardwicke's[6] but the old one I fancy will do.

Y^r friend
CHARLOTTE REYNOLDS.

56

From John Hamilton Reynolds

[4 December 1813]

You seem determined still to surprise me. The return of the Letter I last wrote you—The forcible marks you have made in it and the strange remark at the end of it I cannot account for.[1] It would appear then that my unfortunate delay of sending you the Books has struck you as pointed neglect:—To combat this I have to tell you that many things have been in my mind—I have written 800 Lines of my Tale—In fact I have now finished it.[2] These will surely account for it.

In the first place if you will but coolly consider the case, my conduct will not appear amiss. Your observations in Rylance's letter are—That you feel illnaturedly indignant at my pointed neglect,—That you are astonished that I should not feel a *pleasure* (this stress you made yourself) at doing any thing for you. That in future you would cease to trouble me for any friend would for *Money* procure what you wanted.—Now this certainly appeared to me an unhandsome hint at the Loan;—if I have misunderstood it (which I do not think I have) you will I hope pardon me every expression I have made upon it:—No one is more ready to apologize for a mistake or more ready to confess himself in error than myself when I am convinced that such is the case. I can only say on the subject of the unpleasant business that your warm observations at first led to some warm ones from me—Our friendship has existed as Lord Byron says—'the better half of your Life and the happiest part of mine'[3]—and I cannot feel satisfied that so trifling a cause should occasion an eruption.—I am willing to forget and forgive; I hope you are the same.[4]

I am very much astonished at your resolution to desert the Muses.—You, who have shared their smiles so amply!— You, whose Country situation, Mind & Taste all conspire to favour so much!—Why leave them?—I am rather willing to believe that this is merely an unsettled intention made like the resolves of a Lover to be broken and forgotten. Those who have once sipped at the sacred spring, ever after thirst for its waters. The tongue promises what the heart does not prompt, and thus the words are in direct opposition to the inclinations.

Lord Byron has published another Poem 'The Bride of Abydos'—written with the same fire & originality that so much distinguish his former Works.[5] There is however some intricacy in his Plot, which a first or second reading cannot overcome. I admire very much the simile with which he concludes—Speaking of a flower—

> 'Alone—and dewy—coldly pure and pale,
> Like weeping Beauty's cheek at Sorrow's Tale.'

I have finished my Poem it is not founded on the Ninth Statue[6] but on a simple plot of my own framing. It consists of 1000 Lines; I should like you to see [it] and will certainly contrive to let you have a Copy as soon as time will permit me to make it.[7] I have one or two similes which I think are entirely new or at least treated in a novel manner. Rylance has seen it, and tells me he admires it.

Mr Thomas Moore is engaged in writing an Epic Poem.[8] Campbell is about to publish his Work on the Poets.[9]—Southey has a new Poem in hand[10]——And report says Ld Byron intends giving another Turkish Tale before he leaves England for the Greek Islands which will be in the Spring.[11] This is all the literary news I have Pray remember—'Amantium irae amoris intigrationast,'[12]

and believe Me very faithfully,

Yours

JOHN H. REYNOLDS.

Amicable Soc^{ys} Off.

4 Decr 1813

57

From Mrs Reynolds

[March/April 1814]

To write to an old friend with a new face is awkward especially
when that new face has been occasiond by the absolute neglect of
the old friend, & still further, it is not very wise to write when
you are assurd you will not receive an Answer, but as I am
perfectly easy on this score, & this my letter is not meant as a
concessionary one (myself or family having never given the least
cause for the insults receivd) it needs not that I make an apology
for the same. The reason I address you, is, that both Father &
Mother think it necessary something should be said with respect
to the situation in which John stands with you. The person you
introduced to our Family & to John (Mr Rylance) has taken on
him for some time past to assail John for the 15s due from him to
you & also very unfortunately to forgive him the 5$^{£}$ he unwisely
borrowd of you. He has also been endeavouring to obtain 15
shillings of him for the Index to the Edinborough Review a
book he had *made him a present off* [*sic*]. Many impertinent
scraps have been sent (for we have not for some time admitted
him to our House), but we never have or shall notice them.
However this last week an enclosure came containing a Note to
request our Daughter to give him a character for teaching
french[1] & also a letter from you wher[e]in you invite my Son to
Shakespere's birth day—both were returnd him in a blank cover
—but on the perusal of your letter we found an expression that
was not honorable to the once vaunting friendship held forth to
John—You say thus, or nearly so, that he has 'meanly taken the
advantage of your *Benevolence*'—alas do you as meanly suppose
such an honorable Boy will let you lose five pounds fifteen
Shillings by him—no—nor would his Mother let you—if I had
had my will you had been paid long ago but his Father chose that
he should feel the effects of his folly—for he was not to be
persuaded but that you would do any thing, & every thing for
him. He has had five pounds of experience & twill do him
good—he has been tempted to purchase many expensive Books
which has drain'd his purse & very imprudent to do so but he
will be able to settle with you very shortly—the success of his
Poem has astonished Cauthorne [*sic*] & the elegant letters we

have receivd on account of his Safie is [*sic*] more gratifying than Tongue or Pen can express[2]—I am thankful as Rylance has prov'd such a low creature that he had not any thing to do with his book, I would not take any money for the satisfaction this has afforded me, but John ever after his last visit to you seem'd to think different of this Man than he ever had before. He has broken a friendship of which he is totally incapable of ever forming such a one—& yet has known you but a few short years—

An invitation from *yourself* to John tho it could not have been accepted being too expensive would have met proper attention but convey'd by such a Vehicle cannot be noticd—let this Man dun M[r] Lewis, a concern in which he has a right to act, not take the liberty of asking John for that with which he has *no* concern, in fact I should not at any ra[te] let the Money pass any way but the regular one. He was very high to think you should require him to ask M[r] L for what he ow'd you—yet dares to interfere for the triffle poor Jack stands indebted to you—thus much explained I trust you will feel easy that John will honestly pay you your Money, nor let it perplex you—John is engag'd—indeed is one of the proprietors of a new work which is to come out Quarterly— some of the Gentlemen are literary Men—but it is not quite determind yet, tho pretty certain the Poetical part is given to John[3]——I have been in a very dangerous illness for three weeks or should have sent to you immediately on seeing the letter— John sends remembrances & regret—

CHARLOTTE REYNOLDS.[4]

58

From John Hamilton Reynolds

[19 July, 1814]

My Dear Dovaston,

Your Note by the twopenny Post came to me last night, and I lose not a minutes time in writing to you in terms which were so delightful & refreshing of old and which I hope have rather been slumbering for a time than resting for ever. Our's was no common Friendship it was commenced 'even in our boyish days' —grew with our growth, and strengthened with our strength:[1]

Let it not be severed. I have been long wishing to chase away the mist between us—I have, even from the moment of our misunderstanding, been leaning after our earliest and our best affections—The warmth and goodness that seem to glow in the latter part of y^r Note are proofs that you have not entirely lost the recollection of me—And I think there is no hazard now, that I shall be holding out my hand to one, whose feelings are frozen or even chilled. I will not longer dwell upon this unpleasant business, and assure you that I entertain the same respect & Friendship for you, that I ever did—And for my expression of rudeness or harshness or ingratitude (which hastiness only could dictate) I ask your forgiveness and your forgetfulness. My Father Mother & Family are all anxious that we should again be what we have been:—I am sure you will consider this, as it really is a Letter of Amity—suggested by a lingering of the Heart. If you are inclined to meet me on our first and firmest Friendship, write to me immediately, but say as little as you can help of our lamented misunderstanding, for if it is to be thrust away, the sooner we forget it the better[2]—I will enclose your little volume as you wish and leave it at Mr Turner's[3] the first opportunity.

I am now concerned in a New Quarterly Magazine on the plan of the Reflector, which succeeds tolerably well, and will we hope wriggle itself into Notice—I will send you a Copy of the 1st Number by Longman's Parcel—My contributions in it are—'A Translation of Catullus' Address to his Vessell' (I think Carmen IV). 'An Heroic Measure'—some stanzas—and a long Essay upon Hamlet (10 closely printed pages). Of the rest of the Work I can speak with great praise—It certainly displays very considerable Talent.[4] And I have the pleasure to say that Hunt, (of the Reflector, to whom I have been introduced and can now boast of as a Friend) thinks very highly of it.[5] Of this Gentleman's Genius I entertain very great ideas, and he certainly has the richest fancy (except My Ld Byron & Moore) of any Man living. Hunt has lately published his 'Feast of the Poets' in a Volume by itself with considerable additions and with Notes of much interest & judgement[6]—He will publish a Mask in the course of a Month or two,[7] and has in hand a Poem of some Magnitude.[8] I know of no one who from his intimacy with the Italian Poets and from his own brilliant (and if I may say) Italian Fancy could throw into a Mask so much of its real Poetry, airy sprightliness, delicate wit and fanciful imagery—May I give him a copy of your Poem of FitzGwarine [?].

I thank you for your good opinion of my Safie[9]—It is very defective, I know, in spirit and consequently in interest—But as a first attempt, some allowance will I hope be made. I have hopes, if my health but hold, of doing something better yet[10]— I, however, have some liking for it, in spite of its weaknesses, as it has introduced me to some of the Noblest and Cleverest Men of the Age.[11] I am engaged in another Poem,[12] and have laid vast plans for it, but like many great plans I fear they will not be carried completely into execution.

What are you about?—Do not let your fine genius for Poetry be idle—I hope by this time you have twined many a flowery garland round the antiquities of Owen Glendwyr[13]—It is certainly a fine subject and will allow of your calling up 'Spirits from the vasty deep'[14]—a sort of things, which I long yet fear to meddle with. Perhaps you would indulge me with a Line or two of any thing you may have lately written—I have many things to talk over with you, and it now rests with you, whether our long and Delightful Friendship be again warm'd into action, or be left silent for ever.

    I am yours very sincerely and
      affectionately
       JOHN H. REYNOLDS.
       Amicable Society
        Serjeants' Inn
        Fleet Street[15]

Serjeants Inn
  19 July 1814
I have now to look over a Proof of a Friend's Work, which is just on the Eve of publication—It is 'a Translation of the Popular Poetry of the Hindoos'[16]—Major Broughton the Translator is now in France and I am looking at the Proofs during his absence —Some of the poems are exquisite.

59

From John Hamilton Reynolds

[July–August 1814]

My Dear Dovaston,

Your Letter has been unanswered too long—But I had it in contemplation to have put in a cover the first N.° of the Inquirer with your little Volume & to have written by them:—These intentions have however been frustrated, really not by the idle feelings of the Mind, but by thoughts of too busy a Nature to suffer any other occupations. The fact is I have a new Poem in the Press which though of no great length takes a wonderful delight in engrossing my whole ideas & trespassing on my leisure. I hope by the end of next week or the beginning of the next to have it out. The size of the Poem will be Quarto, and its name is 'The Eden of Imagination.' I have never in the full course of my life found so much pleasure as in the composition of this work, & I rest some small hopes upon its success.[1]

Have you seen Wordsworth's Lyrical Ballads?[2] There are certainly some of the most delightful & delicate ideas—Some of the most deep & philosophical reflections in his Poetry. He is one of those rare Poets who write from actual Feeling & personal observation. It is certainly to be lamented that M.ʳ Wordsworth is known to the generality of Readers only by his inferior Works—by the Weaknesses & peculiarities of his Genius:[3]—They know nothing of his fine feelings & deep thoughtfulness and brilliant Imagination. I hope in a New Poem which he is about to publish, we shall find he has cast away all the small clouds from his Fancy & given us a Work in his best Manner.[4] The chief fault in M.ʳ Wordsworth is a love of speaking as Men in the humbler walks of Life speak: He has mistaken puerility at times for simplicity—and in the Preface to his Ballads holds up as a reason for this familiar tone of expression & unsoaring Style of Poetry—That Poetry & Prose are more intimately connected than is generally imagined. This, though it is apparently open to cavil, is literally true—in the same manner that simplicity is the very foundation of sublimity . . . But I am now, instead of writing a Letter, penning a Lecture, and I have got into a most unmerciful seriousness on things which it is very likely you do not coincide with me upon, or have long been acquainted with, & do not consider of any importance.

I pass over your cottage inspections, and come at once to you Alcaic Stanzas which are really beautiful, they are, in every sense of the word, full of flowers. You have contrived to give a sweeter turn to the last lines of each Stanza—at least to my ear;—But why or wherefore this appears I know not, unless it is the exquisite melody which hangs round the words—'rosas, violasque' at the end of the first, & the alliteration in the last.[5] There really is an elegance, an easiness & a simplicity quite enchanting. I will not run the risk of leaving them fade, by transplanting them into another garden. The Madrigal is a very lively little thing, 'and sweetly & nimbly recommends itself unto our gentle senses.'[6]

Minora Canamus.[7]

What I have written of late in the small way is very uninteresting, and really would not reward you for the trouble of reading. To be sure I have been dribbling pretty plentifully, but then they are of a most washy nature. However when I have time & patience to copy (which of all earthly things is the most tormenting) I will send you a few doses to be take[n] occasionally.

Have you any prose Essays by you of a serious or Mirthful sort? If you have, will you send one for the Inquirer? I am in great hopes that the Second Number will be of a very superior Quality. We begin now to get articles from Strangers, & it is very amusing to read over their opinions. We shall have a very excellent Review of Copplestone's Prelectiones[8] &c., some very pleasing Latin Poems & an excellent Article on the Fine Arts. I am about an Essay on Poetry but fear that it will not be ready for this number a sheet is to be kept open however, to give me a chance, till the latest moment.

By the bye have you seen the Review of Fitzgwarine, which I wrote for the European about 3 Months ago?[9]—If not I will send it [to] you.

You cannot conceive how much I long for a few country pleasures—How much I thirst to renew my acquaintance with Hills & woods & Brooks, I long to be staring with anxiety upon a Pystill Rhaidar, or dangling my legs over a Jerusalem Poney.— To refresh my recollections with a few notes of the Blackbird, which are always so delightful to me. In short, I wish I was now hunting Owls or squinting after Peahens.[10]

Yours very sincerely
JOHN H. REYNOLDS.

I have sent by Watton's Parcel you will receive a No. of the Inquirer & your little Vol.[11]

60

From John Hamilton Reynolds

Serj^{ts} Inn 23^{d} Augt 1814

My Dear Dovaston,

I have been wondering for this last week at your silence and have received great pleasure in hearing from you at last. Your letter has had much the same effect on me, that Coriolanus's had upon Menenius,[1] so that with a fresh stock of health and plenty of spirits, I shall proceed to chatter away to the tune of four sides of paper. Your opinion of the Inquirer is very gratifying to me, but have you not taken the Coces Robiniad as a serious review of the Ballad? The Author meant it as a fling at Black-Letter-Hunters—Lovers of the Old Writings—And on Critics in general. I think its great fault is being too labour[ed]. There is too great a shew of learning for so unimportant a subject—I am no friend to toiling at trifles:—The Essay is however exceedingly ingenious & in many parts witty. You speak well of my Essay upon Hamlet—too well—It wants polish and connection. —I certainly was not aware to whom I was indebted for the remark on the willow or how my mind became fond of the passage (for I have long & often admired it) so it is very likely you pointed it out.——The Latin verses are very good; they are from the same person who wrote on 'Translations of the Dead Languages.' What do you think of the 2^{d} paper? it is written by a Gentleman who thinks highly of your Talents by your Letters (parts of which I have occasionally read him) and who would I am sure be very pleased to hear your opinion.[2] I wish my Fate had led me to Bala when yourself & fair friend were there—Pray let me have a Copy of the Poem written to it which I shall have great pleasure in giving to the 3^{d} N^{o} of the Inquirer (the 2^{d} being made and now in the Press)[3]—I love descriptive Poetry such as is written on the spot, or from immediate observation. It then possesses every attraction. Poetry then advances close to the Side of Painting, and we see how truly they are Sister Arts. Nothing but a love of Nature and a Minute attention to her works can make a Poet—And it may always be seen whether he writes from the ideas of others or from his own. Pray send me a copy of the Poem; for really I long to read it.

I am now pretty well at leisure, as the last sheet of my new Poem crawled through the Press on Saturday[4]—It now only waits for hot-pressing (which by the bye is needless considering what hands it will fall into, when the Critics begin to grind their teeth) and then forth into the World my dignified Quarto marches. I long to be reading the praises some of the genteel and *well-judging* part of the Critic-fraternity will spit over me; and to listen to the snarling and grumbling over my poor bone from the worse sort. You cannot imagine to what a calm temperature I have brought my mind. When my Safie was first published I went one night to sup with a few Gentlemen at a Booksellers, and they had a Review in which the Work was most unmercifully mawled—in which I was pointed out as a dangerous character—the Poem held up as an immoral one—& all the abuse launched at me & it that was possible:[5]—They read it to me, and I never felt less ruffled in my life—perhaps like Sir F Plagiary[6] I felt rather pleased than otherwise! Unfortunately the World does not know that a Critique is written but by one—that tis only the opinion of One Person—so that the condemnation however unfair finds many believers, and the abuse however violent mets with many approvers . . .

Have you seen Ld Byron's New Poem of 'Lara' which is a continuation of 'The Corsair'?[7]—It is in the heroic measure, and is excellent. For a full and nervous style of expression—a depth and brilliancy and originality of thought—a gaiety and richness of Fancy—and for truth of Character, his Lordship certainly stands above all Poets of the present day and equal to most & superior to many of the earliest Bards. His works will be read, I have no doubt, by Posterity with unmixed delight—his Memory will be cherished by future ages when those who are now passing their poor unasked judgements against him, are forgotten. It is a lamentable case that no Author's fame gets warm till his body gets cold;—that admiration wavers so much during life and only settles to steadiness and truth over the grave:—But so it is—And those who have ever most merited applause & attention after death in life have received the most black & rugged treatment. D'Israeli furnishes a melancholy collection of misfortunes of Authors in 'The Calamities &c.'[8]—Enough to stagger one.

I long to visit you this summer, as I have so much to talk over. I long to recruit my ideas with some of your border images and give them a feed on your Mountains and Lakes and Streams; and to make them as Fresh and vernal as your Meadows. I owe many a pleasing recollection to my last visit—My Mind never throws away a flower it has once gathered, but wears it for ever, even though the beauty is faded and the perfume gone: Memory keeps it alive with a delighting attention. I shall have a week's holidays for a country jaunt in the early part of September, and if I can bring it to bear, will try to see you for a day or two;—I have some things to shew you & much to talk over. I should like to chat with you upon the Poem you once had in idea upon Owen Glendwyr;[9]—it is certainly a fine subject, and you might make very much of it, and could. You might adopt the Heroic Measure— Write it in the manner of Rogers' 'Voyage of Columbus,'[10] or on the plan of Ld Byron's 'Giaour,'[11] in fragments—giving enough of them to form a story. You could also enrich the Work with many interesting notes on the times & mysteries and manners of Owen's day. The Spirits would give you an excellent opportunity of picturing rugged and Midnight scenery—Bold and uncouth Characters—And of introducing Incantations, prophetic songs and the dark and gloomy agitations of the Mind.[12] I cannot well express by letter what I conceive of this plan;—But your ardent genius will catch even from my imperfect hints the outline of this idea. The heroic Measure is undoubtedly the best, and is open to a variety of cadence[s]—to the expression of the softness or ardency or tenderness of affection —the violence and blackness of hate— the rooted rancour of Revenge—in fact to all the changes of mental passion. Much as Pope has been admired, I think he nearly ruined this Measure, by his unvaried gentleness and regular unbroken melody—His verses run from the tongue like oil. Remember I am here only speaking of the harmony of his Verse.

I now conclude this rambling Letter, as my paper vows it can bear no more.

> Yours very sincerely
> J. H. REYNOLDS.

61

From John Hamilton Reynolds

Banbury, Oxon, 25th Sept 1814.

My Dear Dovaston,

You will be surprized to hear from me at Banbury. The truth is
I have been making a complete tour of most of the inland
Counties and have been in the first place so harassed & hurried
in preparing for my journey & in the next so situated in the
midst of bustle & confusion in it—that I have hardly com-
manded ½ an hour to let my Mother know that such a being as
myself exists. Will you therefore excuse my long silence—my
neglecting to acknowledge the receipt of your Excellent little
Poem[1] with which I am highly delighted—but of this anon.—
Your letter (inclosed to Lord Cholmondeley)[2] did not come to
my hands for 8 or ten days on account of his Lordship being out
of Town . . . I started so suddenly that I had not time even to see
my Poem from the Press, though it was all printed—One copy
alone excepted which I procured for a young Lady in Devonshire[3] From which place I have received an earnest invitation to
spend a week or two, but albeit considerations infinite do speak
against it.[4] Having now said all I can in explanation of my
silence I will proceed to other matters. Your Poem is written in
the Measure which best suits you—the Ballad. You have given it
all the pleasing simplicity & conciseness which are its chief
ornaments, and have gone back to the purer style of expression
which marked the earlier Poets, taking with you the elegant
smoothness which Moderns have acquired. The Ballad measure
or rather Style, is beautifully calculated for the pictures of tender
& generous love, enthusiastic valour and faithful description of
Nature. It may be rugged or smooth as the occasion demands,
and never fails to keep pace with the thought be it ever so bold or
ever so gentle:—I never rise from the perusal of any one of the
Ancient Ballads without feeling my taste refreshed and my heart
bettered. After these long & tedious remarks upon a Style which
you so well understand and so pleasingly adopt, I will say something generally of your Ballad;—particulars I must leave till my
return to Town as I have not your Letter with me, and as my
Memory will not bear me into them:—Remember, if I make any
error in judgement, that I am judgeing from recollection only.

The Story is very sweet and simple which I very much admire—The versification is correct, and the Melody prettily varied—The Thoughts are in all parts good and natural and in most parts brilliant & beautiful. The expression is for the greater part worthy the thought, but one exception I make to it, which is the continual repetition of the epithet or the adverb as 'sweetly, sweetly.' I read this ballad to some excellent Judges an Evening or two before I came away, and they all admired it except in this instance. The repetition is good when used sparingly—3 or four times in the course of such a Poem as this (to my mind) would be quite enough. However you may think otherwise—opinions will vary.

I have seen some sweet scenery on my journey, and given my thoughts a holiday in order that they may work the better. I shall be busy with them many an evening on my return to Town; half my pleasures spring from recollection, and I do not know whether the contemplation of past joys gives not a more inward satisfaction than the joys themselves—They certainly play upon the mind more undisturbed, and acquire a sweetness which reflection alone can bestow.—

Kean I find has been performing at the Shrewsbury Theatre——Of course you have witnessed his acting. Such a Hamlet I never saw![5] So graceful yet so melancholy, so sarcastic, and so thoughtful. He gives many passages the most exquisite readings and very different from the commonplaces . . . But I may be telling you what you have seen—'He is a *Man*!—take him for all in all; we shall not look upon his like again.' (Mr K's reading).[6]

Pray write to me soon for I am anxious to hear from you;—I shall be at home immediately and shall hope to find a Letter waiting my arrival—

Yours most truly
J. H. REYNOLDS.

62

From John Hamilton Reynolds

Lambeth 30 Sept 1814

My Dear Dovaston,

Although time will not allow me to write you a letter of any great length; yet I cannot send the accompanying Poems without assuring you, in my own hand, what pleasure I have in dedicating to you one of my earliest publications[1]—It is pleasing to me to reflect upon the many happy literary hours I have spent in your Company; and to know that I am offering my Sketch not only to an ardent admirer and excellent judge of Poetry but also to one who is powerful and brilliant in the Art itself. I need not, I believe, say, how much I shall be pleased to hear your candid opinion and any of your admirable suggestions as to its improvement, intreating you at the same time not to let the in[s]cription have any weight with you.—

The Poem though printed will not be published for a Month or two, as the Town is very dull at present. I could not however refrain from sending you a copy.

I only returned to Town last night—And today Walton's parcel leaves for Shrewsbury—This will account for the shortness of my Letter

Yours most truly
    J. H. REYNOLDS.

63

From John Hamilton Reynolds

Serj^{ts} Inn 10 Oct 1814.

My Dear Dovaston,

The true end of Poetry is to please and by so much the more is a Poem worthy of existence—the more it conduces to the pleasure of its author, his friends or the world. I am become much fonder of my little bantling since you admire its features and dress—Your admiration has placed it higher in mine—And

I look upon it as a sort of link in our friendship's chain—which may make our affections faster & better. The truth is I never found such pleasure in the whole course of my existence as I have in composing this little work. It has called forth all my recollections—it has revived my acquaintance with fields & trees —with rivers, rocks & flowers—It has made me examine the images which a contemplation of Nature left upon my Mind. And I really think more lasting good—more exquisite feeling is acquired in resigning Memory to the favourite recollections of early enjoyments than in any actual engagement in what the world calls pleasure—At least I find it so. There is however a difference, and a dreadful one, between reflection upon pictur-esque scenery, with the feeling springing from its varieties, and the contemplation of human Nature & human actions—The first betters the heart—the last saddens the Mind. I have experienced it so every way. I have hours of inward examination & thought, which the World perhaps does not give me credit for, and which I do not desire it to do. The gaiety of my disposition in society subsides into the very opposite in retirement.[1] And the apathy of Memory which the bustle and noise of Company occasion, is amply made up by the activity of my mind in Solitude. But to quit this long essay upon my own feelings & oddities—I heartily thank you for the good opinion you have professed of my fancy's Eden[2]—And I beg of you to consider the dedication as coming from the heart—I say this, because I know it is not always the case.

Of the Mistakes I cannot say much—Both of them stand more however against me than [y]ou and yet I hope, in spite of the blunders I have made, that both your name and the 'amicitia'[3] are written right upon my heart. I trust there are no errata there. Pray send me your 'Rural Walks'[4]—My eye longs to be feasting my mind:—You, with such powers, & living in (what Hunt calls) 'the very thick of the lustre'[5] must needs give a description faithfully beautiful.—I should have mentioned Kirke White; but if you observe all my allusions are only to our first 3 great Poets generally & to the living ones in particular—I speak not also of their moral lives only.—Your Madrigal is what it should be—beautiful & light.—I would fain apply it, as your hint might direct me, if egotism did not forbid it.—

Your letters are sources of such pleasure to my Mind, that I hope you will never enlarge your handwriting or shorten your paper. And do not give your pen too much idle time, it can do so well, that I only grieve it does so little.—By the bye—(to return again to self—) you say that the Poem should have been longer —so it might have been, but hardly so without trespassing on Akenside's property.—[6]

The following Poem was written to a Young Lady (at her desire) upon the death of a youthful friend of hers & mine—[7]

To —— ——

Lady I will not ask thee to recall
Thy wonted calmness at thy Anna's fall
Sisters in Love & youth,—I ask it not.
With thee a grief is not so soon forgot:—
'Tis otherwise of me so us'd of late
To hear the dark effects of mystic Fate,
I scarcely shudder at the sounds that say,
Another much lov'd form is swept away.
Tis Autumn with my friends—they fall like leaves,—
Yet this deserted bosom barely grieves;—
But much of sorrow fortifies the mind,
And worn out feelings get at last resign'd.

Anna was young—alas! too young to fade,
Snatch'd ere her youthful hopes had been betray'd;—
While yet the sun of life was full & bright,
Warm in its joy & cloudless in its light;—
She passed from Earth—while Earth had much to give
Of gentle mirth—and while 'twas bliss to live.

Had years past on—To that too dreadful time,
When breasts prove false, & hearts are stain'd with crime—
When friendship, which in earlier days was sweet,
Shrinks into nought, or blackens to deceit:—
To that dark time, which over comes, when life,
Changes to gloomy sloth, or heartless strife:—
When hopes which all the gaiety of youth,
Gave to the Mind & fondly gave as truth,
Are thwarted—broken—chill'd within the breast,
And only sadden life & poison rest.—
Had she felt these—Her only wish had been,
Weary of all, to moulder from the scene;—
Sick of the World—Unfit its storms to brave,—
She might have crav'd the stillness of the grave.
But in her youth, when every hope was fair,
And Beauty lov'd her cheek and linger'd there;—

When her dark eyes, beneath each darker tress,
Laugh'd in their light, & beam'd of happiness:—
To fade so soon—Her form, How delicate!
To bow in youth before so dark a fate,—
While friends were faithful—while her thoughts were young,—
And truth & sweetness liv'd upon her tongue:—
Might ask the bosom's mournfulness,—but mine
Hath almost ceas'd to wonder or repine.
Tis nearly harden'd—Hourly from my sight,
My early friends are fading into night;—
My ears are now familiar with the sound,
That tells some form hath mingled with the ground:—
And yet I live, and revel with the gay—
Associate with the breathing things of clay,
Who, to drown thought & fear & sorrow, quaff
The madd'ning wine & raise the bitter laugh;—
In drinking health to others—lose their own—
Promise a faith their hearts have earlier known—
Sing the wild song, and pass the wilder jest,
Till Feeling agitates itself to rest.

For her,—Poor faded one!—whose bosom now,
Dead to the world's unkindness, sleeps below,
No dull cold stone, inscribed with colder rhymes,
Shall bear her name & fate to distant times;—
No verse shall bid the stranger ne'er forget
Virtues,—He comes to read & not regret:—
No tortured lines shall tell him that, resign'd,
Affliction touch'd her form & not her mind—
That to the pious, hope is never dim,—
And that a fate like hers remains for him.
No—in the few warm friends that yet have breath,
Shall live the memory of her charms—her death,—
Her virtues, feeling bosoms shall recall,
And those who lov'd her life, shall weep her fall.
In thy young breast, oh lady, cherish well,
The soft remembrance of thy friend that fell;—
And yet let this reflection soothe thy care
'She is at rest'—Tis more than many are!
Oct. 1814.

My excellent Friend Hunt is very kind to me—He lends me
his books, and the observations in them (by his hand) are most
useful—He has in the press a Mask called 'The Descent of

Liberty' prefaced with observations on the origin of Masks.[8]—I find M[r] Roscoe's two sons called on him in Prison.[9]

Pray write to me a speedy & a long letter—[10]

64

From John Hamilton Reynolds

Feb. 25th 1815.

My Dear Dovaston,

You must have been very much astonished at not hearing from me for so long a time—To be plain with you (for how otherwise am I to redeem myself from the charge of neglecting you) My Father has been very much plagued in his Situation by a party that wanted to displace him but which happily we have triumphed over.[1] I have been so much engaged with it as to be incapable of giving up myself to Letter-Writing I do not mean the time but the Mind, which is absolutely requisite. I shall not proceed further in calling up excuses but shall proceed to chat with you . . .

So far from London as you are now all sorts of literary news must be given to you & will I am sure be the most acceptable. My Friend Hunt is again at Liberty,[2] And his freedom is welcomed by his Muse with one of the most spirited Poems that has come before the Public for many years. 'The Descent of Liberty' is a Mask in which he has loosed his Fancy to revel as gaily as she can & wherever she may choose.[3] He sent me a Copy last week with a very handsome Note and I sat up half the Night to read what was so suited to my taste—it enraptured me! And before I went to rest my feelings embodied themselves in a Letter to him of thanks & congratulations. This he has with his usual kind-heartedness thanked me for in the Examiner.[4]—His descriptions of flowers are as fresh as growing flowers & as brilliant. His personfications are amazingly fine—in short the Poem (to give it a proper praise) has very much of the sunny richness of fancy which beams in Comus. I have given him a Poem for his Examiner according to a promise I made him, and it will be inserted in next Sunday's Number—The Subject will be doubly interesting to you—it is 'The Fairies.' Composed from the idea of a Moonlight Scene in your beautiful Field of Fairy-land[5]—Hunt likes it greatly and I think you will—A copy of the Paper shall be sent to you. Lord Byron is married![6]—Alas! where now is the devoted faithfulness to silent virtue and kind beauty—Where is the respect for what was lovely & generous & gentle—Alas! why has he falsified his once favourite sentiment—'Heu quanto peius est cum reliquis versari quam tui meminisse.'[7]—I very much dread that it is a sacrifice to Necessity. His Lordship has a long poem in hand.

I had a very friendly letter from Wordsworth last Week—and highly do I feel the honour of it.[8]—He congratulated me on the love of the country which my Poetry evinces & expresses a hope that I may realize my wishes by a peaceful retirement—Heaven knows how very far I am from expecting it!—His seal is a Head of Shakespeare & the finest I ever saw.—Poor Coleridge! I understand he is out of his Mind!—Or at least in that state of dejectedness which is akin to it—Good God! What a Genius is lost! What a Mind is overthrown! Did you ever read his Poems of 'Love' and 'The Nightingale' in the Lyrical Ballads or his sublime translation of Schiller's Plays of Wallenstein & Piccolomini?—if not—Pray read them & you will see how delicately he can write & how strongly. It has been hinted that a Subscription will be started—I hope there will—[9]

In a few days I shall publish 'an Ode' singly—[10] It will not take more than a sheet & will I hope ride free in a frank. I shall send you one either so or through Longmans. I can vouch for no one merit except the excellence of the printing which I think you will say is what schoolboys call 'something like.'

What think you of the Little stanzas I send you now—they take a poetical view of a little incident which you may remember.[11] It is very odd, but I can always write better on Times that are gone than on pleasures that are present—I know not why it is so.

You have never sent me the Blank Verse Poem which you once mentioned to me & promised me a copy of. I should like very much to have it.—And any other little pieces which you may have by you.

Did you ever in your perusal of Comus notice that a line which is most assuredly one of [the] finest may be understood two ways & in both is beautiful—This it is—'Held up their pearly wrists & took her in.'—The *pearly* wrists might be so called from the E[x]quisite hue of the flesh, or from the Water trickling down from the hand when held up from the Waves forming pearls;—These struck me one night when I had given myself up to a Night of luxury[12]—Milton doubtless meant the former. I really doat upon Comus:—It has such a Wild growth of fancy such an unrestrained flowing of the Mind—It is so full of sense & soul I declare that I would rather have been the author of a scene in Comus than of [any] line of Poetry that has been written since it.—[13]

[I supp]ose Spring will quickly begin to peep over your Fi[elds and bid] good-day to your flowers. The leaves will soon spread their green couches for idle sun beams—and the Blackbird bustle through your walks with his full quick Notes. I long to be twining myself through your walks—gazing at the monument to Shenstone—lying full length at the foot of the Sundial, content to let it keep time for me—Sitting at Breakfast under your Arbour whilest the friendly Robin chaunted his good morning or sitting face to face at the Library Window with an army of apple Trees before our Eyes—a blue sky above—and a volume of Milton or Shakespeare in Our hands & hearts. Thus much for wishing:—Some Autumn may yet s[ee] me by you—some deep, quiet—rich Autumn when the following lines of Hunt will be realized—They are from the Descent of Liberty—

> 'While the bees about their treasure,
> Hum & twitch with tipsy pleasure,
> And the decoying butterflies,
> Drest with all their summer dies,
> Flutter about from every part,
> Tickled, as it were, at heart.'[14]

Most beautiful!

So you had a [word illegible] from Smyth of Cambridge—[15] He is an Elegant writer with no great wildness of Fancy and no great power of Mind—But he is elegant. And Rogers proves what Elegance can do,[16] nor can we expect to have strength & polish together always—Refinements can but be had at the sacrifice of Power—If Achilles had ever visited a Grecian Rout he would have found his muscles & sinews of but little use.—

I shall be glad to hear from you soon.

Yours to the end of the Chapter.

J. H. REYNOLDS.

If you have never read Dryden's dedication to his Translations of Virgil, I would recommend them to you, as being full of his crispness of style.[17] Dryden could write prose almost superior to poetry—I think looking away from the Cecilian Ode that his judgement was greater than his genius—It must ever be remembered what a turn & finish he gave to the English [word illegible]. His wit too was astonishing:—But Alexander's Feast is delicious indeed,—and 'decies repetita placebit.'[18]

I opened this letter to make the enclosure which I at first forgot.

The Song of a Spanish Lover, to his Mistress.

'When for the light Bolero ready stand
'The mozo blithe, with gay Muchacha met,
'He conscious of his broider'd cap & band,
'She of her netted locks & light corsette,
'Each tiptoe perch'd to spring & shake the Castanet.'

Scott.

I

The day is done, the drum is still,
    No more are Ranks retiring;—
No longer echoes up the hill,
    The shouting wild, the firing:—
The Evening Sunbeam glows awhile
    On Wood—and stream—and steep;
And lovely is the God's last smile
    Before he seeks the Deep.

2

Come from the Cot—and bring with thee,
    The cheerful castanet;
And join the evening dance with me,
    The War—the Waste forget:—
That dear dark eye of thine hath seen,
    When none had cause to grieve;—
When every vale was gay & green,
    And Lovers laugh'd at Eve.

3

The peaceful Eve is here once more,
    And Man may quit his thatch,
Nor dread the Cannon's dreadful roar,
    Nor hear the pacing Watch:—
No more, the Stream in furious haste,
    Red Ranks are seen to ford;
Nor now are setting sunbeams cast
    To flash upon the Sword.

This hour is still—And we may pass
  In dance the time till Night;
No columns now will crush the grass,
  And struggle in our sight;—
The peaceful shade shall gently steal,
  And warn from Mirth to rest;
Nor startling Gun nor clashing steel
  Will point the Midnight Guest.

Alas! How long, since foot like thine,
  So lovely, and so light!
Hath kist the vale at day's decline,
  When lingering beam was bright:
The War-steed's hoof,—the soldier's tread,
  Have mark'd the Spanish plain;—
But Desolation's form is fled—
  And thou may'st dance again.

How sweet to gaze once more—and mark
  Thy flowing locks of jet;
Spread to the breeze their tresses dark—
  And hear the castanet:—
How sweet to see the playful feet,
  The flowerets lightly press:—
The glance so bright, the smile so sweet,
  That beam to win & bless.

The grass, my Love! is free from dew,
  Kiss'd by the summer sigh;
And many a gay and golden hue,
  Adorns the Evening sky:
So soft the breeze, it breathes of heaven,
  And whispers our release;
It seems as if the airs were given
  Fresh from the wings of Peace.

Then come, my Love!—The fields are free
  The sun-rays tremble still;

They gild the mountain orange-trees,
  And sparkle in the rill:—
Come from thy cot,—While summer gale
  Breathes light o'er waving flowers;
The Dance again shall cheer the Vale,
  And Laughter light the hours.

J. H. REYNOLDS.

I have inclosed you the copy of a Song written immediately after the liberation of Spain:—its present disturbed state has cast a mist over the truth.—However when it was composed, Freedom seem'd to promise all that I have written.

I now make you an extract from a Poem which I have in my possession, quite unconnected and but roughly planned. It is likely so to remain, for my affections have certainly chilled towards it. I have a long Poem in contemplation, if health and Reading & observation will but assist me.[19]

Extracts from   (These extracts are from
    A Tale   different parts)

'I only ask for Heaven to grant a gale,
'Such as may fret the sea, & swell my sail;—
'Make the high tap'ring mast its streamers lave,
'And almost shew the keel above the wave.
'I know my bark—She lags not on her way—
'The breasting surge will curl itself to spray;—
'And fling its foam to glitter in the light,
'Our fav'ring Moon bestows to charm the Night.'

———

'And should I bleed; with thee to bind my wound,
'A pangless wound when once by thy hands bound;—
'Thy lip to breathe the melodies to cheer,
'Then what were left to wish—Or what to fear.'

———

'Give me the Maid that in Despair can soothe,
'And make life's rugged path of Sorrow smooth;—
'Smile in the hour of joy—In grief be kind,—
'And show the firmness of a Woman's Mind—
'Mournful in absence—mindful of her vow,—
'Free—Fair—& faithful—Zelia such art thou.'

———

'The eyes of Heaven are on us—For each Star
'Lights the wide ocean,—gems the sea afar;—
'Casts a pale light upon the showery spray,
'Plays on the glassy wave—and points the way.'

———————————

'This kiss—my Peri!—which I fondly sip;—
'Will linger with me, then reseek thy lip,
'And on its rosy resting place remain,
''Till I shall fondly snatch it back again.
'That smile hath reconciled the worst of ill,
'Which Fate may frame & force to cross my will:—
'That smile, which gilds each moment as it flies,
'And gives a speaking spirit to thine eyes,
'That single smile of love thy faith endears
'Makes promise to my hopes of golden years.—
'Beams like a sun-light on my heart—and gives
'A summer vision, which in fancy lives.
'Sahmed will wait to welcome from the tide,
'My Eastern Beauty, and his Brother's bride!
'Mark not his roughness—Shrink not from his eye,
'(Though dimm'd with tears it looks despondingly)
'Note not his silence, Zilia—Sorrow now
'Lives on his lip, and frowns upon his brow;—
'His heart, which once was gentle, still is good,
'Though worn with grief and sour'd by Solitude.
'Fix'd on one woe his thoughts to mirth ne'er stray,—
'His feelings are too deep & keen to play.
'He ponders ever on a passion crost,
'He lov'd—The lady left him & was lost.
'Not that tame love which frets awhile, & then
'Calms in the breast and leaves it free again:—
'Not that tame love, which, any form, if fair,
'Could raise;—Not open to distress, despair,—
'No cool, wild, fondness which exists awhile—
'Flies at a frown or revels in a smile:—
'But one resistless passion of the heart,
'Which kindled once, liv'd, never to depart;
'It fed on hopes and wishes,—till betray'd
'In its full strength by the deceitful Maid;—
'It wither'd in his breast, but linger'd still,
'To sadden every thought, and every will.
'Death threw a melancholy sweetness o'er,
'The form he lov'd, it could deceive no more.

'The grave had snatch'd the cause of his distress,
'And turn'd the current of his wretchedness
'His bosom which had at her falsehood griev'd,
'Wept at her loss,—forgot she had deceived,—
'But traced her charms & found excuse for all,
'Forgave her falsehood & bemoan'd her fall.
'His was a noble passion that could find
'A heart of mercy, and a strength of mind.
'But he has suffer'd—And his frame declares,
'That thought ne'er flies, and sorrow never spares.
'His breast indeed is but a living tomb,
'Where all his wither'd hopes lie hid in gloom.
'Should I be gentler, Zilia, if a fate,
'Like his, had left me to bewail or hate:—
'The Spirits darken when the hope is weak,
'And sorrow paints her Image on the cheek.'

&c. &c. &c.[20]

There I think I have given you a sufficient portion of my tale:—What think you of it?—I have scraps written of beginnings—Middles & endings. In fact I have all the bricks made & they only want cementing into form. Must I make it large or small?—Shall I build a Mansion or a Cot?[21]

J. H. REYNOLDS.

EPILOGUE

On this final letter Dovaston noted: 'Wrote to Reynolds 21 March 1815.' There, inexplicably, the correspondence ends. Perhaps the rest has been destroyed; perhaps the letters from Lambeth had been too frequent and too pressing. Dovaston had once cruelly implied that he was cultivated for his money. The implication seems mean and baseless. But the Reynolds family had tried too hard to bind him to themselves; as time went on, one feels that he had grown tired of their insistence. He found them unsophisticated, over-eager, immature. John Hamilton Reynolds was to live for another thirty-seven years, and Dovaston for another thirty-nine; but, as far as is known, they did not see or write to one another again.

One single reference suggests that they remained concerned about each other. In about 1823 Dovaston printed a dozen copies of *The Dove. Scraps of Poetry selected for the OSWESTRY HERALD.* Each poem was accompanied by an anecdote or comment. On 15 August 1822, under the pseudonym Musiphilus, he had explained:

> My little residence is often visited by youths who try their 'prentice han'' at this mystery and calling [poetry]; and some few years agone, I took one to view Llynellys, the Ogo, and Rocks of Blodwell, perhaps not surpassed in all Wales for beauty and variety of prospect. While I was adjusting our gig at the alehouse, his eye caught the flounced frock and white stocking of *Peg o' the Pant*. The youth, no less a body than John Hamilton Reynolds, who has since so largely and lightly flourished in the middle circle of letters, in the Theatres, Magazines, Reviews, and Newspapers, (where indeed he has not spared *me*) on his return to London soon after, sent me the

following lively and fanciful effusion on the 'Lightsome Margarett.'

This pleasant comment on the young Reynolds was followed by the poem which had appeared (with an extra stanza) as 'Margaret' in his *Naiad* volume of 1816.[1]

Dovaston himself did not entirely disappear from record.[2] A second edition of *FitzGwarine* appeared in 1816; a third edition was published in 1825. This included a collection of 'British Melodies.' Twenty-six of these songs had originally been published in 1817, under the patronage of Princess Charlotte, with music by Clementi. 'Florabella,' a poem, followed. In 1822 came the minuscule edition of *The Dove*. In 1839 appeared *Lectures on Natural History and National Melody*.

The title was significant. Though Dovaston was a minor Romantic poet, he had a much stronger claim to remembrance as a naturalist. The Victoria County History of Shropshire records that he was a close friend of the Rev. W. A. Leighton, with whom he studied botany and other branches of natural history. It was, wrote Leighton, 'my friend Dovaston who first directed my attention to our wild cherries'; they grew in the orange-grove at West Felton. It was Dovaston who told him that buckthorn was found nearby, at Cupid's Ramble. Dovaston discovered the variety of yew which came to be known as the Dovaston yew; he grew it on his estate. After Dovaston's death, Leighton published the fourth edition of his *Guide, descriptive and historical, through the Town of Shrewsbury*. For his list of local birds he was 'indebted to the kindness of the late John F. M. Dovaston, Esq., A.M. of Westfelton, near Shrewsbury: . . . a gentleman who, with enthusiastic ardour, devoted many years of unceasing attention and observation, to an accurate investigation of the varieties and habits of the feathered tribes.'[3] Dovaston was a pioneer of field ornithology.[4]

In October 1823 he had ended a tour of the Lake District with a pilgrimage to Newcastle; he had gone to do homage to Thomas Bewick, already famous for his woodcuts and his immensely popular *History of British Birds*.[5] The two men had become friends at once, and over the next year Dovaston sent 'large heaps' of additions and corrections to the fifth edition of the book. He procured many orders for Bewick's work among his friends; he sent him specimens and notes from his naturalist neighbours. He even drafted the preface for the sixth edition of the work, which appeared in 1826 (the last edition to appear during Bewick's lifetime). In August 1825 he visited Bewick once again; it was about now that Bewick engraved a likeness of the 'fat Chubby head' which Eliza Reynolds had once described.

Natural history was not the only bond between the two men; they shared radical views on politics and religion, a great interest in folk music, and a Rabelaisian sense of humour. Perhaps they shared a deeper feeling still, for Dovaston seems to have been in love with Bewick's daughter, Jane:

> Of his eldest daughter, Jane, whom he called his 'right hand,' I feel it difficult to speak in print, lest even the gentlest truth offend her unaffected modesty . . . Her greatest delight was in his fame, and she looked on him almost with adoration, as he did on her. The formation of her person and deportment was particularly graceful and fascinating; her features lovely, and brilliantly animated with intelligence; and her gentle spirit gave a glow to all her excellencies . . .[6]

This portrait in Dovaston's journal in October 1823, and Jane's own letters to him, clearly suggest an attachment between them. Yet perhaps Dovaston's portrait of Jane was deceptive, and she was less angelic than she seemed. When her father died in 1828, she refused to let Dovaston edit his autobiographical *Memoir*. Perhaps he was importunate, perhaps she herself behaved like a dragon. Whatever the truth, their correspondence and their relationship ended. The *Memoir* was published in 1862, eight years after Dovaston had died. Jane herself died, unmarried, in 1881.

Unable to edit Bewick's *Memoir*, Dovaston published his own. In September 1829 *The Magazine of Natural History* published *Some Account of the Life, Genius, and Personal Habits of the late Thomas Bewick, the celebrated Artist and Engraver on Wood. By his Friend John F. M. Dovaston, Esq., A.M. of Westfelton, near Shrewsbury.*[7] It was the first of four instalments.

The Magazine of Natural History records not only recollections of Thomas Bewick, but the observations of a versatile and eager naturalist. Dovaston contributes 'Some Account of the Water-Shrew: a Mouse supposed to have been lost for about a Century.' He discusses the pied flycatcher, or coldfinch; he writes on fairy rings, and on the little, or barred, woodpecker. He observes hares taking the water, and turtledoves, the nightingale, the blackcap and greater titmouse. (He also records—a Romantic touch to delight J. H. Reynolds—'I frequently, on fine nights, place an Æolian harp in my chamber window').[8]

Dovaston devised a field-glass—or, as he called it, an orthoscope. He also invented an ornithotrope: the first recorded feeding device for wild birds. He insisted that birds were never shot at or molested within the bounds of his estate. He encouraged them to nest round The Nursery by providing artificial nesting-holes and nesting-boxes. His concern with natural history was inexhaustible. He tried growing mistletoe 'with tolerable success' on 23 different sorts of trees; he enclosed a piece of grassland in order to make observations on hares; he attempted to record bird songs by musical notation—but he found the task impossible. His ultimate achievement was to stumble upon the phenomenon of bird territory. During the eighteenth century, natural history had grown into a fashionable cult among country gentlemen. In 1789 Gilbert White had published his *National History and Antiquities of Selborne*; in 1790 Thomas Bewick had published his *Quadrupeds*. They had done more to popularize natural history than any other Englishmen; Dovaston followed in their tradition.

He spent nearly all his adult life at West Felton, happy in his country pursuits. He left home very rarely. As late as 1838 he proclaimed that he had never been on a railway train, and that he had no great desire to go on one. Yet in his middle years, at least, he was no recluse. He seems to have led an active social life, and he sat for some years on Shrewsbury Town Council. In 1814, when he was still only thirty-two, he had been presented with the Freedom of the Borough of Oswestry, presumably on the strength of his personal popularity and perhaps the reputation which he had won with his *FitzGwarine*.[9]

Like John Hamilton Reynolds, Dovaston wrote his 'Farewell to the Muse,' but nonetheless continued his writing. He wrote an 'Inscription on a root-seat, under a large Purple-Beech, dedicated to Thomas Yates, at Nursery, West Felton.' He devised an inscription on melancholy, in Old English characters, for another root-seat in his garden. He wrote an 'Inscription for an Urn to Linnaeus, under a Lime-tree, in the grounds of John Clavering Wood, Esq., of Marsh Hall, Salop.' He turned to religion and philosophy, and composed a 'Hymn for the Ladies' Club, or Female Friendly Society, Oswestry, 1817'; he also wrote a 'Prologue to a Play for the Benefit of a Public LIBRARY—Oswestry Theatre, 1822.' The promising young barrister, the widely-read man of letters, the dramatic critic, had all faded; in their place remained a retiring country gentleman. In his 'Monody' he tried to explain his isolation:

> I know not why,
> It is not that my temper's shy,
> Nor that my heart is proud;
> But sooth I can not hit the way
> To mix with minds of ev'ry day
> In converse of the crowd. [10]

He had once 'raised a mound of earth' in a grove at West Felton; it was, he said, to be his grave, 'whenever it shall please the Almighty to call me from this state, where He has so very largely blessed me with happiness.' [11] The happiness was not to last. The bachelor to whom Miss Mackay had often sent remembrances, whom Mrs. Reynolds had carefully cultivated, whom perhaps Jane Bewick had loved, became in time a sombre recluse. As *The Gentleman's Magazine* observed: 'The evening of his life was unfortunately clouded with ill health and depression of spirits, which for the last few years confined him to his chamber.' He died, unmarried, at West Felton on 8 August 1854. He was buried in the village churchyard. [12]

For all his advantages of birth and wealth and education, Dovaston had led a somewhat undistinguished literary career. Already, in 1815, when their correspondence ended, John Hamilton Reynolds had outstripped his mentor. He had earned praise from Byron, a letter from Wordsworth, and the friendship of Leigh Hunt. By 1815 he had met Benjamin Bailey and James Rice; and that year he joined the staff of an influential paper, *The Champion*. By 1816 he felt secure enough to abandon his clerical work, and to embark on a literary career. That year his poem *The Naiad* was published by Taylor and Hessey. It was dedicated 'To Benjamin Robert Haydon, Esq., . . . by one who admires his genius, and values his friendship.' By October 1816 Reynolds had come to know the man whom he instinctively recognised as the greatest poet of his generation. Hunt, in *The Examiner*, classed Reynolds with Keats and Shelley. Reynolds himself never confused his own talent with Keats's genius. 'Do you get Fame,' he told him, '—and I shall have it in being your affectionate and steady friend.' [13]

By 22 November 1816 the Reynolds family had moved from Lambeth to 19, Lamb's Conduit Street. In 1817 George Reynolds was appointed writing master to his old school, Christ's Hospital, and early in 1818 the family moved to one of the masters' houses in Little Britain. In both these houses Keats became a familiar visitor. He had been quickly welcomed by Jane and Marianne, and he wrote more than once to his 'dear friends,' the 'kind sisters';[14] indeed, when Benjamin Bailey jilted Marianne, Keats broke his friendship with him.[15] He sent Mrs Reynolds a bound copy of *Endymion*,[16] and he addressed a sonnet to her cat:

> Cat! who hast past thy grand climacteric,
> How many mice and rats hast in thy days
> Destroy'd?—How many tit bits stolen? Gaze
> With those bright languid segments green, and prick
> Those velvet ears—but prythee do not stick
> Thy latent talons in me . . .[17]

The request was justified; perhaps it was the cat which had once put its claws through a letter to Dovaston.

But the Reynolds household was dominated by women, and Keats grew tired of 'the strife of women's tongues.'[18] By October 1818 he was weary of the Reynolds's gossip and malice. He was enthralled by their cousin, Jane Cox (the Charmian of his letters), and he noticed their jealous treatment of her.[19] When he fell in love with Fanny Brawne, Mrs Reynolds and her daughters showed marked disapproval of his choice. Their hostility to her estranged him from Little Britain. Writing to Fanny, he dismissed them as 'these Laughers, who do not like you, who envy you for your Beauty, who would have God-bless'd me from you for ever: who were plying me with disencouragements with respect to you eternally.'[20] 'Every day I live,' Fanny Brawne was to write, a year later, 'I find out more of their malice against me.'[21]

However he came to dislike Mrs Reynolds and her daughters, Keats remained a close friend of John Hamilton Reynolds—at least until his last months in England. Reynolds did much for Keats. Through Reynolds, directly or indirectly, Keats met many other friends who are now familiar members of his circle. By 17 March 1817 he knew the Dilkes, and through the Dilkes he met Charles Brown. By April 1817 he had left his first unsatisfactory publisher for Reynolds's friends and publishers, Taylor and Hessey. He had also met James Rice and Benjamin Bailey, and by August he had met John Martin. Through Reynolds or Taylor and Hessey he met Richard Woodhouse.

Reynolds, who had shown devotion to Dovaston, found his true place as a friend of Keats. He reviewed his *Poems* (1817) in *The Champion*; he talked poetry with him, and he prevented him from publishing his first reckless preface to *Endymion*. He defended this poem against the critics. He inspired Keats to write 'Robin Hood' and 'Isabella': indeed, they planned to publish a joint volume of metrical versions from Boccaccio. By July 1818 Keats assured Reynolds that,' upon my soul, I have been getting more and more close to you every day, ever since I knew you.'[22] Some of his finest and most significant letters were written to him.

Yet one must not forget Charles Brown's insistence, in 1821, that 'Reynolds was no dear friend to Keats, nor did Keats think him so."[23] Keats was aware of Reynolds's opinion of Fanny Brawne, 'that poor idle Thing of woman-kind.'[24] Reynolds though Severn an unsuitable companion for Keats in Italy, but he did not try to find a substitute, and he did not consider going himself. He did not—like other friends—sail with Keats as far as Gravesend, on the departing *Maria Crowther*. He did not—like other friends—contribute towards his expenses in Italy. He was on the list of those who were to be given some of Keats's books; but it is perhaps significant that, as far as we know, Keats last wrote to Reynolds on 28 February 1820.

When Reynolds's friendship with Dovaston faded, others had grown brighter. More important, he knew love. He seems to have been enamoured of a girl, now unknown, who died before January 1815. Perhaps she was the 'young Lady in Devonshire' to whom he had sent the first copy of his poem.[25] He also became a friend of the three Leigh sisters at Slade, near Sidmouth. But it was another Devonshire girl who captured his affections. He had probably met her through her relation, Mrs Butler, who was a friend and neighbour in Lambeth. In the summer of 1816 he was already in love with Eliza Powell Drewe, his future wife. In about 1817 he determined to marry her; she asked him to abandon literature, and to take up a solid profession. His mother had dominated his youth; Eliza was to shape his later life. On 4 November 1817 he duly became an articled pupil in the office of Francis Fladgate, a solicitor and a relative of James Rice. On St Valentine's Day, 1818, he wrote his 'Farewell to the Muses.'

> My boat is trimm'd—my sail is set—And I
> Shall coast the shallows of the tide of Time
> And rest me happily—where others lie,
> Who pass oblivious days. No feelings climb

Ambitiously within me. Sweet Farewell
Be to the Nymphs that on the old Hill dwell.[26]

He could not abandon literature. In 1821 he published his best-known book of poetry, *The Garden of Florence*; he wrote sparkling essays for *The London Magazine*. He contributed to *The Edinburgh Review*, *The Retrospective Review*, *The Westminster* and *The Athenaeum*. In the summer of 1822 an opera called *Gil Blas*, the joint production of Reynolds and his future brother-in-law, Tom Hood, was brought out at the English Opera House. In 1815 'that united Beaumont & Fletcher brotherhood'[27] brought out the anonymous *Odes and Addresses to Great People*. 'I think the thing is likely to be a hit,' Hood had confided to Reynolds, 'but if you do some I shall expect it to run like wild-fire.'[28] Hood had a high opinion of his collaborator's talents; he had once written to Mrs Reynolds of 'your son John, dear to the Muses.'[29] Reynolds was, alas, less dear to the Muses now. He remained divided between his profession and his vocation. He became an indifferent lawyer, and he never achieved the literary fame which Leigh Hunt had predicted for him.

His domestic life was, alas, to be far from fortunate. In 1822, the year he became a qualified solicitor, he finally married Eliza Powell Drewe. His marriage was saddened by the death of both his children. A warmly affectionate, innocent man, he became, as he told Monckton Milnes, a 'poor baffled Thing.'[30]

Perhaps the patent inequality of his parents had helped to flaw his character; perhaps he had suffered as the only son in a household of women, the son of a strong-minded, ambitious mother. He had always suffered from ill-health, he suffered from it still, and his financial problems became acute. In 1839 he went bankrupt. Finally he abandoned the law and decided to leave London. R. E. Prothero (later Lord Ernle), the son of Canon Prothero, Rector of Whippingham, recorded:

> Some political services rendered by him to the Liberal cause gave him a claim upon Lord John Russell, who, in 1847, appointed him assistant clerk of the newly established County Court at Newport in the Isle of Wight. In Newport Reynolds lived for the five years that elapsed before his death in 1852. He was buried in the churchyard of the town,—a broken-down, discontented man, whose great literary abilities had brought him no success in life. Few, probably, of the islanders were aware that the assistant County Court clerk,

who professed himself a Unitarian and a bitter Radical, and whose drunken habits placed him beyond the pale of society, had promised to be one of the stars of English literature at the period of its poetic revival.[31]

John Hamilton Reynolds died at Newport on 15 November 1852. He was fifty-eight. On his tombstone in Church Litten are the words 'The Friend of Keats.' He had written his 'Farewell to the Muses' in a copy of Shakespeare; he had later given the book to Keats. Keats gave the book to Fanny Brawne; and in it he wrote out his Bright Star Sonnet. This copy of Shakespeare—now at Keats House, Hampstead—measures the distance which divides talent from genius. It is an appropriate symbol of a literary friendship.

NOTES

1. Gittings: 'The Poetry of John Hamilton Reynolds' (*Ariel*, October 1970, pp. 7 sqq.)
2. *The Gentleman's Magazine*, January 1790, p. 83.
3. Marsh: *John Hamilton Reynolds. Poetry and Prose*, 10 sqq.; Walter Jerrold: *Thomas Hood, His Life and Times*. (Alston Rivers. 1907), passim.
4. Gittings: loc. cit. Phyllis G. Mann: 'The Reynolds Family' (*Keats-Shelley Journal*, Vol. V, Winter 1956.)
5. Information from the Librarian, Shrewsbury School, and the Shropshire County Archivist.
6. Reynolds: *The Fancy*. Preface, iii.
7. Ibid, iv–v.
8. 'Stanzas on revisiting Shrewsbury.' *The Fancy*, 77.
9. Southey: *The Life of the Rev. Andrew Bell* (Murray. 1844), II, 183–4, 185. See also J. M. D. Meiklejohn: *An Old Educational Reformer. Dr. Andrew Bell*. (Blackwood. 1881.)
10. *The Gentleman's Magazine*, June 1808, pp. 563–4. The obituary is published in full in the present book, pp. 156–7. According to *The Beauties of England and Wales*, XIII, 271, it was written by Mr Parkes (presumably Mr David Parkes, who figures in the Reynolds correspondence).
11. For accounts of Dovaston, see *The Gentleman's Magazine*, October 1854, pp. 395–6, and the *Dictionary of National Biography*.
12. 'Monody. Myself.' *FitzGwarine*, 35–7.
13. *The Gentleman's Magazine*, loc. cit.

9 March 1808

1. Mrs Reynolds was a woman of literary tastes. In 1827, under the pen-name of Mrs Hamerton, she published *Mrs Leslie and her Grandchildren: a Tale for Young People*. It earned the warm approval of Charles Lamb. She is said to have been a composer of album verses.
2. The Shorter Oxford English Dictionary gives Mountain as 'a variety of Malaga wine, made from grapes grown on the mountains.' When Keats was ill in February 1820, Mrs Reynolds was among the first to call. One can hear her repeating this advice.
3. Jane Reynolds, born on 6 November 1791, was the eldest of the Reynolds children; she was to be a 'dear friend' of Keats until she showed her jealousy of Jane Cox and her hostility to Fanny Brawne. On 5 May 1825 she married Thomas Hood, and, despite their financial problems and Hood's indifferent health, the marriage

proved to be happy. Hood died on 3 May 1845, and his wife survived him only a year, dying on 4 December 1846.

4 *Guida di Musica. Being a complete book of instructions for beginners on the grand & small piano forte. With progressive lessons ... principally taken from the 37th opera of James Hook. To which is added a collection of familiar subjects, etc.* (T. Cooke & Co. Dublin. 1810.)

5 Scotland was much helped in the preservation of its folk tunes by the work of Robert Burns (1759–96), who wrote new poems to the old tunes. In 1810 Cadell & Davies were to publish two volumes of *Select Scottish Songs, ancient and modern; with critical observations and biographical notices, by Robert Burns.* The work was edited by R. H. Cromek.

6 Nicoli is not recorded in the British Library Music catalogue. Possibly this is a reference to Giuseppe Nicolini, some of whose songs were published in the early years of the nineteenth century.

7 Unidentified. Possibly a servant.

8 The Sans Pareil was a minor London theatre, in the Strand.

9 George Reynolds was now master of the Lambeth Boys' Parochial School and writing master to the Lambeth Female Asylum. In time he became writing master to his old school, Christ's Hospital. He retired in March 1835, at the age of seventy, and died on 29 July 1853.

10 Mrs Reynolds knew something about such a voyage. Her only brother, Captain William Beckford Cox, of the Invalid Establishment of the Native Infantry, spent most of his army career in Sumatra; he died there, at Fort Marlborough, in 1814. His daughter, Jane, was the 'Charmian' who enthralled Keats in the autumn of 1818.

11 Dovaston did as he was asked. On a blank space in the letter he wrote his own words to the music:

1

Near Pinkey house aboon the brae,
  'Mang birks & osiers slender,
In hawthorn days I love to stray,
  And pipe my wild notes tender:
But little boots the gowan'd plain
  Unless my Lassie's near me,
And sadly flows my sweetest strain
  Unless she's there to hear me.

2

O Nature, keep the nectar'd cup,
  Gin I *alane* maun take it,
For sweeter far's a cozie drop
  When those we love partake it:

152

Then lassie seek you hawthorns gay,
And hear my wild notes tender,
Near Pinkey house aboon the brae
'Mang birks & osiers slender.

J. M. D. March 12, 1808.

Dovaston's *FitzGwarine* volume includes (p. 193): *SONG: Scotch air.—Pinkey house*. It is given exactly as above.

[12] Mrs Cox appears to have lived in Bristol. *Matthews's Bristol Directory*, 1793–4, gives Samuel Cox, Esq., Southwell Street; no contemporary directory is available in the British Library, but *The Bristol Index*, 1818, gives Ann Cox, 2, Beaufort Crescent, among the nobility and gentry. Among other possible Cox relations were Joseph Mason Cox, M.D., of Stapleton, William Cox (attorney-at-law), and John Cox, wholesale and retail grocer and tea-dealer.

[13] The Reynolds family were fond of Shrewsbury cakes, as will appear more than once in these letters. No doubt Keats knew of their predilection. Writing to Jane and Marianne on 5 September 1817, he observed that 'the Life of Man is like a great Mountain—his breath is like a Shrewsbury Cake' (*Letters*, 36).

21 April 1808

[1] Mrs Reynolds often alluded to her indifferent health, but she was to live for another forty years.

[2] John Dovaston senior had died on 31 March. In *The Beauties of England and Wales*, Vol. XIII, p. 269, the writer warmly maintained that the son was worthy of the father.

To the great and estimable qualities which adorn the mind and heart of this gentleman; to his high genius, his lively fancy, and his ardent benevolence, were we to obey the grateful impulse of our feelings, we would pour forth an ample eulogy; yet perhaps none more proper can at present be given, than to say that he has inherited his father's virtues.

[3] Presumably a school examination. Reynolds was to remain at St Paul's until 1810.

[4] Astley's latest amphitheatre had opened in 1803, and it was famous for its equestrian spectacles. Philip Astley was to build similar places of entertainment all over Britain, France and Ireland before he died in 1814.

[5] One cannot diagnose this illness, but it was clearly more than the common problem of adolescence.

[6] The music catalogue in the British Library lists *Handel's Water Piece, for the Harpsichord or Piano Forte*. (Edinburgh. Urbani &

Liston. 1802.) *Handel's Water Piece. Arranged as a Duet for Two Performers on one Piano Forte.* (G. Walker, 1808?)

[7] In the Introduction to his *Complete Dictionary of Music* (see notes to next letter), Thomas Busby writes (p. xxix): 'The principal Graces used in Music are . . . the Turn, Back Turn, Passing Shake, Beat, Turned Shake, Appogiature . . .'

[8] Dovaston was much interested in music. On 5 January 1812, writing to *The Gentleman's Magazine*, he recorded: 'When at the University of Oxford, one of my amusements was making as large a collection as I could of the popular and national airs of all countries . . .' He reflected that 'had poor Mungo Park, amid the inhospitable wilds of Africa, heard but the simplest British air, it might have enraptured his heart more than all the flimsy *eye-music* of a modern sonata, or even, perhaps, the soul-searching wonders of the divine Handel.' (*The Gentleman's Magazine*, February 1812, pp. 129 sqq.)

[9] Dovaston noted: 'Answ$^{\underline{d}}$ 27$^{\underline{th}}$'.

9 June 1808

[1] In *The Magazine of Natural History*, July 1832, p. 500, Dovaston writes: 'One lichen is already used as a blessed medicine in asthma.'

[2] In *Some Account of the English Stage* (Rodd. 1832), Vol. VIII, John Genest records several performances of *Ella Rosenberg*, given by the Drury Lane company between 1808–10. He also records performances at Covent Garden of a musical farce: *Who Wins? Or, the Widow's Choice.* The overture and music composed by Mr Condell.

[3] In *The History and Antiquities of the Parish of Lambeth*, published in 1826, Thomas Allen describes the St John's district. He records:

> In Church-street, adjoining the churchyard, are the new charity schools, erected for the instruction of the poor children of this district. It is a neat brick building, the upper room being appropriated to the girls' school, and the lower for the boys. At each end of the building are commodious apartments for the master and mistress . . . The children are instructed on Dr Bell's plan, the number of boys are 250, the girls 200; present master and mistress Mr Green, and Mrs Gilmour.

[4] For Dr Bell's opinion of Mr Reynolds, see also Introduction, p. 4. Dr. Bell's system of education was not to be forgotten by J. H. Reynolds; when he published his parody of Wordsworth, *Peter Bell. A Lyrical Ballad*, in 1819, he observed:

> Peter Bell, he readeth ably,
> All his letters he can tell;
> Roman W,—Roman S,

In a minute he can guess,
Without the aid of Dr Bell.

5 The large 8vo edition of Dr Bell's *Elements of Tuition* does not appear in the catalogue of the British Library. A two-volume edition of the work was published by Rivingtons in 1813–15.

6 Thomas Busby, Mus. Doc. (1755–1838) was an active minor composer and the author of *A complete dictionary of music. To which is prefixed, a familiar introduction to the first principles of that science.* The second edition of this work was published by Richard Phillips in 1806.

7 Dovaston notes: 'Ansd. July 5th 1808.'

24 August 1808

1 Reynolds suffered much from ill-health. Writing to Haydon on 5 February 1818, Keats told him: 'The fact is Reynolds is very unwell —he has all sorts of distressing Symptons.' On 18 March George Keats reported that Reynolds had 'a very bad rheumatic Fever'; on 9 August he still had what Keats called his 'confounded Rheumatism' (*Letters*, 99 and *passim*).

2 'Shenstone's Yew.' *Brought a seedling from the Leasowes, August 1806.* The poem was reprinted in the *FitzGwarine* volume, 2nd edition, 1816.

3 Joseph Bonaparte, Napoleon's brother, had been made King of Spain by the Constitution of Bayonne. The Spaniards were now rebelling against him, and early in 1808 Napoleon had been obliged to send French troops to Spain.

4 In June 1808 (pp. 563–4), *The Gentleman's Magazine* published an obituary of Dovaston's father:

> *Lately*, at his elegant villa, 'The Nursery,' West Felton, in Oswestry, co. Salop, aged 68, John Dovaston, esq., a gentleman of learning, science, and ingenuity. He was born in the year 1740, of humble though respectable parents, who lived on their small estate at West-Felton. He was taught to read by an old woman in the village, and that was the whole of his education; every other acquirement, which he afterwards possessed in so eminent a degree, was entirely his own acquisition. He was the eldest of seven children, all of whom he brought up to respectable professions, who might otherwise have drudged in servitude. From his father he received his little estate, almost swallowed up by mortgages and incumbrances, which he redeemed at a very early period of life by two voyages to the West Indies, and afterwards considerably increased by prudence and industry. Though he left scarcely any sciences untouched, his turn of mind was principally

directed to Antiquities, Natural Philosophy, Music, Mechanism, and Planting. Of the first he has left a large collection of MSS.; historical observations relating to Shropshire, and the Welsh borders; on Druidical relicks, and Stonehenge, tracing many traditional vulgar errors from the remote ages of Superstition. In Mechanism he has left a set of philosophical and musical instruments made by his own hands; among which are a large reflecting telescope, solar miscroscope, and an organ on a new principle; an electrical machine on the plan of Dr Franklin; and just before his death he projected an Orrery to show the Satellites, on a new method. In Planting he has cloathed the country round him with forest and fruit trees; and his little villa (which from his partiality to planting he called 'The Nursery') is laid out with much taste and rural elegance. He was well versed in the Hebrew, Anglo-Saxon, British, and Latin tongues; and had some knowledge of Greek. His reading was very extensive, and his application intense: to the very last day of his life he rose at five in the morning. He has never appeared as an Author before the publick; but the writer of this article was informed by his son, that, though he ordered that none of his works be published, his library is always open for the inspection of the curious, and any information from his MSS at their service. He was remarkable for his plainness of dress, yet his person always appeared dignified; his mind was vigorous and his memory retentive; both of which remained unimpaired to the last hour of his life. Though the Writer of this article was warmly his friend, there is no reader who knew him but will be aware of the strictest adherence to truth; and will remember the subject of it with affection and esteem. He has left one son, just called to the Bar, from the University of Oxford.

P.

[5] This work is not listed in the British Library music catalogue.
[6] Dovaston noted: 'Answd. Septr. 2, 1808.'

11 September 1808

[1] Keats, too, enjoyed *Don Quixote*. He referred to it in a letter to Miss Jeffery on 31 May 1819 (*Letters*, 343).
[2] This is the first reference to Marianne Reynolds (b. 1797), Eliza (b. 1799), and Charlotte (b. 1802). Marianne was to be a friend and correspondent of Keats. Jilted by Benjamin Bailey, she married Henry Gibson Green, and became the mother of the artists Charles and Towneley Green. She died on 7 January 1874. For Eliza and Charlotte, see letter of 7–8 October 1810, note 1, p. 172.
[3] Ten years later, on his way to Brighton, Reynolds was 'neatly

canted' out of a carriage outside Coldbath Fields (where Leigh Hunt had once been imprisoned). Writing to Jane Reynolds on 1 September 1818, Keats noted: 'I am glad John is not hurt' (*Letters*, 214).

4 Dovaston notes on this letter: 'Ans^d Oct. 15.'

23 September 1808

1 Reynolds may be forgiven for his erratic spelling of this name. Caldecote Hill, in Hertfordshire, has been variously known as Kerricott, Carricott, Curicut, and Catcot Hill.

2 Covent Garden Theatre had caught fire within a week of the opening of the new season. It had been gutted in four hours; twenty-two people had lost their lives, a huge musical library was destroyed, and Kemble's personal loss had been almost irreparable. An account of the fire appeared in *The Gentleman's Magazine*, September 1808, pp. 846–7. In *Some Account of the English Stage*, Vol. VIII, p. 126, John Genest recorded: 'The cause of the fire was never ascertained— but it was thought probable that the wadding of the gun fired in *Pizarro* might have occasioned it.'

3 Henry Erskine Johnstone (1777–1845), an English actor, had gone to Covent Garden in 1797, and he was at his best in melodrama.

4 Reynolds had not 'spelt it right.' No doubt he meant 'the romantic village of Uffington' mentioned in a Shrewsbury guide. Mr Lawrence recurs elsewhere in these letters, but he remains unidentified.

5 Hecate appears in *Macbeth* to congratulate the witches on their spell. One recalls the threat of the First Witch, who had been crossed by a sailor's wife:

> Her husband's to Aleppo gone, master o' th' Tiger;
> But in a sieve I'll thither sail,
> And, like a rat without a tail,
> I'll do, I'll do, and I'll do.

Reynolds was no doubt aware of the Shakespearean connotation; but one suspects that this Hecate is the family cat, or the nickname of an unwelcome visitor.

6 Possibly *Ovid's Metamorphoses, translated into English Prose . . . For the use of schools as well as private gentlemen.* 4th edition, corrected. (Law, Johnson, &c. 1797.)

7
> See, Winter comes, to rule the varied year,
> Sullen, and sad, with all his rising train,
> Vapours, and Clouds, and Storms . . .
> (James Thomson: *The Seasons*.)

¹ In *FitzGwarine, ... with other Poems*, Dovaston published an engaging poem 'To Mrs Reynolds, of Lambeth, with a GOOSE.' It is given here as a sign of his affection for her, and as a comment on her happy marriage.

> As I oft have been told
> By the poets of old
> Of the swans at their death singing once,
> I ask'd of my Muse
> A few rhymes for my goose,
> For she knew that 'my geese were all swans.'
>
> But on learning to whom
> My poor rhymes were to come
> She told me *your* happier Muse
> Would declare with shrewd wit
> That *my note* was scarce fit
> To *accompany* that of my goose.
>
> But i'faith (replied I)
> My poor efforts I'll try,
> And if they should fail to amuse,
> Give my paper the fire
> That my verses require,
> And they'll shine—when they're singeing the goose.
>
> Old historians describe
> How this cackling tribe
> One night sav'd a city from plunder;
> But more laurels shall shine
> Over this goose of mine
> That one day saves a lady from hunger.
>
> 'Mother Goose' and her eggs,
> And Grimaldi's long legs,
> Suit a cockney's theatrical rage;
> But such jokes who'd not quit
> To partake of your wit,
> And my goose—stuff'd with onions and sage?
>
> Was my goose but a speaker
> (As good int'rest might make her)
> To your social table when carried
> She'd exclaim—''tis now clear
> 'Why my master comes here,
> '—'Tis to learn to live happy when married.
>
> 'May each unmarried pair
> 'See how happy ye are,

'Admire the sweet lesson, and learn it;
  'For without it 'tis plain
  'Life's a straw without grain,
'The veriest gander would spurn it.

  'Then O long may ye live
  'The example to give,
'And its influence widely diffuse;
  'And may all who despise
  'Be referr'd for advice
'To the last dying speech of a goose.'

2 It is perhaps worth noting that *Kent's Original London Directory*, 1814, records 'Reynolds, Blakemore & Co., *tin-pl. manuf.*, Hambro-wf, U. Thames-st.'; *The Bristol Index* for 1818 records Reynolds, Blakemore, & Co., Redcliff Back, among the tin-plate manufacturers and merchants.

3 The *Shrewsbury Chronicle*, 5 April 1811, refers to 'J. Evans, M.D., of this town.' See also p. 46, note 1.

4 Mrs Reynolds was forty-seven.

5 Unidentified.

6 The Oxford English Dictionary does not record the meaning of Cochnit.

7 Apparently unpublished.

8 Apparently unpublished.

9 'Adieu, adieu, adieu! remember me.' The words of the ghost to Hamlet (*Hamlet*, I, v). The quotation will re-appear, in various forms, in these letters.

10 Dovaston noted: 'Answ$^{\underline{d}}$ in a letter to her son, Jan$^{\underline{y}}$ 3, 1809.'

31 December 1808

1 An early indication that Reynolds had literary gifts. The essay remains unknown.

2 *The Farmer's Boy*, by Robert Bloomfield (1766–1823) had been published in 1800; it is said that 26,000 copies were sold in less than three years. *The Gentleman's Magazine*, December 1808 (pp. 1100–1101), reviewed *The Fisher-Boy, a Poem; comprising his several Avocations during the Four Seasons of the Year. By H. C. Esq.* The critic observed that 'such a description of artless, unsophisticated Nature . . . must ever be perused with interest and satisfaction.'

3 Richard Edwards, the son of Thomas Edwards, linen-draper, late of Broad Street, Carnaby Market, was admitted to St Paul's School on 21 September 1770, at the age of ten. He later went to Trinity College, Cambridge (B.A., 1782), and he became chaplain at his old school in 1783. He took his M.A. in 1785, became surmaster at St

Paul's in 1806, and resigned his post at Christmas, 1823. He died in London in 1841. There was also an usher, Richard Edwards, appointed at St Paul's in 1783. R. B. Gardiner lists the namesakes as different people in *Admission Registers of St Paul's School, from 1748 to 1876* (Bell. 1884).

4   Keats was later to attend Hazlitt's lectures on English poetry at the Surrey Institution.

5   A useful statement of fact.

6   Literally: 'I prefer, I prefer, I prefer, rather than live, I prefer, I prefer.'

7   The Prince of Wales laid the foundation-stone of the new Covent Garden Theatre on 31 December 1808; the theatre was opened—with commendable speed—on 18 September 1809.

8   It was in fact Icarus, son of Daedalus, who attempted to fly; his wings were melted by the sun, he plunged into the sea, and he was drowned:

> When the youth began to aspire at a more daring flight, forsook his guide, and fond to trace the skies, soars aloft in air. The rapid sun now nearer softened the fragrant wax that held together his pinions: it melts away; he shakes his naked arms, and stripped of his oary wings, feels no resistance from the air. Then calling his father, plunges in the sea-green waves, which from him derived their name.

Ovid, op. cit., p. 286.

9   Dovaston noted: 'Answ$^{\underline{d}}$ Jany. 3 1809.'

10 Keats owned a copy of Burns's poems; on his Scottish tour of 1818, he wrote a sonnet in Burns's cottage, another on visiting his tomb, and lines after visiting his country.

10 February 1809 (1)

1   This is clearly 'Cooper the once Coachmaster's son' mentioned in the letter of March-April 1809.

2   *Pizarro; a tragedy in 5 acts ... taken from the German drama of Kotzebue and adapted to the English stage by R. B. Sheridan.* It was published by J. Ridgway in 1799, and a twentieth edition appeared the same year. Herschel Baker, in his life of John Philip Kemble, records that *Pizarro* was a wild success when it was first performed at Drury Lane Theatre; it was 'one of the most brilliantly and patently theatrical pieces in English drama.' *The Gentleman's Magazine* for 1808 records that *Pizarro* was performed in May and June at Covent Garden.

   Reynolds himself was to write more than once for the stage. *One, Two, Three, Four, Five: by Advertisement, a Musical Entertainment in One Act* was brought out at the English Opera on 17 July 1819. 'So Reynold's Piece succeeded,' wrote Keats to Dilke, from the Isle of Wight. 'That is all well.' (*Letters*, 365.) Reynolds was also a dramatic critic; and in the winter of 1817–18 Keats briefly took over his task (*Letters*, 72).

3   An honest comment on his old headmaster. The anonymous *Guide through the Town of Shrewsbury* (1836) records (pp. 25, 27): 'Nearly opposite the Castle are THE FREE SCHOOLS, founded by Edward VI, by letters patent, dated 10th February, 1552, by the title of the 'Free Grammar School of King Edward the Sixth' . . . The present headmaster is the Venerable Samuel Butler, D.D., F.R.S., Arch-deacon of Derby; by whose indefatigable exertions and learning the institution has attained an unrivalled celebrity and repute, and un-doubtedly, and most deservedly, ranks as the first public school in England.'

4   The Leasowes was a small property near Birmingham inherited by the poet William Shenstone (1714–63), friend of Robert Dodsley, poet, publisher and playwright (1703—64). Dodsley often visited the Leasowes, and his description of it was prefixed to many editions of Shenstone's poems.

10 February 1809 (2)

1   Dovaston's *Poems* include 'Inscription for the Cottage in Porking-ton grounds.'

2   No doubt the Hecate mentioned in Reynolds's letter of 23 September 1808.

3   The rumour proved to be unfounded. Dovaston was to remain a bachelor.

4   Unidentified.

5   *The Shrewsbury Guide* (1809) lists 'the Fox, for Travellers,' among the principal inns.

[March/April 1809]

1   Porkington is a hamlet a mile and a half north-west of Oswestry. Porkington House was described in 1870 as 'the beautiful seat of W. Ormsby-Gore, Esq.' (Murray's *Handbook for Shropshire, Cheshire, and Lancashire.*)

2   Unidentified.

3   The friends in Stanmore remain unidentified.

4   *The Gentleman's Magazine* for April 1809 reported (p. 373):

Friday, April 7.

This evening a benefit for that eminent Professor Dr. Callcott, under the patronage of his Royal Highness the Prince of Wales, took place at the Opera House, and was most nobly attended. There were nearly four thousand persons in that beautiful theatre enlisted in the cause of charity, and more than a hundred of the first musical professors England could produce, vying with each other which should most effectually serve a large and helpless family, labouring under severe affliction.

5 One wonders if this energetic kitten inspired the sonnet 'To Mrs Reynolds's Cat,' which Keats wrote on 16 January 1818. He was careful to remind the animal:

> . . . pr'ythee do not stick
> Thy latent talons in me . . .

(*Poetical Works*, 532).

6 Dovaston was not indolent: he answered this letter on 11 April, 1809.

11 August 1809

1 Mardol: a street in Shrewsbury. The residents remain unidentified.
2 The Reynolds family were to be renowned for their tendency to quarrel. Keats deplored 'the strife of women's tongues' in Little Britain (*Letters*, 106).
3 It is difficult to establish the truth of this statement. Reynolds refers to 'my friend Mr Sheil' on 3 November 1809, but Mrs Reynolds records in November 1810 that she has 'struggled to restore a broken friendship.' Sheil appears more than once in these letters; he seems to have been a Shrewsbury friend with a classical education and inadequate means.
4 In 1798 John Dovaston of West Felton, the father of the Reynolds's friend, had founded the Breidden Society. Its purpose was to celebrate an annual summer festival on Breidden Hill, near Shrewsbury, with eating, drinking, smoking, poetry reading, singing and dancing. If the record is to be believed, there was also much kissing, inspired by the traditional kissing of a stone. Until his death in 1808, John Dovaston conducted the festival informally every year. In 1809 Thomas Yates, who succeeded him as president, arranged for written rules, which were recorded by J. F. M. Dovaston. Every year thereafter the president named his successor for the following year. The president had, however, to pay for such prerogatives, since he was 'at the whole Expence, and Trouble of providing a plain cold dinner; Rum, Brandy, and Beer.' Since laurels did not grow on the hill, there was no poet laureate; but the abundance of ferns led to

the creation of a poet ferneate. Dovaston was president, poet ferneate, and recorder in 1810; vice-president and poet-ferneate in 1811; and poet ferneate in 1812. Reynolds was poet ferneate in 1813. The manuscript book of the constitution, laws, and minutes of the society are in the Houghton Library at Harvard.

5   Not listed in the British Library music catalogue.

6   The *Shrewsbury Chronicle* was 'regularly filed . . . at the following Coffee Houses: viz, London, Chapter, Worcester, Garraway's, and Peel's.'

7   John Wall Calcott (1766–1821) was one of the most prominent London musical practitioners of his time, and especially famous as a composer of glees and catches. In 1787 he entered a competition organized by the famous Noblemen and Gentlemen's Catch Club. He submitted nearly 100 glees, and it was decided that three should in future be the maximum to be received from any one competitor at any one competition. See also p. 35.

8   See p. 29.

[18 August 1809]

1   See pp. 4, 43–4.

2   It is clear from this correspondence, and from all we know of his life, that Reynolds would have liked to devote himself to literature and the theatre; but his parents—who were far from rich—were anxious that he should earn his living in some solid career. They were aware of his gifts and spirit; they were aware, even now, of his tendency to vacillate, his inability to work intensely. Reynolds was to try more than one occupation before he entered a solicitor's office.

3   *Canzonets. Set 1. No. 3.* Italian and English. (Printed by Wilkinson & Co., 1808.) See also *The Royal Musical Magazine*, 1809.

4   Dovaston noted: 'Ansd. Augt. 20.'

[Late August or early September, 1809]

1   This letter gives some insight into the relationship between mother and son. It is remarkable that a youth who had just left school to earn his living should have had his correspondence read and censored—and even signed—by his mother. One wonders how much Mrs Reynolds's forceful personality explains the sometimes inadequate nature of her son. It is worth observing that her husband remains almost unnoticed in the wings, while she herself figures

prominently in the letters of Keats and her son-in-law, Thomas Hood.

2 See. p. 25.

3 This anticipates Richard Abbey's comments to Keats, on reading his *Poems* (1817): 'Your Book is hard to understand & good for nothing when it is understood.' (KC, I, 308.)

10 October 1809

1 Dovaston was to abandon his practice as a barrister.

2 The British Library lists the following works by George Reynolds: *The Teacher's Arithmetic* (1812); *The Madras School Grammar; or the New System reduced to Questions and Answers* (1812); *The First Elements of Arithmetic* (1818); *The First Class Copy-Down Book of Arithmetic* (1822); *Exercises in Arithmetic* (1828).

3 Possibly a relation of William Morris, the Shrewsbury printer.

4 This is an engaging picture of brothers and sisters; it testifies to Reynolds's interest in art as well as his continuing concern with the theatre.

3 November 1809

1 'Miss Morris of Cheltenham, formerly of Shrewsbury' (see previous letter).

2 Presumably as tutor to Arthur Hill-Trevor, 3rd Viscount Dungannon of the 2nd creation (1798–1862).

3 The Golden Jubilee of George III was celebrated in 1809, his 50th year on the throne: not, as we should expect, on the completion of 50 years' reign. *The Gentleman's Magazine* (July–December 1809, pp. 975–6) recorded the festivities. 'The celebration was announced in this great metropolis by the pealing of bells, the hoisting of flags . . . Daylight was scarcely gone, when the full blaze burst forth upon the eye in all the skill of Art, and in all the radiant splendour and varied magnificence of the general illumination of the British capital. Hands could hardly be procured to light up the innumerable lamps. . . .'

4 The cost of building the new Covent Garden Theatre had led Kemble to raise the prices of admission. This led to the famous O.P. (Old Prices) riots which broke out on the opening night, 18 September 1809. The air was filled with cries of 'Old Prices!' Police and soldiers were called in, the Riot Act was read, but rioting went on for sixty-one nights. The whole town took sides; men wore the letters O.P. on their hats and waistcoats, and women wore medals with the same inscription. Kemble eventually gave way.

Henry Clifford, a barrister, had been seized as a rioter by James Brandon, the box-keeper at Covent Garden, and forcibly carried to Bow Street, where he was dismissed. The unofficial leader of the opposition, Clifford immediately sued Brandon for alleged assault and false imprisonment. The trial was held on 5 December 1809, and it was recognised that it would decide the long struggle. Clifford was awarded £5 damages, but the riots were over.

[18 November 1809]

1 The Chancellorship of Oxford University had become vacant by the death of the Duke of Portland, and the election of the new Chancellor was to take place on 14 December. Dovaston, as a Master of Arts, was entitled to vote, and he planned to visit the Reynolds family on his way to Oxford. There were three contenders for the Chancellorship: Lord Eldon, the Duke of Beaufort, and Lord Grenville, who was elected after a stormy campaign.

2 See p. 46. The *Shrewsbury Chronicle* for 5 April 1811 recorded that one of the two gold medals given annually by the Chancellor of Cambridge University 'to the two best classical scholars among the commencing Bachelors of Arts,' had recently been awarded to R. W. Evans, of Trinity College, son of Dr J. Evans of Shrewsbury, 'and formerly a pupil of the Rev Dr Butler, at the Free Schools.'

14 February 1810

1 On 10 January 1810, in the *Shrewsbury Chronicle*, D. Parkes of Castle Street had 'respectfully informed his friends and the public, that his SCHOOL will be opened again on Monday, the 22d. of this month.' No doubt this was the David Parkes listed in Castle Street in 1828. *FitzGwarine, a ballad of the Welsh Border . . . With other Rhymes . . .* By John F. M. Dovaston, was to be published in December 1812. The engraving on the title-page was signed 'D. Parkes delin.' The second edition of the book (1816) includes '*Inscribed in a Cell*, Discovered in the Town-walls of Shrewsbury, in the garden of Mr Parkes.' It also includes a poem addressed to 'Mr. D. Parkes.' Dovaston's *Poems* (1825) include 'To Miss [Harriet] Parkes, of Shrewsbury, on her going out as Governess.' Mr Nelson has not been identified.

2 A shortened version of her Christian name, Charlotte.

3 There was much rivalry between the educational systems of Andrew Bell and Joseph Lancaster, but Shrewsbury was in time to support them both. *The Salop Directory* (1828) was to list the charitable

institutions of the town, among them 'schools upon Dr Bell's, and the Lancasterian system, &c.'

4   *The New School*, by Thomas Barnard, is not in the British Library catalogue.
5   Mrs Sarah Trimmer (1741–1810), author of exemplary tales and educational works.
6   Dovaston's dog.
7   Dovaston's servant.

11–14 March 1810

1   'Nothing is truly elegant, but what unites truth with beauty.' *The Citizen of the World; or, Letters from a Chinese Philosopher, residing in London, to his friends in the East.* By Oliver Goldsmith, M. B. 2 vols. (Taylor & Hessey. 1809.) The quotation comes from Letter XIV, Vol. I, p. 50.
2   *Hamlet*, V, i.
3   *Dinarbas: a tale; being a continuation of Rasselas, Prince of Abyssinia.* By Ellis Cornelia Knight. (C. Dilly. London. 1790.) The fifth edition was to be published by T. Cadell and W. Davies in 1811.
4   John Philip Kemble, brother of Mrs Siddons, became successively manager of Drury Lane and of Covent Garden, and earned fame for his own performances in the great tragic parts. It was no doubt his performance as King Lear which Reynolds admired.
5

> . . . that she may feel
> How sharper than a serpent's tooth it is
> To have a thankless child!

(*King Lear*, I, iv.)

6   This news gives an early indication of Reynolds's interest in literature and the theatre.
7   Another reference to Dovaston's dog—and a compliment to Dovaston himself. Among his *Rhymes* (1805) is a rhyme 'To a Friend in the Anglo-Scottish Manner.' It ends:

> The king might wish himsel' wi' me,
> Thy friend and crony.

8   Unidentified.
9   The Post Office annual directory for 1815 gives G. Squibb, auctioneer, Boyle Street, Savile Row. Catalogues in the British Library announce sales by Mr Squibb & Son, at their Great Room, Savile Row, in 1819, 1821 and 1826. No doubt George Squibb was related to the 'Wm Squibs,' 'a younger brother of the Squibs,' whom Keats met with James Rice and Francis Fladgate at the Redhall dance (letter of 5 January 1818; *Letters*, 76). Frank Squibb, as will be seen, was a friend of J. H. Reynolds.

[10] Robert Dodsley (1703–64) was a bookseller, publisher and poet, and the author of several plays; but he is chiefly remembered as a founder of the *Annual Register*, as the publisher of works by Pope, Johnson, Young, Goldsmith and Gray, of the *Select Collection of Old Plays* (1744) and of *A Collection of Poems by several hands* (1748–58). In 1814–1816 Charles Wentworth Dilke was to bring out his six-volume edition of *Old English Plays*, a continuation of Dodsley's work. In April 1737, Dodsley published *Leonidas*, an epic of Miltonian proportions by Richard Glover (1702–85). It went through several editions and was praised by Fielding and Chatham.

[11] See. p. 63.

[12] A reference to the convergence of the vertical lines of Doric columns.

[13] Keats was also to tire of puns. 'The night we went to Novello's there was a complete set to of Mozart and punning—I was so completely tired of it that if I were to follow my own inclinations I should never meet any one of that set again.' (17 December 1818. *Letters*, 252.)

[14] 'When the gentlemen of the country come to see him, (Sir Roger) only shows me at a distance . . . (I) have heard the knight desiring them not to let me see them, for that I hated to be stared at.' Joseph Addison: *Sir Roger de Coverley at Home*.

[15] Similar, alike.

[16] Father and Mother send their love.

[*10 May 1810*]

[1] The *Shrewsbury Chronicle* of 4 May 1810 had published an account of Shakespeare's birthday celebrations at West Felton the previous week.

[2] The 'Irregular Ode to Shakespeare's Birthday' had appeared in the *Shrewsbury Chronicle* on 4 May, and it was later published in the *FitzGwarine* volume. Dovaston explained that it was 'written and recited on occasion of a few literary friends planting a Walnut-tree (having a wine-bottle buried under the root, with an appropriate inscription cut thereon, with a diamond), in the author's ground, on that day in 1810, and intending to celebrate it annually.' An account of the occasion also appeared in *The Gentleman's Magazine*, June 1810 (pp. 565–6).

[3] *The Day* was printed and published by John Fisher, at 5, Picket Street, Strand, near Temple Bar. The first issue of the paper, on 2 January 1809, bore the explanation:

> No expence shall be spared, no exertion . . . shall be wanting to give to this Paper that high degree of interest, which can alone be excited by early and authentic communication in the various

branches of FOREIGN AND DOMESTIC INTELLIGENCE . . .
The Proprietors have already avowed, that their principal object in
the establishment of a Newspaper was to facilitate the operations
of the Commercial, the Landed, and Monied Interests by communicating, at an early hour each day, those pariculars in which
they are, more or less, respectively concerned.

The British Library has an incomplete run of the newspaper. The
latest issue is dated January 1814.

4 The project of becoming a surveyor has long since faded. Reynolds
is already torn between his affection for literature and his need to
earn a living.

5 One wonders if this could be a reference to Peter de Wint, now
living in London with William Hilton. De Wint was a friend of
Keats and of Reynolds (and he attended Reynolds's wedding in
1822).

6 On 13 February 1809, *The Day* had reported a recent performance at
the Haymarket Theatre.

> On Saturday night, the Historical Play of *King Henry the Eighth*
> was represented with more than usual splendour. The lovers of
> the Drama, and the admirers of Shakspeare, are bound to ack-
> nowledge in Mr. Kemble the sound judgment and good taste
> with which the Plays of this Theatre are generally selected, as
> well as his own peculiar excellence, so often conspicuous in the
> performance of them. MRS SIDDONS in *Queen Catherine* was,
> perhaps, never more impressive, not even when, in those fine
> scenes, she drew forth the warm praise of DR JOHNSON.

7 The letter is unsigned; but Dovaston noted: 'John Reynolds. 10 May
1810. Ans: 8 June.'

12 June 1810

1 Reynolds is already unsettled in his career, but it will be remembered that he is only fifteen. No doubt his age explains his
parents' intervention; but his mother's dominant nature is all too
apparent.

2 *FitzGwarine, a ballad of the Welsh Border*, was to be published in
1812.

3 Jane Mackay rarely failed to send remembrances to this eligible
bachelor.

4 *The Gentleman's Magazine*, June 1810, pp. 582–3, records: 'Thursday, May 31. A most extraordinary and atrocious attempt was made
early this morning to assassinate the Duke of Cumberland . . .'

5 Dovaston noted on this letter: 'Wrote to Mrs R. 4 Aug⸱ 1810.' He was
clearly anxious to space out the correspondence.

¹ A reference to the Breidden Festival. On 13 July the *Shrewsbury Chronicle* had recorded:

> The convivial Society of Breiddenites held their twenty-first festivity on Breidden Hill, last Friday; John F. M. Dovaston, Esq., President. The company, both in members and strangers was very numerous, and the day particularly favourable.—They dined at the Well in the Valley, at one, and at three adjourned to the pillar, in commemoration of Rodney, where the new annual comic song, composed for the occasion by their poet *Ferneat* (the present president), was sung with much humour and spirit by Mr Thomas Yates, the Vice-president; the general glee and chorus was also sung, with a variety of songs, catches, and recitations.— A dance then took place, on a small flat westward of the pillar; after which the following gentlemen were elected to fill the respective offices for the next year; John Clavering Wood, Esq., to be President; John F. M. Dovaston, Esq., Poet *Ferneat*, and Mr Thomas Yates, Recorder. An adjournment was then made back to the Well, where again the song, dance, and glass went merrily round.—It was almost nine when the ladies and gentlemen left the mountain.

² Reynolds entered the service of the Amicable Assurance Office, as a junior clerk, in July 1810; he remained there at least until April 1816, and in November 1817 he was studying law.

³ *The Iron Chest* (1796) was a dramatisation by George Colman the younger of William Godwin's novel *Adventures of Caleb Williams*, which had appeared in 1794.

⁴ 'Another yet?—A seventh?—I'll see no more.' *Macbeth*, IV, i.

⁵ In the Shropshire volume of *The Beauties of England and Wales* (1813), p. 274, Nightingale published a poem on Whittington Castle, 'justly and poetically described by John F. M. Dovaston, Esq. in one of his legendary ballads yet in manuscript, with a sight of which we were favoured by a friend of his:

> In ancient days of high renown
> Not always did yon castle frown
> With ivy-crested brow . . .'

⁶ *The Lady of the Lake*, a poem in six cantos by Sir Walter Scott, was published this year. See also p. 61.

⁷ William Squibb, 'a younger brother of the Squibs,' was to make himself 'very conspicuous' at Redhall's dance, and earn two mentions in Keats's letter of 5 January 1818 (*Letters*, 77). The triennial London directory, 1817–9, includes Squibb and Seymour (attorneys), 12, Little Portland Street, Cavendish Square; it lists

'William Squib, Esq.,' among the gentry, and gives his address as 19, Margaret Street, Cavendish Square.

8 A reference to a part which Dovaston had played in some amateur theatricals. Mrs Bruin is a character in Samuel Foote's play, *The Mayor of Garratt* (1763).

9 In an open letter addressed to the Lord Chamberlain, on 2 May 1818, R. W. Elliston referred to 'Mr Astley's *Blood-red Knight*, . . . a very attractive description of stage performance.' (*Copy of a Memorial presented to the Lord Chamberlain, by the Committee of Management of the Theatre-Royal, Drury-Lane, and the Proprietors of the Theatre-Royal, Covent Garden, against the Olympic and Sans Pareil Theatres*. With copies of two letters, in reply to the contents of such memorial, addressed to the Lord Chamberlain, by Robert William Elliston, comedian. (Miller. 1818.))

10 Lord Grenville had been installed as Chancellor of Oxford University after a controversial election (see pp. 46, 55, 166). On 6 July the *Shrewsbury Chronicle* had reported:

> Oxford, July 2. Ancient Rome in the zenith of a Saturnalia never exhibited more unequivocal symptoms of confusion and hilarity than this city upon the occasion of the Installation. Lord Grenville arrived privately, but his entrance was soon announced by the bells . . . The prices demanded for the hire of houses, lodgings, and beds only, exceed belief . . .

The recent Encaenia at Oxford had been described in *The Gentleman's Magazine*, July 1810, pp. 69 sqq.

11 Reynolds is jocular here; but see letter of 24 August 1808, note 1, p. 156.

[27 September 1810]

1 Possibly an early reference to *FitzGwarine*, which was in the style of *Marmion*.

2 One recalls Keats's letter to his publisher, John Taylor, on 21 June 1818: 'I promised Mrs Reynolds one of my books bound. As I cannot write in it let the opposite be pasted in . . . Mrs Reynolds with J. K.'s respects.' (*Letters*, 153, 154).

3 See p. 45.

4 *All in the Wrong*, a comedy, performed at the Theatre Royal in Drury Lane, was written by Arthur Murphy, and published by Cadell in 1787. It was performed at the new Theatre Royal, Covent Garden, on Friday 28 September 1810.

5 See p. 55.

6 The Grand Pageant had first been performed on 6 August. Elliston clearly had a high opinion of it, and of his own function in popu-

larising Shakespeare. His feelings were echoed in *The Times* on 15 August:

> Those worthy inhabitants of distant villages, who from daily occupation and difference of habits, have hitherto had no time or inclination to peruse the works of our immortal bard, SHAKE-SPEARE, have, on their coming to town and paying a visit to the Surrey Theatre, imbibed, from the sample exhibited in the Grand Pageant, such a taste for Shakespearian productions, and so much curiosity to peruse plays of which they have just seen enough to make them wish for more, that the demand for pocket editions and other sets of the Poet's works is so great, that the booksellers have of late been obliged to reprint them in all forms and sizes.

[7] See p. 55.

[8] Dovaston noted: 'Ans. 12 Nov.'

7–8 October, 1810

[1] Eliza Beckford, the third daughter of George and Charlotte Reynolds, was born in Shrewsbury in 1799, and baptised at St Mary's Church on 20 November. On 27 December 1821 she married Dr George Longmore, of Upwell, Norfolk. Her great-granddaughter, Mrs G. D. Hessell, writes that the Longmores came back to London in about 1823, 'and lived in Thavies Inn, Holborn (abode of the Jellybys—there are several suggestions of Longmore incidents in *Bleak House*) and later in Lansdowne Place, Brunswick Square.' The marriage ended sadly. George Longmore,

> as heir to the considerable estate of his mother (*née* Mary Anne Skinner) seemed to do little to support his family of eleven children (some of whom died in infancy) and borrowed heavily from his brothers. He was finally forced by them to sell the entailed property, Carpenders Park in Hertfordshire, to redeem his debts. The Longmores had to leave their home and the family was scattered. Lizzy, the eldest daughter, who had married, emigrated with her husband and two sons to Australia in 1850. George Moody Longmore travelled about the country to find work, then emigrated in 1854, only to die in Lizzy's home at the age of 31. William, the architect, was in poor lodgings, working with Vulliamy. The remaining son, Edward Reynolds Longmore, went to sea and was rumoured to have deserted his ship and 'sloped to the diggings' in Australia, but nothing further seems to be known of him. Of the three youngest children, all daughters, one died at the age of ten about this time. Eliza was able to place Mary Anne (11) and Dora (6) in a little school in Cheyne Walk. Ill and sad, she lived in lodgings and died in 1854.

The father did his best to shelve responsibility for these two children; he was doing something in Liverpool (all very vague) and managed to get a woman to look after them. Then he had the idea of taking them to Lizzy in Sydney, but instead of this he sent them off by sailing ship on their own (they were then 16 and 12). They spent the rest of their lives in Australia.

Charlotte, the fourth and youngest daughter of George and Charlotte Reynolds, was to remain unmarried. Before she died in 1884, she talked about Keats and her family to Harry Buxton Forman. 'She had,' he wrote, 'up to the month of her death, a vivid recollection of him as he was when he frequented her father's house . . . The song 'Hush, hush! tread softly!' was composed to a Spanish air played by Charlotte Reynolds on one of the many occasions when Keats listened, as he would for hours, to her playing on the pianoforte.' Writing in *The Athenaeum* on 13 December 1884, Mr Forman added:

> Only a few weeks ago her appearance and manner were such as to justify the hope that she might live for years yet, and her faculties were wholly unimpaired; but she caught a cold in the chest on one of the coldest days of October, and this speedily took so serious a turn that after a very short illness she passed peacefully away. Miss Reynolds was born on 12 May 1802 . . . , so that at the time of her death she had reached the advanced age of eighty-two. She died at Hampstead, at the residence of her nephew, Mr. C. Green, the well-known watercolourist.

This, one might add, was Charlecote, Hampstead Hill Gardens.

2 On 23 March 1810, the *Shrewsbury Chronicle* had noted: 'In compliance with a request from the Baptist congregation in this town, Mr Lancaster has sent a person to organize their Sunday school on his system.' On 1 November 1811, the same paper recorded: 'Last night Mr Lancaster delivered a Lecture, at the County Hall in this Town, on the errors of the present mode of Education.' A long and heated correspondence followed in the *Chronicle* about the rival merits of the Bell and Lancaster systems. However, *A Guide through the Town of Shrewsbury* (1836) recorded that 'immediately opposite the Gaol are the Royal Lancasterian Schools, established in 1812, for the purpose of affording an useful education to poor children of all religious denominations, on the plan recommended by the ingenious Mr Lancaster. They are supported by voluntary annual subscriptions.'

3 William Waldegrave, first Baron Radstock (1753–1825), was the patron of the poet John Clare. He was the author of *The Cottager's Friend; or, a Word in Season to him who is so fortunate as to possess a Bible or New Testament, and a Book of Common Prayer* . . . The twentieth edition of this book was published by Rivington in 1816.

The Magdalen hospital was a charitable institution for fallen women. It was originally opened, as Magdalen House, in Prescott Street, Goodman's Fields, in 1758. It stood for just a century near the southern end of Blackfriars Road. Thousands of young women who had 'strayed from the path of virtue' were, we are told, admitted, restored to their friends, or placed in service. The only recommendation was that of repentant guilt.

⁵ Dovaston noted: 'Wrote to Mrs R., 18 November 1810. Sent a hare, brace of birds & 2 fowls, and a fine hare afterwards.'

⁶ Mrs Reynolds was forty-eight.

[November 1810]

¹ Mrs Reynolds had no doubt read the *Genuine and Authentic account of the Life, Trial, and Execution, of Elizabeth Brownrigg, who was executed on Monday the 14th of September 1767, for the barbarous Murder of Mary Clifford, her Apprentice Girl. With Her Behaviour while under Sentence of Death, and at the Place of Execution. Together with the Sufferings of Mary Mitchel, and Mary Jones. To which is prefixed, a Frontispiece of Mrs Brownrigg in the Cell in Newgate; and the Manner of her Torturing the Girls; with the Dark Hole where the Girls were confined on Sundays, truly represented.* This anonymous pamphlet was published in 1767.

² The letters of Keats, and those of Thomas Hood, make it plain that the Reynolds family were drawn to gossip, sometimes malicious gossip, and that they were more than once involved in serious quarrels. In 1821 Fanny Brawne reported to Fanny Keats that even the endearing Mrs Dilke had 'quarrelled, I hope for ever with the Reynolds. My dear Fanny if you live [to] the age of the Methuselem and I die tomorrow never be intimate with the Reynolds, for I dare say they will come your way—Mrs Dilke cannot keep up a feud and perhaps one day will be friends again. Every day I live I find out more of their malice against me.' (*Letters of Fanny Brawne to Fanny Keats*, 37). In 1835 Hood quarrelled bitterly with the Reynolds family at the bedside of his desperately ill wife—the former Jane Reynolds.

³ The song by Robert Burns. The quotations which follow are presumably titles of other songs, or familiar phrases from them.

⁴ Unidentified.

⁵ Unidentified.

⁶ The Lawrences of Uffington (see p. 26).

⁷ See p. 27.

⁸ Dovaston noted: 'Wrote to her 6 Jany 1811.'

¹ For Dovaston's 'Prometheus,' see p. 66.

² On 9 December 1815, Reynolds reviewed *The Honeymoon* in *The Champion*, and recorded that 'Mr Kean has appeared as the *Duke Aranza* in the comedy.' The play, by John Tobin (1770–1804), was first performed in 1805.

³ *The Lady of the Lake* had been published this year. On 9 November the *Shrewsbury Chronicle* reported: 'Mr Walter Scott, it is said, has sold the copyright of his poem, *The Lady of the Lake*, for 2000 guineas, which is calculated at the rate of 8s. per line!—Milton sold his *Paradise Lost* for £15 !!!'

⁴ Dovaston noted: 'Wrote 9 Dec^r'

24 December 1810

¹ *Sylvester Daggerwood, or New Hay at the Old Market*, was an occasional drama written by George Colman the younger for the opening of the Haymarket Theatre on 9 June 1795. *The Gentleman's Magazine* for 1808 recorded that *The Honeymoon* was performed in May at Drury Lane, and *Sylvester Daggerwood* in May and June. In *The Life and Enterprises of Robert William Elliston, Comedian* (Routledge. 1857), George Raymond noted (p. 154) that 'on Thursday, 16th March, 1809, the Drury Lane company opened the Opera House, for three nights, as stated, for their common benefit. The first performance was "Man and Wife," "Sylvester Daggerwood," and the ballet of "Quichotte," by the whole force of the Opera corps, producing 549£. The second night was "The Honeymoon," with an occasional address.' Doiley was a character in *Who's the Dupe?*, a play more than once performed at Drury Lane.

² Dovaston complied with the request. He noted on this letter: 'Ansrd 26 Decr with the enclosed prologue.' The verses, which are given here, appeared in his *FitzGwarine* volume as 'Prologue for a FARCE. Written and sent to London at the request of some juvenile actors there.'

Ladies and Gentlemen,

Let me read you a letter that patly now pops here
In the place of a prologue.—'Tis dated from Shropshire.
    Dear Jack,—I have spurr'd my dull Muse to make one try
To tell how we actors get praise in the country,
Where our audience ne'er yawn at the squallings of Naldi,
Never weep at your Kemble nor grin at Grimaldi;
But they fix on *a farce* (for too just are our fears
Since they sleep at our *Hamlets* they'd sneeze at our Lears).

Our bed-quilt is hung, on whose patch-work so gay
Trees, trophies, & temples at once we display;
Our parts are rehears'd, & our playbills indited,
And all good-natur'd friends (but none else) are invited;
To whom, while our players are putting their dress on,
Little Miss thumbs and elbows her only Hook's lesson;
While each Actor by turns thro' a slit in the quilt
His well-raddl'd nose pushes up to the hilt,
Or peeps with importance behind the proscenium,
(—That's a name that we give to two pots of geranium.)
        But hark!—'twas the sheep-bell!—a sure signal that is
That summons to fame our *personae Dramatis.*
See!—the coverlid moves!—like the forest of Birnam!
(Curse the cords & the pullies—how they creak as we turn 'em)
The wit it then wags, and the fun it goes featly,
And 'twixt prompter *and* actor 'tis done most completely.
        Then how from our Audience can plaudits be scarce,
When our Acting is all—(what they fix'd on)—a farce!

3   On 2 November 1810 the King's youngest daughter, Princess
    Amelia, died at the age of twenty-seven. George III was over-
    whelmed, and lapsed into permanent insanity. On 31 December,
    Spencer Perceval moved in the House of Commons that the Regency
    should be offered to the Prince of Wales. On 6 February 1811, before
    the Privy Council, the Prince was sworn in as Prince Regent of the
    United Kingdom.
4   Unidentified.
5   Reynolds's earlier plan to be a surveyor may have owed something
    to the enthusiasm of Frank Squibb.
6   The Shorter OED records: 'FRANK: To sign (a letter, etc.) so as to
    ensure its being sent free of charge; to send or cause to be sent free
    of charge.'

13 May 1811

1   In his *Souvenir of the Bi-Centenary of the Old Amicable Society,* J.
    J. W. Deuchars recorded (pp. 46, 47) that:

        the Anniversary Dinner continued for many years to be an im-
        portant and successful function. It usually took place at Hamp-
        stead, but occasionally it was held at the Freemasons' Tavern. In
        the beginning £5 was considered sufficient to pay for this dinner,
        but later, 'any sum not exceeding £15' was agreed to . . . Minute,
        1756: 'That the £25 allowed to be expended for a Dinner had for
        some time past been exceeded.' Resolved and Ordered:—'That
        the Directors for the Time being be desired to provide such a

dinner for the Members of this Society on the Annual Day of Election of Directors as they shall judge proper.' Ten toasts were drunk at the annual dinner in 1790.

In 1811, John Hamilton Reynolds was only sixteen, and perhaps he was the worse for the experience. In later life he drank excessively. Charles Kemble, when asked about him, always shook his head, and said: 'Brandy & Water! Brandy & Water!'; and in the Isle of Wight, at the end of his life, his drunken habits put him beyond the social pale.

2 Probably a reference to Tassie's imitation gems, which were very popular among Keats's friends. Keats gave some to his sister (*Letters*, 286, 291), and George Keats sealed a letter with a Tassie Shakespeare. Reynolds was to admire the seal that was used by Wordsworth (p. 132).

3 The first suggestion that the friendship was not always smooth.

4 An allusion to the Breidden Festival. The reference to Old Nick and 'his Devilship' recalls Dovaston's festive contribution this year:

> OLD NICK;
> or, the Birth of Breidden;
> Being a Pindaric Grin for the Convivials of Breidden-hill, 1811.
> By their Poet-Ferneat.

For the kissing-stone, see p. 65.

5 Dovaston noted: 'Ans. June 23, 1811.'

14 June 1811

1 The only indication that Reynolds played cricket. The friends of Keats appear to have been unlucky in the game. On 31 July 1815 James Augustus Hessey reported that he had recently found Richard Woodhouse '*perdu* in his Chambers with a formidable Black Eye. He had received a Blow from a Cricket Ball.' (Blunden: *Keats's Publisher*, 38.) Keats himself was no more proficient. On 19 March 1819 he reported to his brother and sister-in-law: 'Yesterday I got a black eye—the first time I took a Cr[icket] bat.' (*Letters*, 314.)

2 The 'small poem in the press' was *The Vision of Don Roderick*. Scott was 'paid a hundred guineas for this trifle,' which appeared in July 1811. The work 'of large dimensions' was no doubt *Rokeby*, which appeared in 1813.

3 Scott paid no recorded visit to the Isle of Wight this year.

4 There are numerous references to Dovaston in *The Gentleman's Magazine*. In August 1808 he writes on the origin of 'The Swan and two necks' (the name of a well-known London public house). In June 1810 there is a reference to his celebration of Shakespeare's birthday. In May 1811 he publishes his lines on the same anniver-

sary, and in January 1812 'My Boxen Bower.' In February 1813 there is a review of his *FitzGwarine*, and in August his poem 'To the Ivy.' November brings his letter about 'the constant tendency of the *Plane tree* to an apparently premature death.' Elsewhere he discusses the music of the *Ranz des vaches*. In February 1814 he publishes a sonnet, and in March a letter on acacias.

[5] No doubt a reference to Dovaston's comic poem, 'The Story of Prometheus done into doggrel.' This appeared in the *FitzGwarine* volume.

[6] See note 1 to previous letter. The printed version of the address is not listed in the British Library catalogue.

[7] Not identified.

[8] Not identified.

2 September 1811 (1)

[1] This comedy by R. B. Sheridan was first produced in 1775.

[2] *Gertrude of Wyoming*, a poem in the Spenserian stanza by Thomas Campbell, was published in 1809.

[3] This is no doubt a reference to the first production, on 26 July 1811, of 'a grand dressed Rehearsal, of a Tragico-Comico-Anglo-Germanico-Hippo-Ono-Dramatico Romance, a new piece (in two acts) called the Quadrupeds of Quedlinburgh, or The Rovers of Weimar,' based by Colman, as the sub-title suggests, on *The Rovers; or, The Double Arrangement*, the burlesque written by George Canning and John Hookham Frere for the *Anti-Jacobin* in 1798.

[4] Presumably *FitzGwarine*, which was to be published in 1812.

[5] For William Squibb, see letter of 1 August 1810, note 7, pp. 170–1.

2 September 1811 (2)

[1] Jane Reynolds was now nearly twenty. It seems that she was giving French lessons to increase the family income (see p. 116).

[2] The postman seems to have come before time.

4 November 1811

[1] The quotation remains unidentified.

[2] *Henry VIII*, III, ii.

[3] Among Mrs Siddons's early parts were Isabella in *The Fatal Marriage* and Belvidera in *Venice Preserved*. She was later out-

standing as Constance in *King John*, Zara in *The Mourning Bride*, and above all as Lady Macbeth, the part in which she made her farewell appearance on 29 June 1812.

4   One of the most lasting triumphs of Kemble's career was his performance as Penruddock, the misanthrope, in Richard Cumberland's *Wheel of Fortune*.

5   Reynolds was commendably continuing his education. His progress with Greek may be judged from some of the following letters. The grammar in question was probably *The Elements of Greek Grammar: with notes for those who have made some progress in the language*. It was the work of Dr Richard Valpy, headmaster of Reading School from 1781–1832. It enjoyed considerable popularity. The second edition had appeared in 1807, and the eighth appeared in 1822.

2 *February 1812*

1   On 14 June 1813, Dovaston wrote to *The Gentleman's Magazine*: 'Some nights ago, . . . crossing the busy little stream of the Morda, near its uniting with the Vyrnwy, I observed a very perfect *ignis fatuus* (Will o'the wisp) coming along the meadows toward the river . . .'

2   Among the poems published in the *FitzGwarine* volume was one about the arbour at West Felton, 'My Boxen Bower.'

3   Keats did not share this opinion of Charles Mayne Young (1777–1856). He found him 'a ranting coxcombical tasteless Actor—A Disgust A Nausea' (*Letters*, 376).

4   During the season of 1811–12, a live elephant made its appearance on the stage of Covent Garden. Henry Harris, the manager, paid £900 for the animal, and introduced it triumphantly in *Harlequin and Padmandba*, the Christmas pantomine. The *Examiner* warned the public that 'elephants are subject to sudden fits of rage, and have no natural forbearance in favour of theatrical amateurs.'

5   Dovaston noted: 'Wrote to her 24 March 1812.'

23 *June 1812*

1   Presumably an error for Brentwood.

2   For an account of Mrs Siddons's last performance, see pp. 180–1.

3   Mrs Siddons played fifty-seven times, recreating almost all her famous roles, in her last season.

4   'In 1812 Kemble revived and adapted, with a splendour, in those days unparalleled, the play of Julius Caesar. No piece was ever more

effectively cast: Brutus had for its representative John Kemble; Cassius, Young; Antony, Charles Kemble; Casca, Terry; First Citizen, Simmons; and Portia, Mrs Siddons. I have never spoken with any one fortunate enough to have seen that play rendered, as it then was, who has not admitted it to have been the greatest intellectual recreation he ever enjoyed.' (J. T. Young: *A Memoir of Charles Mayne Young, Tragedian.* (Macmillan. 1871). Vol. I, pp. 59–60).

5 It is impossible to say which sister Reynolds meant. Marianne lived to be 77, and Charlotte to be 82. Whichever sister he intended, she was no doubt staying with 'Miss Morris (from Cheltenham, formerly of Shrewsbury)': see letter of 10 October 1809, p. 41.

6 See p. 70, note 5.

7 Presumably *FitzGwarine*, which was to be published in December.

8 Dovaston notes: 'Wrote to him 26 June 1812 to invite him here.'

2 July 1812

1 His employer at the Amicable Assurance Society.

2 See p. 50.

11 July 1812

1 George Steevens (1736–1800) was a well-known Shakespeare commentator. In 1773 he published a complete annotated edition (including notes by Dr Johnson) in ten volumes, to which a supplementary volume of the Poems, together with seven plays ascribed to Shakespeare, was added in 1780. Steevens also forged a letter of George Peele describing a meeting with Shakespeare. William Warburton (1698–1779), sometime Bishop of Gloucester, brought out a much criticised edition of Shakespeare in 1747. Edmund Malone (1741–1812) published an edition in 1790; the revised edition, 1821, is said to have been the best to that date. Reynolds's comparison of the various editions says much for the taste of a youth of eighteen.

2 Mrs Siddons, as we have seen, made her farewell appearance, as Lady Macbeth, on 29 June 1812. *The European Magazine* for July 1812 (pp. 45, 46) described how she took leave of the stage:

> In the last scene of the play in which Lady Macbeth appears, that is to say, in the last scene in which she walks in her sleep, the audience became boisterous in their applause: they would hear and see no more—they stopped the progress of the Play, thus paying a compliment of the proudest kind to their distinguished favourite.—Shakespeare, at this moment, had no charms for a British audience.

Mrs Siddons delivered an address. She then

made her reverences with great emotion, and Mr Kemble stepped on to the stage to assist in leading her off. The house took leave of their favourite with reiterated acclamations.

Mr Kemble then came on, and, in a short address, requested to know the pleasure of the house, whether they would hear the remainder of the play . . .; but the universal cry of the house was, that they *could* hear no more; and with this unexampled compliment to the great tragic actress of the age, the scene closed.—It had an unutterable effect on the feelings of the company, who immediately began to retire.

[July–August 1812.]

¹ Presumably Dovaston's horse.
² *The Curse of Kehama* had been published late in 1810.
³ The quotation remains unidentified.

16 August 1812

¹ Unidentified.
² *FitzGwarine, a ballad of the Welsh Border*, was to be published this December. It was an evident imitation of *Marmion*.
³ Murray's *Handbook for Shropshire, Cheshire, and Lancashire* (1870) records, p. 70, that 'the Breidden Hills, the steep wooded sides of which tower over the road, are a singular group, rising to the height of 1199 feet, though they appear more, in consequence of their isolation.'
⁴ There is no Mackay in the Bath directory for 1812, or in the directory corrected to January 1819. The Bath directory, corrected to January 1826, gives the Hon Mrs Mackay, 17, Alfred Street, and W. H. Mackey, esq., solicitor, 4, Paragon Buildings. If Mrs Reynolds's friend belonged to a titled family, it might help to explain her 'superior' nature, and Mrs Reynolds's eager friendship with her.
⁵ These were the days of the Peninsular War. By late July 1812 the French Army of Portugal was completely defeated. On 12 August the Allied army entered Madrid. The capital was free of the French for the first time since December 1808, and it gave Wellington a spontaneous welcome. King Joseph, with his main army, and an enormous train, was already across the Tagus at Aranjuez and heading for Valencia.

1   *Henry VIII*, III, ii.

2   *Macbeth*, I, i.

3   Reynolds's account of his journey is pedestrian. He was to make amends with his essay 'The Inside of a Stage Coach' in *The London Magazine*, August 1822.

4   'Kynaston's Cave' and 'Myself and Echo: a Dialogue,' both appeared in the *FitzGwarine* volume.

5   These are not listed in the British Library music catalogue.

6

> O Grave! where is thy victory?
> O Death! where is thy sting?
> (Pope: 'The Dying Christian to his Soul.')

7   No doubt the Rev Joseph Nightingale, who lived in the Barbican. Nightingale edited *The Beauties of England and Wales*; the Shropshire volume, written by Rylance, was published in 1813. Nightingale acknowledged his debt 'to MR D. PARKES, of Shrewsbury, for several useful hints, and for the very liberal loan of several excellent original drawings. To J. F. M. DOVASTON, of West Felton, ESQ. I would express myself in terms better able to convey my high sense of his politeness, and of the kindness and assistance rendered to my friend, during his late visit to that part of Salop, had I the same facility of communicating my thoughts with which natured has so liberally endued that ingenious and most excellent gentleman.'

8   Reynolds published his first known poem in *The Gentleman's Magazine* this October. It was an 'Ode to Friendship, inscribed to J. F. M. Dovaston, Esq., of West Felton.'

9   *Leonora*. A Ballad translated from the German of Gottfried Augustus Bürgher. By W. R. Spencer, Esq., H. J. Pye. J. T. Stanley, Esq., F.R.S. To which is added the original text. (Vienna. Printed for R. Sammer, Bookseller. 1798.) A second edition of Spencer's translation, 'with Designs by the Right Honorable Lady Diana Beauclerc,' was published by Scott & White in 1809. The British Library catalogue gives the translator as the Hon William Robert Spencer.

10   Dovaston notes: 'Ansd. by Messrs Rylance & self, 4 Septr. 1812.'

11   *Hamlet*, I, iv

12   On 15 August 1822, Dovaston was to explain in the *Oswestry Herald* how, 'some few years agone,' he had taken Reynolds 'to view Llynellys, the Ogo, and Rocks of Blodwell, perhaps not surpassed in all Wales for beauty and variety of prospect. While I was adjusting our gig at the alehouse, his eye caught the flounced frock and white stocking of *Peg o' the Pant* . . .'

13   Unidentified.

¹⁴ Will Wimble, in Addison's *The Spectator*, is a friend of Sir Roger de Coverley, a good-natured man who is generally esteemed for the obliging services that he renders to everyone.

August–September 1812 (2)

¹ *Romeo and Juliet*, II, i.
² *The Anatomy of Melancholy*, by the Rev Robert Burton (1577–1640), was published in 1621.
³ *The Miseries of Human Life; or the Groans of Samuel Sensitive, and Timothy Testy* . . . 3rd edition (Miller. 1806.). The book was published anonymously.
⁴ On St Magdalene's Eve, 22 July 1403, a famous battle near Shrewsbury ended the revolt of the Percies of Northumberland against Henry IV.
⁵ Clarice: the daughter of FitzGwarine, hero of Dovaston's ballad.
⁶ Robert Hartley Cromek. *Reliques of Robert Burns*, collected and published by R. H. Cromek, were brought out by Cadell & Davies in 1808.
⁷ *Macbeth*, I, iv.
⁸ A character in the play *Poor Gentleman*. On 15 May 1809 the play had been given at Drury Lane for Bannister's benefit performance, and Bannister had taken the part of Ollapod.
⁹ The words of this song date from about 1750. They were addressed by Lady Caroline Keppel to Robin Adair, the young Irish surgeon with whom she was in love.
¹⁰ *Rokeby*, a poem in six cantos by Walter Scott, was published in 1813.
¹¹ *Macbeth*, II, iii.
¹²

> Be bloody, bold, and resolute; laugh to scorn
> The power of man, for none of woman born
> Shall harm Macbeth.
> (*Macbeth*, IV, i.)

¹³ Unidentified quotation.
¹⁴ Thomas Moore (1779–1852) was the author of *Irish Melodies*, which established him as the national lyrist of Ireland. In 1813 he issued *The Twopenny Postbag*, a collection of satires directed against the Prince Regent.
¹⁵ The letters which follow are modelled on those in *The Spectator*. It had become a private joke between the friends in West Felton and Lambeth to identify themselves with Addison's characters. On 16 June 1816, Reynolds published an essay 'On the Spectator' in *The Champion*. 'In our boyish days we read *The Spectator* through with the greatest delight, and we remember that no volume of a peri-

odical work ever took such an absolute possession of our hearts, or won so much of our time of leisure, as the second volume of this pleasant book.'

16 The Mohocks were aristocratic ruffians who infested the streets of London at night in the early years of the eighteenth century. The word is taken from *Mohawk*, the name of a North American Indian tribe, formerly supposed to be cannibals.

17 Dovaston noted: 'Mrs Reynolds & Jack. Wrote to her by Rylance 8 Sep.ᵗ 1812.'

2–3 September 1812

1 Robert William Elliston (1774–1831) was one of the most popular actors of his day. Leigh Hunt placed him second only to Garrick in the theatre, and Lamb said: 'Wherever Elliston walked, sat, or stood still, there was the theatre.' In 1809 he became lessee of the Surrey, London; ten years later he became lessee and manager of Drury Lane. In 1819 Keats and Brown submitted their drama, *Otho the Great*, to Elliston, but it was not performed.

2 Once again Mrs Reynolds quotes from *Hamlet*, I, v. This time she does so correctly.

3 *The Merchant of Venice*, III, ii.

[15 September 1812]

1 George Reynolds was the only son of his father's second marriage, and there were no known children of the first. This uncle may therefore be Mrs Reynolds's brother, Captain William Beckford Cox, the father of Keats's Charmian.

2 This poem is apparently unpublished.

3 William Morris of Shrewsbury was printing Dovaston's book of poetry.

4 *FitzGwarine, a ballad of the Welsh Border, in three cantos. With other Poems, Legendary, incidental, and humorous.* By John F. M. Dovaston, A.M. The poem—an evident imitation of *Marmion*—was published in Shrewsbury in December 1812. A second edition appeared in 1816 with numerous additional poems, and a third in 1825. The work was dedicated to the Rev Charles Albany Lloyd, Rector of Whittington, Salop.

The dedication was appropriate. The *Beauties of England and Wales*, Vol. XIII, p. 272, records that 'in the year 1796, in digging a grave in the place where the porch of Whittington Church once stood, there was discovered the remains of a very strong oak coffin, three inches thick, containing probably bones of one of the Fitz-Guarines.' The family figured largely in Dovaston's local history.

5 Probably a reference to the poem which introduced the book: Rylance's poem 'To my friend DOVASTON, On his Metrical Romance of FitzGwarine.' This began in grand romantic style:

> CAMBRIA, they harp too long untouch'd hath been,
>   Save by the mountain-wind's far-roving wing
> That waves the fern on BREIDDEN, light and green,
>   Its sweet notes swelling on each trembling string . . .

One may record here that in August 1808 (p. 727) *The Gentleman's Magazine* had included 'A War-Song, for the Spaniards,' by R. Rylance, among its select poetry. In *The Dove* (p. 57), referring to Ludlow Castle, Dovaston noted that 'Mr. Rylance, the warm-hearted, learned, and ingenious Collector for the "beauties of England and Wales," visited this Castle in 1810, and . . . breathed forth the following SONNET on the spot . . .' Dovaston continued to record his affectionate admiration for his friend. In *The Museum of Natural History*, in January 1833, he announced that he had inscribed an oak-tree at West Felton 'to our learned, gifted, and beloved friend Rylance.'

The British Library tentatively catalogues one book by Ralph Rylance: *Reasons for Christianity; and the hope therein founded* (Bell & Churton. 1833.) It lists one pamphlet under his name: *A Sketch of the Causes and Consequences of the late Emigration to the Brazils*. This was published in 1808 by Longman, Hurst, Rees & Orme. It was dedicated to William Roscoe (see pp. 95, 131).

Among the Dovaston Papers at Shrewsbury is an uncorrected proof of an obituary of Rylance. The author is not known.

"On the 6th June, aged 52, in London, Mr. RALPH RYLANCE, a gentleman who spent almost the whole of his laborious life in the service of Messrs. Longmans, the great publishers. He was the Author and Translator of even multitudinous books, bearing the names of Veterans in literature, and not of one to which his own is affixed. He was a native of Bolton, in Lancashire, where his very brilliant talents were early discovered by the munificent ROSCOE, who put him to school under the celebrated Lempriere, where he acquired the classical languages with astonishing facility; and soon after became so able and extensive a linguist, as to read, write, and speak with fluency about eighteen tongues; and near his death was hard working at the Welsh and Celtic, for the purpose of composing an Ethnic Essay on the affinities of all languages. He had studied English intensely, and formed his style from that of the age of Elizabeth; was extensively acquainted with ancient history and literature, that of Europe, and of his own country: was an ardent admirer and thorough familiar of Our Matchless Poet, and good old 'Chaucer's Well of English undefiled.' He first came into this county

(Shropshire) about 25 years ago, to collect materials for 'The Beauties of England and Wales,' where he gained great admiration for his beautifully elegant sonnet composed in Ludlow Castle, 'HERE Milton sung.' He soon acquired many Salopian friends all round the Wrekin, by his amiable disposition, his fertile glow of conversation, and his racy powers of music and song. In politics he was a liberal whig; and in religion, though differing from his nearest and dearest friends, he was always steadily and faithfully attached to the Church of England; in whose defence he laterally diverted the pure and vigorous stream of his powerful pen, in several neat volumes, which we could readily name, with many others, 'but that we are forbade to tell the secrets of the PRINTING-HOUSE.' In the words of his most favourite and beloved poet, he was—

> 'Ev'n as just a man
> 'As e'er my conversation cop'd withal—
> 'That no revenue had but his good spirits
> 'To feed and clothe him,' &c.

And many who read this short notice, whose convivial tables his wit has set in a roar, will regret his somewhat early death; and remember with cordial fondness, his ardent and grateful friendship, his sweetness of manners, his exuberance of fancy, and his most extraordinary facetious drolleries of humour!—(From a Correspondent)."

6 The British Library catalogue lists five editions of *Childe Harold* for 1812.

7 See p. 81.

8 The Ealing Local History Library has, alas, no reference to the Squibb family.

9 The Zetesophians, or Seekers after Wisdom.

9 April 1813

1 This seems an ambitious theme for a youth of eighteen who is teaching himself Greek.

2 A reminiscence of *Othello*, IV, ii.

3 Unidentified.

4 No review of *FitzGwarine* appears in the index to *The British Critic*, 1813.

5 Presumably J. Hatchard, the publisher and bookseller.

6 For all her ailments and complaints, Mrs Reynolds was to live to her eighty-seventh year (she died on 13 May 1848). Reynolds was to suffer much from ill-health and to die at the age of fifty-eight. It is curious that, even now, he doubts if he will live his normal span.

7 Shakespeare was born on 23 April 1564, and died on 23 April 1616. Dovaston celebrated the day every year. In 1810 he had recited his 'Irregular Ode to Shakespeare's Birthday' (see pp. 50–1); in 1811 he had written a dirge for the anniversary of Shakespeare's death. In 1814 he marked the day with an 'ADDRESS, Spoken to the Literary Friends

assembled at West-felton, on Shakespeare's Birth-Day . . . Formed from his Works.' Reynolds's love of Shakespeare was to last all his life; he was to share the passion with Keats. 'I'll tell you what,' Keats wrote to him in April 1817, '—on the 23rd was Shakespeare born—now if I should receive a Letter from you and another from my Brothers on that day 'twould be a parlous good thing . . .' (*Letters*, 21).

8 An allusion to Nelson's death at the Battle of Trafalgar, 21 October 1805.

9 These verses are apparently unpublished.

30 April 1813

1 The first page of this letter is edged with black. It is a youthful joke, and clearly owes something to Addison's account of the death of Sir Roger de Coverley. Rylance has not of course died, as will be seen from subsequent letters.

2 Unidentified quotation.

3 See p. 82. 'Beautiful name, that Magadalen,' Keats was to write to Reynolds on 14 March 1818 (*Letters*, 114); but the subject did not move him to poetry.

4 *The Lady's Monthly Museum; or Polite Repository of Amusement and Instruction* . . . By a Society of Ladies (1798–1828).

5 In other words, smoking his pipe. In 'The Story of Prometheus done into doggrel,' Dovaston wrote:

> We read in Greek Romances old
> That one Prometheus was so bold
> Smoking with friends and ale jocosely
> At heaven's lamp to light his *Broseley*.

Murray's *Handbook for Shropshire, Cheshire, and Lancashire* (1870) records (p. 30) that Broseley is 'an unattractive [Shropshire] town, principally dependant on its potteries and brick-yards. Tobacco-pipes are also largely made there.'

6 *Hamlet*, III, i.

7 Robert Southey's *Life of Nelson* was published, in two volumes, by John Murray. On 25 September Southey told his wife: 'Of the Nelson 3000 were printed, and a second edition is to be sent to press as soon as I have looked it over and made such improvements as new matter may enable me to make. It will now be compressed by the printer into one volume as originally intended.' *New Letters of Robert Southey*, edited by Kenneth Curry. (Columbia University Press. 1965). Vol. II, 74–5.

8 But see p. 115, note 8.

9 *The World before the Flood*, a poem, in ten cantos; with other occasional pieces; by James Montgomery. (Longman, Hurst, Rees, Orme & Brown. 1813.)

¹⁰ Henry Kirke White (1785–1806), the son of a Nottingham butcher, was articled to a local lawyer. In 1803 he published a volume of verse which won respect from Southey, who thenceforward protected him, and wrote a memoir of him after he died. White obtained a sizarship at St John's College, Cambridge, where overwork brought about his death at the age of twenty-one.

¹¹ The letter is postmarked 30 April 1813. Dovaston has noted: 'Jack Reynolds—wrote to him—3ᵈ May 1813.' On the fold of the letter Reynolds has written 'Dead!—Dead!!—Dead!!!'

24 May 1813

¹ The celebration of Shakespeare's birthday, 23 April.

² *Tales*. By the Rev George Crabbe, LL. B. (Hatchard. 1812.) The fifth of these tales was 'The Patron.'

³ Literally: 'What have I done?' This is a reference to Dovaston's poem: 'Written on the night of my *birthday*.' It appeared in his *Poems* (pp. 207 sqq. of the edition of 1825). The theme reappeared in the same volume (pp. 430–1) in 'Hymn. Tune by the Author.'

> What have I done? that ev'n to me
> Thy gladd'ning gleams are shown!
> For all Thy boundless bounties free,
> O Lord, what have I done? . . .

⁴ *Travelling Sketches in Russia and Sweden during the years 1805, 1806, 1807, 1808*. By Robert Ker Porter. The second edition, with forty-one plates. In two volumes. (Printed for John Stockdale. 1813.)

⁵ *Macbeth*, II, i.

⁶ The poem remains unknown.

⁷ Thomas Moore (1779–1852) became the national lyrist of Ireland by the publication of his *Irish Melodies* (1807–35).

⁸ 'Llunck-Llys. A Ballad' was published by Dovaston with the following note: 'Llunck-Llys Pool is a small but beautiful lake, of extraordinary depth, on the Welsh Border near Oswestry. The name in the Welsh signifies SUNK-PALACE . . . My ingenious friend Mr T. Yates . . . suggested a more fanciful and perhaps more accurate derivation of the name—Llyn-glas, the Blue Lake.'

⁹ Sonnet XI (*Poems*, 1825) begins

> Hark! 'tis that harp whose undulating strings
> Give music to the wind . . .

¹⁰ According to the records at Keats House, Hampstead, these stanzas appear to be unpublished.

¹¹ Dovaston noted: 'Answered 27 May, 1813.'

¹² An abbreviation of the writer's address: Amicable Society Office, Serjeants' Inn, Fleet Street, London.

¹ Presumably a reference to the work of William Roscoe (1753–1831). In *Mount Pleasant: a descriptive poem* (1777), Roscoe had exhorted his fellow poets:

> . . . Sweep the light strings, and louder swell the Lyre!
> For nobler themes a nobler song require.—
> The Heav'n-born Virtues come,—a lovely train;
> They prompt the verse,—be theirs the votive strain . . .

² *The Giaour* was published in 1813. Eight editions of the work appeared in the last seven months of the year. See also p. 100.

³ This poem appears to be unpublished. The Hon C. M. Woodhouse writes: 'The poem contains distinct echoes of Sappho's vocabulary —the breeze, the moonlight, the waves, the light on the sea at night, unrequited love, and so on. But Sappho had no monopoly of these images, and Reynolds could have got them at second hand. Probably he had read and used Pope's poem, *Sappho to Phaon*, which was itself a free translation of Ovid's *Sappho Phaoni*, in his *Heroides*, XV. The basis of the story is that Sappho committed suicide, because Phaon rebuffed her, by jumping from a well-known cliff on the island of Leucas (Santa Mavra, in the Ionian Isles).'

⁴ J. H. Reynolds was himself Poet Ferneate for the Breidden Festival this year, but he was unable to leave London for the occasion. On 12 July, so the minutes recorded, 'the day was fine and the company numerous. At one o'clock upwards of sixty sat down to dinner, soon after which the usual convivialities began. The annual tribute of the Poet Ferneat Mr John Hamilton Reynolds was received with heart-felt applause, and he being absent his cup was crowned with the Ferne [*sic*].' The annual tribute was 'The Reflections of Mirth, On the Eve of the Breidden Festival, for the Year 1813' (see p. 98).

⁵ The loan was clearly to be made without the knowledge of the Reynolds family. As will be seen, it brought about a crisis in the friendship with Dovaston. Reynolds was to be notably unfortunate in money matters.

[*Late June 1813*]

¹ Presumably Reynolds was thanking Dovaston for appointing him poet ferneat of the Breidden Festival this year. Since he was unable to leave London, his poetic offering—given in this letter—was read for him. It was printed in the introduction to Jones: *The Letters of John Hamilton Reynolds*, pp. xv–xvi.

² *Lady Jane Grey. A Tale, in two books; with Miscellaneous Poems, in English and Latin. By Francis Hodgson, A.M. Fellow of King's College, Cambridge; and author of a translation of Juvenal.* (Mackinlay.

1809.) The contents list '*Lady Jane Grey*. Historical Extracts, in Illustration of the above. A gentle Alterative [*sic*] prepared for the same subject . . .' The 'Alterative' is far from gentle, and begins as follows:

> Ye Quacks & Mountebanks of various schools,
> Who vend your trash to London's host of fools;
> But chiefly ye, anonymously wise,
> Who skulk in darkness from Detection's eyes,
> And high on Learning's chair affect to sit,
> The self-rais'd Arbiters of sense and wit,
> Ye paltry Critics!—shall the bard refrain
> From the just vengeance of his scourging strain. . . ?

3 *The Monthly Review*, May 1813, p. 99, notices *FitzGwarine* among other books of poetry:

> The ballad of *FitzGwarine* is by far the best in this collection, and contains some pleasing imagery and poetical touches, although they are disfigured by a want of polish and correctness in the verse.—The humorous poems, however, are far from commendable; and the author's talents must be aided by time and study, if he aspires to the title of a poet: though we question whether, in any case, his compositions would rise above mediocrity, or repay him for neglecting the more solid pursuits to which he seems to be professionally devoted.

An anonymous review of *FitzGwarine* appeared in *The Gentleman's Magazine*, February 1813, p. 137.

4 See p. 107.
5 An adaptation from *Henry IV*, Part I, III, i.

[July 1813]

1 See p. 97.
2 The Breidden Festival this year was celebrated on 12 July.
3 Reynolds is recalling 'Clifton Grove,' in *The Remains of Henry Kirke White*, Vol. II, pp. 11 sqq. This is the passage where Bateman drowns himself:

> He saw the Grove,—in fancy, saw *her* lie,
> *His* Margaret, lull'd in Germain's arms to rest,
> And all the demon rose with his breast.
> Convulsive now, he clench'd his trembling hand,
> Cast his dark eye once more upon the land,
> Then, at one spring he spurn'd the yielding bank,
> And in the calm deceitful current sank . . .

4 *Hamlet*, I, ii.
5 *The Quarterly Review*, March 1813 (pp. 207 sqq.), discussed *Poems*, by Samuel Rogers. These included 'an entirely new performance in

eleven cantos, called "Fragments of a Poem on the Voyage of Columbus."' Whatever Reynolds maintained, the review was far from favourable. The critic merely decided that 'with all its defects both of subject and of execution, the poem is by no means undeserving attention.'

[6] Reynolds may refer to the song:

> Wish'd for gales, the light vane veering,
> Better dreams the dull night cheering . . .

This comes from *The Beacon: a drama*, in *The Dramatic and Poetical Works of Joanna Baillie*. (Longman, Brown, Green & Longmans. 1851), pp. 303–4.

[7] Videlicet: to wit.

[8] According to the records at Keats House, Hampstead, this poem appears to be unpublished.

[9] An adaptation from *Macbeth*, II, iii. See also p. 84.

[10] 'This is not a period for the idle occupations of poetry, and times like the present require talents more active and more useful. Few have now the leisure to read such trifles, and I sincerely regret that I have had the leisure to write them.' So Thomas Moore ended the dedicatory letter of *Epistles, Odes, and other Poems*, addressed to Francis, Earl of Moira. (*The Works of Thomas Moore, Esq.* (Paris. Galignani. 1819.) Vol. III, p. 9.)

[11] Unidentified.

[12] 'My ingenious friend Mr T. Yates' is mentioned more than once in these letters. Dovaston addressed two poems to Thomas Yates, and a sonnet to Mrs Mary Yates. One of the twelve copies of *The Dove*, his collected comments on poetry, was inscribed 'Elizabeth Yates from John F. M. Dovaston.' It is now in the British Library.

[13] Unidentified.

[14] *Othello*, V, v.

2 August 1813

[1] The Ancient Briton ran between the Bull and Mouth, in Holborn, and the Lion Inn, Shrewsbury. *The Shrewsbury Guide* of 1809 records: 'The Ancient Briton Coach to London, every Sunday, Tuesday, and Thursday mornings, at four o'clock.'

[2] William Hayley (1745–1820) was a poet, and the friend of William Cowper, whose life he wrote.

[3] Unidentified.

[4] *Tales from Shakespeare*, by Charles and Mary Lamb, had appeared in 1807; it was designed to make Shakespeare familiar to the young. It is impossible to judge whether this was the book in question, or whether Dovaston proposed to write a volume with the same title.

[5] Dovaston noted: 'Jack Reynolds. Wrote to him to come.—4th. Aug.ᵗ 1813.'

¹ This is a curious remark; few visits to Shrewsbury are mentioned in the present correspondence.

² Perhaps Mrs Reynolds was asking for a compliment. The reference to old age comes strangely from a woman of fifty-one.

³ This is a repetition of her son's criticism.

⁴ Brother and sister seem to have been particularly close. In February *The Gentleman's Magazine* had published Reynolds's poem to Jane: 'Lines to a Sister, on her Birthday.'

⁵ No doubt Mr Squibb of Ealing, the father of Reynolds's friends.

⁶ Dovaston noted on this letter: 'Wrote to her on Jack's return, August 1813.'

⁷ George Squibb—yet another member of the numerous family—was very probably known to Keats. He became a member of The Royal College of Surgeons on 2 February 1821, and a Fellow on 12 August 1852. The *List of the Members of the Royal College of Surgeons in London* gives his name as G. James Squibb, and his address as Orchard Street, Portman Square. In 1855 he has moved to Montague Place, Bryanston Square. He seems to have died by 1859.

Francis Fladgate (1799–1892) was a relative of James Rice, and a boon companion of Keats. For fifty-nine years he was a member of the Garrick Club; a fellow-member found him 'one of the most polished gentlemen and good-natured persons I ever met.'

⁸ On 28 July 1813, at the battle of Sorauren, Soult's general attack was beaten. Wellington had finally stopped the French advance on Pamplona; and Soult was in a dangerous situation. Soult's nine-day offensive failed to relieve San Sebastian or Pamplona. He lost at least 13,500 of his original 60,000 men. The French Army was more disorganized and defeated after the Battles of the Pyrenees than they had been after Vitoria. On 31 August, the British took San Sebastian by storm. That day, on Soult's orders, two French divisions were forced to retire after a day-long fight with a British brigade of the 7th Division near the Bidassoa.

4 September 1813

¹ Keats and Reynolds later planned a joint volume of metrical versions from Boccaccio. When Reynolds read *Isabella*, he urged Keats to publish it, and added: 'I give over all intention, and you ought to be alone. I can never write anything now—my mind is taken the other way.' After Keats had died, however, Reynolds published *The Garden of Florence and other Poems* (1821).

² Isaac d'Israeli (1766–1848), father of Benjamin Disraeli, produced several discursive collections of literary and historical anecdotes. Among them was *Calamities of Authors* (1812–13).

3 A quarterly founded by Leigh Hunt. The first number had appeared in October 1810, the fourth and last at the end of 1811. Its glory lay in its association with Charles Lamb, who contributed several essays to it.

4 Presumably William Morris, the printer and publisher of Dovaston's poetry. See p. 88.

5 Wood & Walton, of St John's Hill, were Shrewsbury booksellers; they also printed the *Shrewsbury Chronicle*.

6 Possibly a relation of the Rector of Whittington, or of Dovaston's neighbour, W. Lloyd, of Aston Park.

7 In an undated letter to Robert Southey about the criticism of 'Clifton Grove,' Henry Kirke White explained: '[I] thought I had been deluding myself into an idea of possessing poetic Genius, when in fact I had only the longing, without the *afflatus*.' (*The Remains of Henry Kirke White, ... with an Account of his life*, by Robert Southey. 2 vols. (Vernor, Hood and Sharpe, etc. 1807). I, 25.)

8 These satirical verses seem to have been unpublished.

9 *Translations chiefly from the Greek Anthology, with tales and miscellaneous poems*. (Phillips. 1806.) This collection, published anonymously, was the work of the Rev Robert Bland, in collaboration with Denman, Francis Hodgson, afterwards Provost of Eton, and John Herman Merivale (1779–1844), sometime Commissioner of Bankruptcy. The book was re-issued several times, and there was a new edition in 1813. Among the translations was one from Sappho: *To an illiterate woman*. Possibly Reynolds had had this in mind when he had recently written his *Sappho*.

10 Literally: 'Blest is the man who looks on you . . .'

11 On 27 April 1818 Keats wrote to Reynolds: '[I] shall learn Greek . . . If you understood Greek, and would read me passages, now and then, explaining their meaning, 'twould be, from its mistiness, perhaps a greater luxury than reading the thing one's self.' (*Letters*, 136.)

12 *The Giaour* was published in 1813. Eight editions of the work appeared in the last seven months of the year, increasing its length from 685 lines to 1334.

13 *Macbeth*, III, ii.

14 Presumably *FitzGwarine*.

15 Octavius G. Gilchrist (1779–1823) was a literary scholar who contributed occasionally to *The Champion* and *The London Magazine*. One might record that Dovaston's *Rhymes* (1805) had been dedicated 'To Horatio Thomas Gilchrist Esq. (of Stamford).'

16 Ralph Rylance.

17 No doubt it was during Reynolds's recent visit to West Felton that Dovaston had written:

To R. Rylance; then in Scotland

Rylance, from sweet Westfelton's lone resorts
　　To thee two bardlings now in union write,
Much wishing thee SPECTATOR of their sports,
　　SIR ROGER this, and that WILL WIMBLE hight . . .

We greet thee cordial: for right well we know
　　Thee not forgetful of the merry glee
When last warm August's ev'ning sun, as now,
　　Spark'd our three glasses thro' the greenwood tree,
Whence we two send, as here our wreaths we twine,
This little friendly flow'r to fade in thine.

[18]　Reynolds had an unfortunate addiction to puns. Possibly he planned
　　　to write a poem on the Nine Muses.
[19]　As his earlier quotation implies (p. 106), Reynolds was thinking of
　　　Macbeth; no doubt he also recalled *Henry IV*, Part One, III, i. Owen
　　　Glendower was a natural subject for a poet who was living on the
　　　Welsh border. Indeed, on the Oswestry road, just outside Shrews-
　　　bury, there stood the shell of what was once a magnificent oak,
　　　known as Glyndwr's Oak, from a tradition that he had climbed up it,
　　　to witness the issue of the Battle of Shrewsbury. However,
　　　Dovaston does not appear to have published a poem about him.

30 September 1813

[1]　See the reference to Boccaccio in the previous letter.
[2]　Reynolds gives no hint as to the nature of the letters. Presumably
　　　they were letters from distinguished literary figures about his own
　　　writing. Dovaston's behaviour seems extraordinary. This is an early
　　　indication of a flaw in the friendship.
[3]　See letter of 23 October 1813, p. 109.
[4]　Presumably Maria Williams, a friend of Dovaston's.

23 October 1813

[1]　A note on this letter reads: 'Am. Soc. Office, 23 Oct. 1813.'
[2]　James Asperne was the publisher of *The European Magazine and
　　　London Review*. Reynolds's review of *FitzGwarine* appeared in the
　　　issue of March 1814, pp. 228–30. Mr Dovaston, he concluded,

　　　has, in this poem, made the style of Mr Scott his model, and has
　　　given to the world a very elegant and interesting production: he
　　　seems particularly happy in describing natural scenery . . . Deli-
　　　cate minds will find, in his volume, much according observation
　　　and similarity of feeling; and we cannot but imagine that *Fitz-
　　　Gwarine* will prove an admired poem: if it should be neglected,
　　　we shall think that popularity is more often gained by chance than

by real desert; and that the unmusical tinklings of idiotic versifiers are more likely to win the smiles of the many, than the pure and animated efforts of superior genius.

[3] An interesting comment from the future friend of Keats. John Gibson Lockhart was to write a savage attack on Keats in *Blackwood's Edinburgh Magazine*, August 1818.

[4] This encouragement of Dovaston anticipates the encouragement which Reynolds was to give to Keats some five years later. Condemning 'all the ignorant malevolence of cold lying Scotchmen and stupid Englishmen,' Reynolds assured him: 'The overweening struggle to oppress you cannot be directed to nothing. Men do not set their muscles, and strain their Sinews to break a straw.' (14 October 1818; *Letters*, 222.)

20 November 1813

[1] Looney Mactwolter, a character in *The Review, or the Wags of Windsor*, a musical farce by George Colman the younger. Mactwolter is 'a raw Irishman,' whose parents have 'died of a whiskey fever.'

[2] Mrs Reynolds was still keeping a watch on her son's correspondence; she was now aware that there were problems in his friendship with Dovaston. Rylance appears to have been making trouble.

[3] Mr J. C. Trewin writes: 'I believe (although this is a surmise) that John Philip Kemble said "What is it you do want?" when addressing a demonstrative audience during the O.P. riots at Covent Garden in the autumn of 1809.'

[4] Presumably an allusion to Byron.

[5] Reynolds had followed Dovaston's lead, and submitted several pieces to *The Gentleman's Magazine* in 1812 and 1813; he was soon to become more ambitious.

[6] A touching sign of Reynolds's youthful affection for Dovaston.

[7] This work is not in the British Library music catalogue.

[8] Dovaston noted: 'Ansd. 23 Novr. 1813.'

29 November 1813

[1] Dovaston, still a bachelor, was aware of the attractions of his income and his Shropshire estate. He was also aware that the Reynolds family had a humbler way of life. He had now implied that they were cultivating him for his money.

[2] Mrs Reynolds shows remarkable forbearance at Dovaston's extraordinary rudeness.

[3] The correspondence does not suggest that Reynolds paid frequent visits to his friend. Dovaston was waiting for the repayment of the £5 which he had lent him; the loan was small, but it had become a source of surprising anger and malice. Reynolds's delay in sending him books had also become a source of contention.

4   The Nine Muses.
5   A correspondent, signing himself W. R., recalled after Reynolds's
     death: 'With splendid dark eyes, a mobile and intelligent counten-
     ance lit up by never-failing good humour, and a quiet, bland, but
     somewhat arch smile, he was goodly to look at as well as to listen
     to.' The tribute, in *The Examiner*, was quoted in *The Hampshire
     Independent* on 4 December 1852.
6   Unidentified.

4 December 1813

1   This letter, written some time since 30 September, is not of course
     among the Dovaston Papers.
2   This is no doubt a reference to *Safie: an Eastern Tale*, which was to
     be published in 1814.
3   The quotation remains unidentified.
4   One is tempted to agree with Reynolds that Dovaston's behaviour
     was 'unhandsome.' Reynolds himself showed a forgiving spirit.
5   Byron, still intent on the East, had published *The Bride of Abydos*
     in 1813.
6   See p. 107.
7   Possibly a further reference to *Safie*.
8   Moore was now working on *Lalla Rookh*, a series of oriental tales in
     verse, connected by a story in prose; it was to be published in 1817.
9   *Specimens of the British Poets*, by Thomas Campbell, was published
     by Murray in seven volumes in 1819.
10   Probably *Roderick, the last of the Goths*, which appeared in 1814.
11   Whatever the report, Byron did not go to the Greek islands in the
     spring of 1814. The Turkish Tale was no doubt *The Corsair*, which
     was published in January 1814. It was dedicated to Thomas Moore,
     who considered it 'a very high niche in the Temple indeed' (*Letters*,
     I, 293).
12   This should be 'amantium irae amoris integratio est': Lovers'
     quarrels are the coalescence of love.

[March–April 1814.]

1   This suggests that Jane Reynolds may herself have given French
     lessons (see p. 69).
2   James Cawthorn, of Cockspur Street, later described by Keats as 'the
     Bookseller and print-virtuoso,' was in partnership with Reynolds's
     friend, the publisher John Martin, of Holles Street, Cavendish
     Square. In 1814 they published *Safie: an Eastern Tale*, by J. H.
     Reynolds. This was an attempt to capitalise on the vogue of Byronic
     oriental tales in verse. It was considered a remarkable achievement
     for a young man who was not yet twenty. It was dedicated, 'with
     every sentiment of gratitude and respect, to the right honourable

Lord Byron.' On 20 February Byron acknowledged his presentation copy from the author. 'The Poem itself, as the work of a young man, is creditable to your talents, and promises better for future efforts than any which I can now recollect. Whether you intend to pursue your poetical career, I do not know and have no right to inquire—but, in whatever channel your abilities are directed, I think it will be your own fault if they do not eventually lead to distinction.' Byron's assessment was sadly prophetic. A copy of *Safie*, inscribed: 'Mrs Reynolds from Her Affectionate Son John H. Reynolds,' is now at Keats House, Hampstead.

[3] Soon after the appearance of *Safie*, John Martin started a periodical called *The Inquirer, or Literary Miscellany*. In the first number, dated May 1814, there are three contributions signed 'J.H.R.' Two of these are poems; the third is an article 'On the Character of Hamlet.' The last number of this short-lived periodical, dated January 1815, contains another poem signed 'J.H.R.'; and in both this and the other numbers there are unsigned articles which George L. Marsh was tempted to ascribe to him. The periodical was seen by Marsh when he edited *John Hamilton Reynolds, Poetry and Prose* (1928); the copy in the British Library was destroyed by bombing during the last war, and it is unlikely that further copies will be found.

[4] Dovaston noted: 'Wrote a hasty and free answer, 10 April 1814.'

[19 July, 1814]

[1] *Othello*, I, iii.

[2] Reynolds's affectionate nature is illuminated by his behaviour.

[3] Not identified.

[4] A reference to *The Inquirer*. The first number had appeared in May. See pp. 196–7.

[5] This is the first reference in these letters to Leigh Hunt (1784–1859). In 1808 Hunt had begun to edit *The Examiner*; and in 1813, with his brother John, he had been fined and imprisoned for a libel on the Prince Regent. At the time this letter was written, he was still imprisoned in Coldbath Fields. In 1815, Keats was to mark his release with the sonnet 'Written on the day that Mr Leigh Hunt left prison'; Keats was later introduced to Hunt, and often visited his Hampstead cottage. In 1816, in *The Examiner*, Hunt predicted three young poets of the future: Keats, Shelley and J. H. Reynolds.

[6] *The Feast of the Poets*, an exercise in verse and criticism, had appeared in *The Reflector* in 1811; in 1814 it was re-issued, with profuse notes, as a book. In 1815 it was published in a new, enlarged version.

[7] *The Descent of Liberty: a Mask*, was dedicated to Thomas Barnes, the future editor of *The Times*. It appeared in 1814.

[8] No doubt *The Story of Rimini*, based on the story of Paolo and Francesca. It was published in 1816.

9 Dovaston made some amends for his behaviour by addressing a sonnet 'To Mr John Hamilton Reynolds, Author of *Safie*, and other Poems.'

> Reynolds, no more as erst two frolic boys
>> By Severn's side our school-day tricks we try,
> For me now holds the love of rural joys,
>> Thee city pomp, light Sock, and Buskin high.
> Yet Distance dares not bid us leave to ply
> The social sheet, or court our mutual Muse,
>> For Distance cannot time-tied souls untie,
> Nor dim the long horizon of their views.
> But never let my woods their leafage lose
>> 'Till thou hast there admired ripe August glow;
> Nor shall in turn my friendly feet refuse
>> To beat thy threshold with December's snow.
> So shalt thou love my rural joys; and I
>> Approve thy scenic pomp, light Sock, and Buskin high.

This poem was published in the second edition of the *FitzGwarine* volume, in 1816.

10 Reynolds was on the eve of his twentieth birthday (9 September 1814); but for some years he had been anxious about his health, and even now he seemed aware that he might die young. One recalls Keats's note to Fanny Brawne: 'If I had had time I would have made myself remember'd' (*Letters*, 468).

11 It was, of course, indirectly responsible for his introduction to Keats.

12 No doubt *The Eden of Imagination*, which appeared later this year.

13 See p. 107.

14 *Henry IV*, Part One, III, i.

15 Dovaston noted: 'Wrote to Jack Reynolds, 21 July 1814.'

16 *Selections from the Popular Poetry of the Hindoos. Arranged and translated by Thomas Duer Broughton, Esq., Major of the Hon East India Company's Service in Bengal; and author of Letters from a Mahratta Camp.* (John Martin. 1814.)

[*July–August 1814.*]

1 In 1814 James Cawthorn and John Martin brought out *The Eden of Imagination*. In this second book by Reynolds, the influence of Wordsworth supersedes that of Byron. Reynolds's admiration for Wordsworth is apparent in the present letter.

2 *Lyrical Ballads*, a collection of poems by Wordsworth and Coleridge, had appeared in 1798. The second edition, with new poems and a preface, had been published in 1800, and a third edition in 1802.

3 The comment is worth noting. In 1819 Reynolds published a skit on Wordsworth's poem, *Peter Bell*, which was soon to appear. It came

out under the same title, and ran through three editions that year. Coleridge declared that it was written by Charles Lamb, because no other person could have written it.

4 Reynolds's hopes were to be fulfilled: Wordsworth's new poem was *The Excursion* (1814).

5 The Alcaic stanza was the four-line stanza particularly associated with Alcaeus of Samos (a contemporary of Sappho). It was also used by Latin poets, especially Horace. *Rosas violasque*: roses and violets.

6 A misquotation from *Macbeth*, I, vi.

7 Literally: 'Let us sing lesser themes.'

8 *Praelectiones Academicae Oxonii Habitae* ab Edvardo Copleston S.T.B. Collegii Orielensis socio et poeticae publico praelectore nunc ecclesiae cathedralis Londinensis praebendario. (Oxonii. Typis academicis impensis auctoris. Prostant venales apud J. Parker, Oxonii, . . . 1813.) This learned work, by the future Bishop of Llandaff, was dedicated 'Nobilissimo viro Baroni Grenville Academiae Oxoniensis Cancellario S.P.D. Edvardus Copleston.'

9 See p. 108.

10 This is an unmistakable hint that Reynolds would like to be invited to West Felton.

11 Dovaston noted: 'Wrote to Jack Reynolds, 18 August 1814.'

23 August 1814

1 'I will make my very house reel to-night:—a letter for me!' (*Coriolanus*, II, i).

2 See letter of March–April 1814, p.??, note 3.

3 Dovaston notes: 'Wrote to Reynolds, 26 Aug.ͭ 1814—& sent him a Copy of Bala Water for his Inquirer.' The ballad appeared in the second edition of *FitzGwarine*, in 1816.

4 *The Eden of Imagination.* Reynolds sent Dovaston a copy on 30 September (see p. 127).

5 Byron, to whom it was dedicated, had, however, praised it. See letter of March–April 1814, p. ??, note 2.

6 Sir Fretful Plagiary, the poetaster: a character in Sheridan's *The Critic* (1779).

7 'The reader,' said the publisher's advertisement, 'may probably regard [*Lara*] as a sequel to *The Corsair*.' Lara was in fact Conrad, the pirate chief in the earlier poem, returned to his domains in Spain. In the character of Lara one may see Byron's conception of himself. Both poems were published in 1814.

8 See p. 105, note 2.

9 See p. 119.

[10] See p. 100; *Columbus*, a fragmentary epic by Samuel Rogers (1763–1855), was published in 1810.

[11] See p. 100.

[12] Reynolds seems to be thinking again of *Macbeth*.

25 September 1814

[1] The poem remains unidentified.

[2] George James Cholmondeley, K.G., 4th Earl Cholmondeley (1749–1827).

[3] Possibly a reference to Eliza Powell Drewe, of Exeter. Reynolds had probably met her and her family through their London relative, Mrs Butler, who was a friend of his own family in Lambeth. He was to marry her in 1822. It is also possible that he already refers to Mary. Sarah or Thomasine: one of the Leigh sisters, of Slade Hall, near Sidmouth. They were already the 'adopted sisters' of James Rice and Benjamin Bailey. Eliza is known to have joined the group by March 1815; Reynolds and Rice visited Slade Hall from 31 August—11 September 1816. All three young men addressed poems to the sisters, and Bailey fell in love with the youngest, Thomasine, his adored 'Zilia.' She did not return his love, and in 1817 she married Lieutenant John Carslake of the Royal Navy. In his extracts from a tale (pp. 136–8), Reynolds refers to Zelia and Zilia.

[4] An adaptation of lines in *Henry IV*, Part One, V, i.

[5] Writing in *The Champion* on 27 October 1816, Reynolds professed his admiration for Kean's Hamlet. 'Mr Kean's performance of Hamlet is a very noble work . . . The great beauty of Mr Kean's acting is its mental energy. He plays directly and intensely from his mind.'

[6] *Hamlet*, I, ii.

30 September 1814

[1] *The Eden of Imagination* was dedicated

To
John Freeman Milward Dovaston, Esq.,
of West Felton, Shropshire.

My Dear Dovaston,
    As a slight but sincere token of the pleasure I feel in our long friendship, allow me to dedicate to you the following little sketch. Few are possessed of minds so capable of enjoying the scenes it attempts to describe, and I know of no one whose judgment I would sooner rely on, as to its Poetical merits.
        Your's very faithfully,
            John Hamilton Reynolds.
August 1814.

1 'I know three witty people all distinct in their excellence—Rice, Reynolds and Richards,' Keats was to write on 17 January 1820. 'Rice is the wisest, Reynolds the playfullest, Richards the out o' the wayest . . .' (*Letters*, 453).
2 *The Eden of Imagination.*
3 Amicitia: friendship.
4 These were not included in Dovaston's *Poems* (1825).
5 The quotation remains unidentified.
6 Mark Akenside (1721–70) was the author of *The Pleasures of Imagination* (1744), rewritten and published in 1757 as *The Pleasures of the Imagination.*
7 In *John Hamilton Reynolds. Poetry and Prose*, George L. Marsh refers to the death, late in 1814, of 'an unidentified girl whom he loved, a tragedy over which he grieved repeatedly in numerous poems dating from January 1815.' This conventional poem does not suggest that its author had been in love with Anna, the 'youthful friend.' Perhaps the 'Young Lady' who asked him to write it was Eliza Powell Drewe, or one of the Leigh sisters. It appears to be unpublished.
8 *The Descent of Liberty: A Mask*, was published in 1814. It was prefaced by an account of the 'Origin and Nature of Masks,' in which Hunt revealed how the Elizabethans were now recapturing the English imagination.
9 Presumably the sons of William Roscoe (see pp. 95, 131, 185), among whose works was *The Butterfly's Ball and the Grasshopper's Feast* (1807), now a children's classic. Roscoe was not only an author, but a bibliophile, an attorney, and—from 1806—one of the two Members of Parliament for Liverpool. He was a fierce opponent of the slave trade. Rylance had dedicated his pamphlet on the Brazils 'to one whose whole life, public and private, is a consistent and uniform example of that moral principle, and of those virtues which ought to actuate nations as well as individuals.'

   Reynolds himself was clearly among those who visited Leigh Hunt—who was still in prison at Coldbath Fields.
10 Dovaston noted: 'Wrote to Reynolds, 20 Oct⁻ 1814.'

1 This was not to be Mr Reynolds's only professional problem. On 4 July 1820, Reynolds asked John Taylor (by then Keats's publisher and his own) to intervene with Lord Radstock on behalf of his father. Some of the managers of the Female Asylum, Lambeth, were 'preparing to lop his trifling salary of £50 per annum down to £30' (Rollins: KC, I, 119–20).

2   Keats marked Hunt's release with the sonnet 'Written on the day that Mr Leigh Hunt left Prison' (*Poetical Works*, 40).

3   See pp. 130–1.

4   Hunt's appreciation of Reynolds was also expressed in an indifferent sonnet (Hunt: *Poetical Works*, Vol. III, p. cxxx):

> To John Hamilton Reynolds,
> on his lines upon the Story of Rimini.
>
> Reynolds, whose Muse, from out thy gentle embraces,
> Holding a little crisp and dewy flower,
> Came to me in my close-entwined bower,
> Where many fine-eyed Friendships and glad Graces,
> Parting the boughs, have looked in with like faces,
> And thanked the song which had sufficient power
> With Phoebus to bring back a warmer hour,
> And turn his southern eye to our green places:
> Not for this only, but that thou dost long
> For all men's welfare, may there be a throng
> Of kind regards, wherever thou appearest;
> And in thy home, firm-handed Health, a song
> Girt with rich-hearted friends, and she the nearest
> To whom the warble of thy lip is dearest.

5   Dovaston himself had written a poem on the place:

> There is a field in Felton's woodland vale,
> Maids call it Fairyland . . .

The poem appeared in his *FitzGwarine* volume in 1816.

6   Byron had married on 2 January 1815. On 15 January 1816, Lady Byron left with her infant daughter, and she never saw him again.

7   'Alas, how much worse it is to be in the company of others than to remember thee!'

8   Reynolds was already moving in literary circles far above those of Dovaston, his former mentor.

9   Coleridge had not in fact ended his literary career. In 1817 he published his *Biographica literaria* and in 1825 his *Aids to Reflection*. However, he spent much of the latter part of his life in the houses of friends, and after 1816 he lived with a kindly surgeon, James Gillman, at Highgate. Keats met him on Hampstead Heath in April 1819, and was invited to call on him.

10   In *Notes and Queries* T.M.T. ascribes to Reynolds 'an Ode on the overthrow of Napoleon.' This appears to be it.

11   'The Song of a Spanish Lover to his Mistress,' signed J.H.R., had appeared in *The Inquirer* in January 1815. One might add that in the same month *The Gentleman's Magazine* (pp. 63–4) had published Reynolds's poem 'The Hand.'

12   Reynolds anticipates Keats's phrase to Fanny Brawne: 'I have two

luxuries to brood over in my walks, your Loveliness and the hour of my death . . .' (25 July 1819. *Letters*, 362).

[13] Reynolds apparently came to change his views. In 1817 he wrote 'Milton and Spenser. Sonnet to a Friend.'

> We both are lovers of the poets old!
> But Milton hath your heart,—and Spenser mine!—
> So let us love them:—you, the song divine,
> And I, the tale of times gallant and bold . . .

The poem appeared in *The Athenaeum* on 4 July 1832.

[13] Reynolds had presumably quoted from memory. The correct lines appeared in Hunt's *Poetical Works* (C. & J. Ollier. 1819), p. 27:

> While the bees, about their treasure,
> Hum and pitch with tipsy pleasure,
> And the coying butterflies,
> Drest in all their summer dyes,
> Flutter up, from every part,
> Tickled, as it were, at heart.

[15] William Smyth, Professor of Modern History in the University of Cambridge, was the author of *English Lyrics*. The second edition had appeared in 1798, the fourth appeared this year, and the fifth was to be published in 1850.

[16] Samuel Rogers (1763–1855), had published his *Pleasures of Memory* in 1792.

[17] John Dryden (1631–1700) translated the whole of Virgil into verse. The complete work appeared in 1697. In was very successful, and according to Pope brought him in £1,200.

[18] 'It will please at the tenth repetition.'

[19] Reynolds is only twenty, but he has continued fears for his health.

[20] These extracts do not appear to have been published.

[21] Dovaston notes: 'Wrote to Reynolds 21 March 1815.' However, this is the last dated letter in the correspondence which survives.

Epilogue

[1] See letter of August–September 1812, No. 1 and note, p. 182. Dovaston's pseudonym, Musiphilus, means Lover of the Muses.

[2] For the most complete accounts of Dovaston, see the *Dictionary of National Biography*, and *The Gentleman's Magazine*, October 1854, pp. 395–6.

[3] *A Flora of Shropshire*. W. A. Leighton, B.A. (Van Voorst. 1841), pp. 114, 523, and *passim*; *A Guide, descriptive and historical, through the town of Shrewsbury*. W. A. Leighton, B.A. 4th edition. (Shrewsbury. Davies. 1855?), p. 190.

4   See D. E. Allen: 'J. F. M. Dovaston: an overlooked pioneer of field ornithology.' (*The Journal of the Society for the Bibliography of Natural History*. Vol. 4, Part 6. July 1967, pp. 277 sqq.)

5   For Bewick and Dovaston, see: *The Life and Works of Thomas Bewick*. David Croal Thomson. ('The Art Journal' Office. 1882.); *Bewick to Dovaston. Letters 1824–1828*. Edited by Gordon Williams. Introduction by Montague Weekley. (Nattali & Maurice. 1968.); *A Memoir of Thomas Bewick*. Written by himself. Edited with an introduction by Iain Bain. (Oxford University Press. 1979.).

6   Quoted in *Bewick to Dovaston*, 135.

7   *The Magazine of Natural History*. Conducted by J. C. Loudon, F.L.S., G.S., &c. September 1829, pp. 313–9.

8   Ibid, July 1829, 219 sqq.; January 1832, 83–4; March 1832, 113–8, 147–9; April 1832, 293, 299; June 1832, 425–8; September 1832, 660–1; June 1832, 427.

9   Allen: op. cit., 278.

10 'Monody. Myself.' *FitzGwarine*, 35–7.

11 *The Magazine of Natural History*, February 1832, 111–2.

12 *The Gentleman's Magazine*, October 1854, p. 396.

13 [14 October 1818.] *Letters*, 223–4, note.

14 Ibid, 35, 41, 58, 214.

15 14 February—3 May 1819. Ibid, 303–5.

16 21 June 1818. Ibid, 153.

17 'To Mrs. Reynolds's Cat.' *Poetical Works*, 532.

18 21 February 1818. *Letters*, 106.

19 14–31 October 1818. Ibid, 232–4.

20 [July 1820]. Ibid, 500.

21 [15 November 1821.] *Letters of Fanny Brawne to Fanny Keats*, 37.

22 11–13 July, 1818. *Letters*, 178.

23 [1821.] Sharp: *Life and Letters of Joseph Severn*, 109.

24 21 September 1820. KC, I, 156.

25 See letter of.

26 Quoted in Keats: *Letters*, 177, note.

27 Gosse (ed.): *The Letters of Thomas Lovell Beddoes*, 54.

28 Shelley: op. cit., 324.

29 Ibid, 330.

30 17 April 1848. Quoted by Marsh: op. cit., 42.

31 Quoted in KC, I, cxxiii.

SELECT BIBLIOGRAPHY

The list of books on Keats and his circle is so large that I have restricted the present list to books by and about J. H. Reynolds, books by J. F. M. Dovaston, and articles on Reynolds and his family. I have included the editions of Keats's poems and letters which I have used, and Professor Rollins' edition of the letters and papers of the Keats Circle (referred to, in the notes, as KC). Other publications are specified in the notes themselves.

DOVASTON, J. F. M.   *Rhymes.* (London. No publisher given. 1805.) Twenty-five copies only were printed.
——, *FitzGwarine, a ballad of the Welsh Border; in three cantos. With other Rhymes, Legendary, Incidental and Humorous.* By John F. M. Dovaston, A.M. (Printed and published by and for W. Morris, Shrewsbury. December, 1812.) *FitzGwarine* was republished in 1816 and 1825.
——, *The Dove. Scraps of Poetry.* Selected by John F. M. Dovaston, A.M. For the *Oswestry Herald*, 1823. Twelve copies only were printed for presentation.
——, *Poems, Legendary, Incidental, and Humorous.* (Printed and republished by and for W. Morris, Shrewsbury, 23 April 1825.)

KEATS, John.   *Poetical Works.* Edited by H. W. Garrod. (Oxford. The Clarendon Press. 1939.)
——, *Letters.* Edited by Maurice Buxton Forman. (O.U.P. 1942.)

REYNOLDS, John Hamilton.   *Safie, An Eastern Tale.* (James Cawthorn & John Martin. 1814.)
——. *The Eden of Imagination. A Poem.* (James Cawthorn & John Martin. 1814.)
——, *The Naiad: a Tale. With other Poems.* (Taylor & Hessey. 1816.)
——, *Peter Bell. A Lyrical Ballad.* 3rd edition. (Taylor & Hessey. 1819.)
——, *The Fancy.* A Selection from the Poetical Remains of the late

Peter Corcoran, of Gray's Inn, Student at Law. With a brief memoir of his life. (Taylor & Hessey. 1820.)

——, *The Fancy.* With a Prefatory Memoir and Notes by John Masefield and thirteen illustrations by Jack B. Yeats. (Elkin Mathews. 1905.)

——, *The Garden of Florence; and other Poems.* (John Warren. 1821.)

——, *Selected Poems of John Hamilton Reynolds.* Edited by Leonidas M. Jones. (Cambridge, Mass. Harvard University Press. 1966.)

——, *The Letters of John Hamilton Reynolds.* Edited with an Introduction by Leonidas M. Jones. (Lincoln, Nebraska. University of Nebraska Press. 1973.)

——, *John Hamilton Reynolds. Poetry and Prose.* With an introduction and notes by George L. Marsh. (O.U.P. 1928.)

REYNOLDS, John Hamilton, and HOOD, Thomas. *Odes and Addresses to Great People.* 3rd edition. (Colburn. 1826.)

ROLLINS, Hyder Edward (ed.) *The Keats Circle. Letters and Papers, 1816–1848.* 2 volumes. (Cambridge, Mass. Harvard University Press. 1948.)

ARTICLES

GITTINGS, Robert 'The Poetry of John Hamilton Reynolds.' (Alberta, Canada. *Ariel*, Vol. I, No. 4. October 1970.)

KAUFMAN, Paul 'The Reynolds–Hood Commonplace Book: A Fresh Appraisal.' (*Keats–Shelley Journal*, Vol. X, Winter 1961.)

MANN, Phyllis G. 'The Reynolds Family.' (*Keats–Shelley Journal*, Vol. V, Winter 1956.)

MARSH, George L. 'New Data on Keats's Friend Reynolds.' (*Modern Philology*, Vol. XXV, No. 3. February 1928.)

——, 'The Writings of Keats's Friend Reynolds.' (*Studies in philology*, Vol. XXV, No. 4, October 1928.)

POPE, Willard B. 'John Hamilton Reynolds, the Friend of Keats.' (Reprint from *Wessex*, 1935.)

206

INDEX